Social Media Marketing for Small Business Owners

How to Use Paid Advertising and Sales Funnels on Facebook & Instagram for Maximum Revenue Growth in 2020

Mark Warner

book.

By reading this document, the reader agrees that under no circumstances is the author responsible for any losses, direct or indirect, which are incurred as a result of the use of information contained within this document, including, but not limited to, — errors, omissions, or inaccuracies.

Table of Contents

Dear Reader,

As an independent author,
  and one-man operation
  - my marketing budget is next to zero.

As such, the only way
  I can get my books in front of valued customers
  is with reviews.

Unfortunately, I'm competing against authors and
  giant publishing companies
  with multi-million-dollar marketing teams.

These behemoths can afford
  to give away hundreds of free books
  to boost their ranking and success.

Which as much as I'd love to –
  I simply can't afford to do.

That's why your honest review
  will not only be invaluable to me,
  but also to other readers on Amazon.

Yours sincerely,

Mark Warner

Sales Funnel Management for Small Business Owners in 2019

Strategies on How to Setup a Highly Automated Funnel for Your Business (That Actually Makes Money)

Introduction

I want to thank you for choosing this book, Sales Funnel Management for Small Business Owners in 2019: Strategies on How to Setup a Highly Automated Funnel for Your Business (That Actually Makes Money).

Common problems that a lot of small business owners face is a lack of time, a loosely targeted social media marketing strategy, and the lack of proper understanding of their target customers. These problems can affect your bottom line, and you might not even be aware of it. The good news is, these can be easily remedied by corrective action, and this is where this book comes in. The goal of this book is to help you solve these issues effectively and efficiently without burning a hole in your pocket. The actionable steps and tips given in this book are practical, easy to implement, scalable, and cost-effective. Do you wish to increase the efficiency of your marketing efforts but aren't sure where to begin? If yes, then this is the perfect book for you.

In this book, you will learn about different strategies you can use to create a highly functional and automated sales funnel, which will help the efficiency and the productivity of your business. The information given in this book is backed by research done by eminent personalities like Robert Cialdini, whose principles of persuasion are commonly used in marketing.

If you want to turn things around for your business, then it is time to take some action. Go through the information given in this book and implement the suggestions given so that you don't get left behind your competitors. In business, time is money, so it is essential to act quickly.

So, let us get started without further ado!

Chapter 1: Customer Buyer Persona

Unless you have never dealt with marketing before, it is quite unlikely that you aren't aware of the need to define your target audience. Having a detailed and thorough idea of your average customer improves the focus and target your marketing campaigns. You might think that a basic demographic profile of your existing customers will suffice, but that's not the case, and this is where the concept of buyer personas comes into the picture. A buyer persona is derived from your target customers. Instead of including just numbers and figures, a buyer persona takes into account the audience's research and is presented in the form of a hypothetical profile of an ideal customer. Think of it as a semi-fictional depiction of your ideal audience. For instance, instead of merely targeting your marketing efforts toward women in the age group of 25-35 years with an income between $45,000 and $80,000, you will be targeting Olivia, a 27-year old fashion designer.

Understanding your customers is quintessential for any business. A successful business owner not only understands what their customers want but also knows the most efficient means of making their products or services available to those customers. It means knowing more about their customers than their age, name, or income. As a business owner, you must know about your customer's interests, tastes, preferences, what they watch, where they spend their time, and the kind of content they read. All these things can be leveraged to increase the business's profits.

It is also essential to understand their buying behavior, too. As a business owner, you must try to understand the types of individuals who will need or want the products or services your business provides. Here are a couple of simple questions you must keep asking yourself daily to become a successful business owner.

- What is the reason for buying the products or services you offer?
- How frequently will they need to purchase that product or avail the service? If you take steps to be proactive in your marketing efforts around the time when the customers need to buy something, chances are they will not look elsewhere for the same.
- Is the buyer your ultimate consumer, or are they buying it for someone? The messaging and promotional strategies you design will depend on the ultimate consumer of the product or service.
- Where will they purchase the product from? Will they buy it from a brick and mortar store, or can it be ordered online, too?

Businesses that are aware of what their customers want and what their expectations are can use this information for customizing the buyer's experience to establish brand loyalty.

A simple means to do this is by increasing the length of customer interaction your business usually has. By simply listening to what your customers want, and by answering the questions they typically have or solving any of their problems, you can create a better customer experience. To do this, you must be aware of what the customers are looking for. As a business owner, it is quintessential that you not only provide excellent quality services and products, but you must stand out from the other competitors in your niche. Your customer knowledge, along with relationships, gives you this advantage. So, developing a customer persona is the first step to create a successful marketing strategy. This, in turn, helps increase your profitability.

You might be thinking that you already have customer personas in place. Well, it is a common misconception that customer segments, and customer personas, are synonyms. Most businesses tend to create customer segments instead of personas. Segmentation enables a business to understand the various sets or groups of customers in the market. It might give you an idea of where a specific group resides, their age, or even their usual buying behavior. A customer persona enables you to understand these groups and recognize certain key traits present within which are favorable for your business.

To create an ideal representation of your sample audience, you need to create customer personas that are based on the analysis of your real customers. It helps create a detailed and thorough representation of your ideal customer which includes information like their personal motivations, the value they look for in a business, the kind of content they like, the communication they expect, etc. Businesses can use all these insights and incorporate them to create a customer experience, which is no longer one-dimensional.

Benefits of Creating Customer Personas

A characteristic of a good marketing campaign is that it focuses on your target audience. So, before you can develop a marketing strategy, it is essential to create a customer or a buyer persona. There are different benefits you can reap by creating customer personas, and they are as follows.

Right time and place

Having detailed customer personas while designing your marketing campaign is quintessential, especially because most businesses are client-oriented these days. It helps identify where your ideal customers spend most of their time. Instead of wasting your time on platforms seldom used by your target audience, wouldn't it be better if you target those platforms they do spend time on? Instead of blowing your budget on unwanted ads, you can create such content which will help solve a buyer's needs. Instead of spending money marketing on platforms where you think you can find your potential customers, you can now be sure of the platforms you must target. Being present at the right place at the right time is an invaluable resource for businesses these days.

Develop brilliant content

What business wouldn't want to develop brilliant content? The idea of marketing is to transform the "wants" of a potential customer and make them seem like "needs." Content is king when it comes to marketing. If the content isn't exceptional, it will become rather difficult to attract your target audience. To create such content, you must have a thorough understanding of your customer base. You must be aware of the questions they ask, the challenges they face, and the possible solutions they are seeking. By being aware of all these things, you can create content which will instantly appeal to your audience.

Prioritizing leads

Having established your customer personas, it gives a marketer a glance into the lives and minds of your potential customers. You can redirect your marketing efforts toward those customers and leads who are in sync with your business's customer personas. When you are aware of the customer personas and where they usually spend their time, you can target the digital ads in those areas instead of generating random ads.

Stand out from the crowd

By spending the necessary time on researching, building customer personas, and creating good content, your business can easily stand out from your competitors. A lot of businesses tend to spend a lot of time talking about their business, but only a few spend time answering the questions which their potential customers might be asking. When you shift your focus to your potential customers, you will be able to reach them before they even realize they need your business. By acknowledging specific problems your target customers might be facing and giving solutions to the same, your business essentially becomes a trustworthy source of information the customers come to rely on.

Once you create the customer personas, your job doesn't end there. You must keep updating the personas from time to time. We live in a dynamic world, and you cannot expect any different from your customers. When you keep updating the customer personas, it helps ensure that your marketing efforts are generating the returns you expect.

Customer Persona Examples

Now that you are aware of the different benefits you can reap by creating customer personas, let us look at a couple of examples, so you know what an ideal customer persona looks like. A customer persona doesn't have to be lengthy, as long as it includes all the necessary information.

Online shopping has become quite popular these days, and rightly so. Online shopping helps customers save time, energy, effort, and even offers attractive deals. Here is an example of a customer persona for an online business selling shoes.

Name: Rachel Smith

Gender: Female

Age: 35

Occupation: Receptionist

Earnings: Over $35,000

Location: Los Angeles, California

Motivation: Rachel tends to get rather emotional while shopping for shoes in regular retail stores since her feet are quite narrow, and she seldom finds any that fit her perfectly. Dejected with her offline shopping experience, she turns to online shopping. Online shopping allows her to filter her requirements and find an ideal pair. Apart from this, she can also compare the prices of shoes across different sites and read the reviews posted before making a purchase.

Goals: She needs a SS (4A) width shoe. Is keen to purchase multiple pairs for different occasions. Hopes to find shoes that provide both style and comfort without compromising on either.

Frustrations: Limited choice available when the width-filter is applied. No other recommended shoe option is shown to simplify the shopping process.

When the business is aware of what their target customer is

looking for, it becomes relatively easier to deliver what the customer needs.

Here is an example of a customer persona a coffee shop can use.

Name: Sarah Geller

Gender: Female

Age: 20

Occupation: Student/ Freelancer

Earnings: $15,000

Location: Ohio

Motivation: Sarah is a student at the local university, and she likes to freelance as a content writer. She is looking for a place where she can work as well as study. Aims to find the ideal work and study environment which offers comfort along with good coffee and food.

Goals: She needs a place that serves good coffee at a reasonable price. A place that offers free Wi-Fi and offers good deals or coupons. It offers cozy and comfortable seating with plenty of charging stations and isn't noisy.

Frustrations: Inability to find all her requirements in one place.

Questions to Ask

Questions about the customer's background

Briefly describe the customer's personal demographics.

The best place to start developing your customer profile is by obtaining demographic information. It is not only easy to get but is the starting point of painting a more precise and accurate picture of your ideal customer. What is their marital status? What is their age group? What is their average income, and where do they reside? What is their gender? Do they have any children?

Write about their educational background.

What is their level of education? Which schools, colleges, or universities did they attend? Try to include specific names of the educational institutions.

Write about their career path.

How did they end up in their current job? Is the subject they majored in at school similar to their job profile, or is it different? Is their career path conventional or did they shift from one industry to another?

Questions about their work

What is their job profile or title?

How long has the customer held onto their current title or role? Does their job description include managing other employees, or are they an individual contributor?

Whom do they report to and who reports to them?

The seniority level of the customer in relation to developing the customer persona will depend on the product or service you are offering. If you are a B2C business, then this piece of information will help you gain insight into your customer's daily life. However, if you are a B2B organization, then this information comes in handy. Is your customer persona present at a director or a managerial position? The higher up in the organizational hierarchy your persona is, the more autonomy they have while making any purchase decisions.

How to measure their job?

What are the different metrics that your persona deals with? Which charts, numbers, or graphs does your ideal customer persona look at day after day? This information will help you understand what makes them successful and the things they might be anxious about when it comes to obtaining specific numbers at work.

What does a typical day in their life look like?

What time do they leave their homes to go to work, and what time does their workday end? What are their most productive hours during the day? What does a typical day at work look like? This information must include details about the way they spend their day at and outside their place of work. Do they spend more time at work or at home? Do they like their work? Is there any other place they would rather be? What are their hobbies, or what do they do in their spare time? What kind of vehicle do they own? Are there any specific TV series they like to watch? What kinds of clothes they usually wear? You get the gist, don't you? You can ask them personal questions as long as it pertains to their daily life.

What skills do they need to do their job?

If they had to hire someone as their replacement, then what are the skills required? What are the skills they possess to do their job? What are the ideal skills required to do the job and how well does your persona measure up? Where did they acquire these skills from? Did they get on-the-job training, have any previous experience, or undergo a certification course?

What knowledge and tools do they usually use in their job?

Are there any specific applications and tools they use daily? Getting to know about the products they like to use can help you understand how your products will fare.

Questions about their issues or challenges

What are their biggest obstacles?

You are in business because the products or services you offer a help solve a problem for your target customers. If that problem wasn't solved, how would it affect their daily lives? Try to elucidate how the said problem makes your target audience feel. For instance, if your business deals in personal taxation software, which is directly sold to the customers, one of the customer personas you create might be a first-time taxpayer. What are the different challenges a first-time taxpayer might face? Make a list of all the likely hurdles they might run into and offer an explanation as to how your business can solve the same.

Questions about their buying habits

Ask them to describe their recent purchase.
What were their reasons for making the purchase? What evaluation process did they undergo while selecting the product to buy? How was their buying experience? Would they buy a similar product in the future? Is there anything they would want to change about the buying process?

Do they search for products or services online before making a purchase?

Does your customer persona spend any time online to look for products and services and to compare the prices? If yes, then what are the different online portals they refer to? Do you ask others for their opinions before buying a product or availing a service?

Do they spend any time online on social media sites?

What is their go-to social media networking site? How frequently do they check their social media accounts, and what are their favorite pages? Do they read any online magazines and blogs?

Create Your Own Buyer Persona

Now, it is time to create customer personas for your business. Here are some questions you can ask while creating customer personas.

- Describe their personal demographics.
- Describe their educational background.
- Describe their career path.
- Where do they work and what is their job profile?
- What does a typical day in their life look like?
- What are their unique skills?
- Does their job require any special skills?
- What are their biggest challenges?
- What are their goals?
- What are their fears?
- What triggers them?
- What encourages them to buy?
- What is their buying behavior?
- Are there any obstacles they face?
- What is their online behavior?
- What platforms or apps do they frequently use?
- Do they have any brand affinities? If yes, then what are

their favorite brands?

- What are they looking for?
- What will make their life easier?

Once you complete this exercise and work out all these details, you will have a thorough idea of what your target customers are looking for. You can also go through the different stock photos available online and find one that fits your customer profile perfectly. It helps provide a clear image of your ideal customer for your business. Once you have a customer persona in place, it becomes easier to concentrate on your marketing efforts and make the necessary changes.

Chapter 2: Sales Funnel

About a Sales Funnel

A sales funnel is a marketing term that's used to describe the journey that a potential customer goes through on their way to making a purchase. There are various steps in a sales funnel which are generally referred to as the top, middle, and the bottom of the sales funnel. The names of these steps differ depending on the model of the sales funnel. The pain of missing out on a sale is something that all business owners are familiar with. At times, even after a couple of weeks of sales pitches, demos, conversations, and chatter, a prospective customer can drop out of a sales funnel without making a purchase. This is quite common. However, the chances of this can be reduced drastically by using the proper sales funnel. The sales funnels used by small businesses are like sieves with gaps left by barely held together spreadsheets, sticky notes, forgotten follow-up calls, and missed appointments.

There is a simple way to fix it, and that's by developing a good sales funnel that doesn't leave any holes. The different steps involved in the sales funnel help filter out people so that only the interested customers are in the funnel. As you go along, the process keeps narrowing the field of interested parties, and you will be left with a funnel-like structure.

The first phase of the sales funnel is referred to as the

"awareness" stage. This is the phase wherein people become aware of your business and the products or services you offer for the first time. They might have heard about your business from others, through social media, or even advertisements. The reasons for why and how such people move further along the sales funnel solely depends on your sales and marketing efforts. The leads formed along the middle and lower stages of a sales funnel are those that you must concentrate the most on since it consists of individuals who have moved from the phase of awareness to that of "interest."

Now you will be able to see the importance of a sales funnel. Even if the leads are quite good, they can easily slip out of the funnel if you don't nurture them carefully. The best way to minimize or even prevent such loss is by having a clear idea of all the steps that you must include in the sales process. You will learn about the different steps involved in the subsequent sections.

Sales funnels are necessary for all those businesses which depend on interaction and engagement with prospects for closing sales. Their sales process might be complicated, or they might merely be dealing with high-ticket items that require consideration and deliberation by the customer before making a purchase. All businesses which have either B2B or B2C models can use sales funnels. Businesses, as well as sales professionals, can use sales funnels. Sales managers and professionals tend to use sales funnels to plan their sales activities to improve their leads from the beginning of the funnel to its end. Marketing managers tend to use sales funnels for creating leads, which are in alignment with the business's brand and for establishing good customer relations for a higher rate of conversions. Business owners use sales funnels for a similar reason as marketing managers.

Different Stages

The stages in a sales funnel include all the steps that a prospective customer goes through, and they determine how close the lead is to being converted into a customer. There are five stages in a sales funnel, and they can be easily customized according to your business needs. The different stages are as follows.

Awareness

The first stage is that of awareness. This stage refers to the first time when your prospective customers become aware of your business, products or services, and your brand. It is primarily an introductory phase wherein they learn about who you are, what your business is about, and the factors which make your business unique.

Discovery

Once the prospective customer's interest is piqued, they move into the next stage, and that's discovery. Now, the prospects are quite curious about your business and the products you offer. The prospects are quite eager to learn more about your business. In this stage, you will need to provide them with valuable and educational content which is related to a problem or a need your prospects have. This stage takes place when you are qualifying a lead and are defining their needs.

Evaluation

Now, your prospects are armed with all the information they need. Once they have all the information they need, it is time for them to evaluate your business along with the products or services you offer. They will also be actively seeking out other options and comparing the different alternatives to see how you fare. At this stage, it is time to send your initial proposal or even a quote to them.

Purchase

In this stage, the prospect has decided to make a purchase, but the deal hasn't been finalized yet. They intend to buy but will want a proposal or a quote from your business regarding the price they are willing to pay. In this stage, you can negotiate the terms or even finalize the proposal. Once this is done, the prospect is ready to take the next step and seal the deal. Voila! Now your business has acquired a new customer. This is a sweet step, and it gives you a chance to ask the customer for referrals.

Loyalty

If your business deals with such products or services which will be delivered over a period, then it gives you a chance to offer other products which the customer might need. Essentially, it gives you the time to identify other needs and make any additional sales. However, if it is a one-time purchase, then this is the opportunity your business needs to establish loyalty and ensure repeat business. Most small business owners tend to combine the purchase and loyalty stages of a sales funnel and place them as a single stage.

Importance of a Sales Funnel

Selecting a marketing strategy

Most often, small businesses tend to blow their marketing budget on strategies that only yield minimal results. To avoid this, you need a sales funnel. It helps you understand the different marketing strategies and tools your business model needs to ensure success. For instance, if most of the prospects of your business are in the awareness stage, then you need to develop a marketing campaign that focuses on moving them along to the next stages of the sales funnel. Some marketers tend to focus on those leads which are in the decision phase of the sales funnel. If the marketers know which stage the leads are in, then they can take the necessary steps to move them further along the sales funnel and drive them to the goal-making a purchase.

Relate to the customer

Did you know that most businesses tend to operate in their own jargon? At times, the way the business describes its products, the content produced, or the way you talk to your clients helps move them further along the sales funnel. Once you can identify the stage within which most of the leads are present, then you can readily change the tone and content of your copy and create well-targeted content which will help convince the leads to move along the sales funnel.

Generating more sales

When you can select a good marketing strategy, the right marketing tools, and are aware of how you can relate to your prospects, you can drive more prospects toward the purchase stage. If you have good sales funnel management in place, then you will be able to generate more sales in the long run for your business. The fundamental principle of a sales funnel is to learn how you can methodically draw the outcome you desire from your prospects.

Standout from other entrepreneurs

A common problem faced by entrepreneurs, especially the newbies, is the lack of proper direction. They might have a ton of great ideas, but they aren't capable of executing those ideas since they don't have a system in place to implement them for making sales. Having a thorough understanding of a sales funnel gives you a competitive advantage over all those present in your chosen niche.

Grow your business

When it comes to business, there is no such thing as a perfect business model. A lot of those overnight success stories you hear about in business don't necessarily happen overnight. A sales funnel can help you obtain the essential feedback about all those marketing strategies which can help improve your sales. Not just your sales, but it also paves the way for developing and strengthening customer relations and loyalty. A combination of all these things helps in the growth of your business. For instance, you might have noticed that a lot of your leads who are keen on making a purchase don't finalize the deal because of the product pricing. When you have such insights available, you can easily use them to restructure your product pricing model and choose a price that works favorably for the business as well as the customers.

A sales funnel is certainly an integral part of a successful marketing strategy. As you begin to identify each potential customer's stage in the sales funnel, you will start to become adept at generating and converting those leads to improve your sales.

Possible Leaks to Plug

Once you are aware of the different stages you want to include in your sales funnel, it is time to analyze where you end up losing your potential customers. As a small business owner, you must sit down with your team at work and ask the following questions.

- What are the different obstructions in the sales process?
- Where does your business lose track of prospective customers?
- Are there any positive triggers that can help increase sales?

Take a close look at the different cracks present in the funnel, then fix them. There are three primary causes of such leaks, and they are as follows.

Moving over the "no's"

When it comes to sales, a "no" usually means "maybe not now, but later." For instance, a usual objection for a business that is selling customer relationship management software is, "I don't have the necessary time to get all the content finalized for making the platform useful." An objection like this means the prospect is interested in the product being offered but isn't ready at the moment. While working on leads, it might be rather tempting to ignore such leads and move onto a more viable one.

Instead of throwing away the prospects the moment they raise an objection to purchasing, you need to find a solution. You can develop an automated email follow-up system that addresses their objections directly. Whenever you encounter such an objection in the future, you can merely send the predesigned information to the prospect. It will certainly take some time and effort to convince the prospect to become a customer, but it will eventually happen if you are persistent.

Make a note of all the common objections you receive from your leads and think of how you can turn them around with useful content and an automated follow-up system. Identify the stages in your sales funnel wherein you are easily and quickly dismissing any prospects and work to fix the leak.

Failure to follow-up

Are you following up with your prospects as often as you should be? Well, a majority of businesses usually fail to follow up with their prospective customers. According to the National Sales Executive Association, about 80% of the sales are finalized between the fifth and the twelfth contact a business makes with the prospective customers. So, that's a lot of ground to cover. The challenge is quite simple - do you need to call new leads, or do you need to follow up with an existing lead for the fifth time? Persistence might feel like nothing more than a waste of time, but that's not what the data suggests. Automating your sales funnel is a good idea for small businesses. Instead of debating about whether to call existing or new leads, an automated funnel will help you do both. All your leads will receive regular, consistent, and friendly emails at all stages of the sales funnel. Take some time and analyze the last twenty leads you had and count the number of times you had to contact to enable conversion. This will help you arrive at an average number of follow-ups you will need to do to convert a lead into a customer successfully.

Being too slow

The data provided by the National Sales Executive Association also shows that a new lead is nine times more likely to convert provided you go ahead with a follow-up within the first five minutes of their expressing interest. Waiting for over thirty minutes brings this number down, and the lead is twenty-one times less likely to convert into a paying customer. You might be thinking it sounds impossible to be able to contact that lead within the first five minutes of them expressing their interest in your products. This is where an automated sales funnel management system comes into the picture. You must set up the system such that it generates an automatic response as you desire, which will be immediately sent to the prospects as soon as they express any interest. As the lead moves further along the sales funnel, you can program the automation system to send personalized emails that are in sync with the lead's movement in the sales funnel. Take some time and analyze the time that's usually taken to respond to a new prospect. Once you have this number, you can draft a mass personalized email that can be sent to all prospects readily.

Value Ladder

Imagine if there was a means you could use to maximize the purchases made by every customer of your business. Yes, this can be done, with the help of a value ladder. If you have never heard of this term, then it is quite likely that you have been letting go of several sales opportunities for your business. It can be rather tricky to precisely understand how much a customer is willing to spend without asking them this question directly. Usually, a lot of buyers tend to underestimate or even lie about their buying power, and most leads don't convert when they are faced with an entry price point.

Let us look at what a business without a value ladder looks like. For instance, you have three possible leads who want to purchase your product. The three potential customers are Customer A, B, and C, and each of them has $20, $50, and $250 to spend. Your business offers a variety of products between the price range of $30 to $70. Customer A cannot afford to purchase anything from your business and will therefore not spend anything. B is capable of spending $50 and might, therefore, ask for a discounted or a lower-priced product that will fulfill his need. If he gets a good deal, he will spend $50. Customer C will realize that even the most costly item available is well within his budget and will spend $70 readily. So, the total sales made add up to $120. If you had a value ladder, you would have been able to earn $320 from the sales. So, by adding a value ladder to your business, you can work on maximizing the purchases made by the customers.

Now you are aware of what happens to businesses that don't have a value ladder. So, what does a value ladder mean? It refers to a wide range of products or services listed in ascending order of their price from the lowest value offer to the highest-priced or premium category products. The customers are guided to make their way through each of these stages of the value ladder and maximize their spending. To fully understand the usefulness of a value ladder, let us go back to the previous example. You once again have three prospects, but your business operates quite differently in this situation. Instead of giving the prospects a price range of all the products available, you give them a free service or an extremely low-price product. Once this is done, you make an offer to the next tier of the value ladder in place. This will go on indefinitely - the best value ladders either have no endpoint or end such that it increases the chances of a repeat purchase.

In this case, the business starts its value ladder from $0, then adds products along with the price range of $5, $15, $30, $75, $125, $250, $500, and so on. So, what will happen to the three customers now? Customer A will accept the first free product, and this might go on to impress him so much that he goes on to spend his money on the next two tiers, too. The same happens to customer B, and he spends his budget on three tiers of products. Customer C walks away buying four tiers in the ladder - $5, $15, $30, $75 and spends $125. He is so happy that he got more than what he had bargained for and therefore, ends up spending the rest of his budget, too. Essentially, you end up with $320 in the form of sales, and your business has managed to maximize the customer's purchasing power.

The structure, along with the staging of the value ladder, is incredibly important in determining its success. In the previous example, the value ladder is structured rather perfectly, and this seldom happens in reality. Before you can start planning the different tiers of the ladder, you must understand one thing- the very first offer cannot be a sales meeting or a consultation. The first offer needs to be appealing and irresistible; it must be something that the leads usually pay for and are now getting for free. When you do this, the prospect is given a chance to see the value that your business is offering. This tends to influence and goad them into purchasing from your business.

Essentially, the free or low-cost offer is the bait you are setting. It helps increase the number of leads who step onto the value ladder. Not just that, it also helps increase awareness about your business, and you can create a list of potential customers, too. The tier after this one needs to be priced such that it covers the costs of the previous offer along with the current one. For instance, if the first offer costs you $2 and the second one costs $3, then the second offer needs to be priced at $5. Until now, you have done nothing but break even.

39

However, you have managed to provide two products to your customers at an incredibly competitive price, and the value they derive from your business has them hooked. Once you breakeven, every offer from now on will help your business earn a profit. You must ensure that the customers don't skip any stages because a value ladder helps maximize the customer's purchases only if they proceed in the desired order of spending.

Value ladders are quite common, and a lot of industries use different types of value ladders to attract and retain customers. For instance, a business selling snacks might offer the first box of snacks for free. The next step consists of offering a discount coupon for single-use at a supermarket. The third tier of the ladder consists of purchasing the product at its full price. The fourth tier consists of subscribing to receive the product once every month, and the final tier consists of upgrading this service to increase the frequency of the deliveries.

Chapter 3: Customer Journey

How do you determine what the customers want? What happens when you believe that you are offering your customers all that they need, but they end up shopping at your competitor's business? The simplest means of understanding what your business is missing is to go through a customer journey.

So, what is a customer journey? It is essentially a roadmap that shows you how a customer tends to become aware of your business, and the interactions they have with your business and your brand. Instead of merely concentrating on one part of the customer experience, the customer journey is a documentation of the entire experience of being a customer. That does sound like a lot to cover, but understanding the customer journey is not tricky as long as you stay organized.

By understanding the customer journey, you can help nurture and enhance the experience your customers have. Usually, whenever a customer purchases a product or uses a service, they expect that a pleasant feeling of happiness or satisfaction will accompany their purchase. This sense of satisfaction that people experience when they find something they want, and finally purchase and enjoy it is something a business must not discount. Customers tend to pay attention to how easy or problematic their entire experience was. If they have a positive experience, it is quite likely that they will either repeat their purchase or even tell others about the wonderful experience they have had. To get a better understanding of the customer journey, it is time to think about it from a customer's perspective. Whenever there is any scope to learn or explore, you will notice the word "(ping)" mentioned.

For instance, your potential customer is out shopping, and she sees your store along with all the signage (ping). She walks into the store and observes the store layout (ping). One of your employees goes to greet her (ping) and offers her assistance (ping). The employee is quite friendly (ping) as well as knowledgeable (ping) about the store and helps the customer choose something that meets her requirements. The potential customer is now ready to make a purchase, and she is assured that even if she does change her mind about the purchase, she can return the same within a week without any questions asked (ping). In the evening, your customer posts a picture of her new purchase on Facebook and also mentions your business (ping). She even recommends your store to all her followers on yelp.com (ping) because of the wonderful experience she had at the store. Now, you have acquired a loyal customer. After a couple of weeks, you send her a promotional email (ping) which gives her an exclusive discount (ping), and it reminds her of the pleasant feelings she had at the store and the values your business promotes (ping). This is just one instance. However, if you don't pay any attention and don't try to understand the mindset of your customers, then you will not be able to do your business any justice. If the potential customer has an unpleasant experience, then she might not even make a purchase. Or if her shopping experience was frustrating, then she will end up associating all those negative emotions with your brand and business. For instance, if she had to deal with rude employees, unhelpful employees, or couldn't find the product she was looking for, they all amount to a negative experience. If she ever has to buy the same product again, she will opt to go to your competitor's store because of the frustrating experience she had at your store. She might even convey her negative experience to others, and this can discourage other potential customers from doing business with you. You can certainly see the importance of paying attention to the customer journey now!

Benefits It Offers

Understanding the perspective of the customer is quite important when you want to understand the experience they have with your business. This is the primary reason why businesses concentrate on mapping out the customer journey for studying the customer experience and learning the places where there is scope for improvement. By analyzing the quantitative data and taking into account the feedback from customers and employees, a business can develop comprehensive maps that reflect the motivation and sentiments a potential customer undergoes on their way to becoming loyal customers. Here are all the different benefits of understanding the customer journey.

Understand underlying emotions

As potential customers go from one point to another, a map shows how easily they can do this. For instance, is your prospect able to get in touch with an agent quickly by using the IVR menu? Can the prospect switch from the business's social media page to the official page easily? What is the level of customer satisfaction after the contact is made? The answers to all these questions show how the prospect feels about every step of the journey and helps businesses improve their practices by identifying which ones tend to cause ambiguity or even frustration. Businesses can also learn about the different aspects of their workings which satisfy their customers and can divert their time and resources on perfecting such practices.

Identify any gaps

Mapping the customer's journey can also help identify any gaps which exist in the customer service you provide. For instance, you may be able to identify channels that are frequently used by the customer but are understaffed, which results in frustration on the part of the customer. Similarly, switching from the desktop to the mobile versions of your website might not be fully optimized, and this causes a communication gap. Any problems regarding the lines of communication between employees can also be discovered if the employees aren't able to receive the necessary support they need during customer interactions. So, mapping the customer journey helps you identify any gaps that exist in your internal routes of communication in your business.

Reduction of costs

Businesses that use customer journey analysis can also reduce their costs according to the research conducted by the Aberdeen Group. It is reported that brands which map customer journey can experience ten times the improvement in their costs of customer service when compared to those brands that don't. Also, an increase in the word of mouth publicity helps decrease customer turnover, which in turn reduces the costs involved in acquiring new customers for the business.

Better sales

If you are well versed in the customer journey and are aware of the different things you can do to make the customer experience better, it increases your sales. In fact, it helps increase the revenue generated from any upselling and cross-selling efforts of your business. Also, it helps in improving your marketing efforts, which in turn improves the ROI on your marketing practices. So, you can optimize your sales as well as marketing strategies with the help of the customer journey map.

Improved levels of satisfaction

As the customers get the experience they desire, the level of customer satisfaction will naturally increase. Also, when you work on improving the communication problems within the business, it improves employee satisfaction, too. When you are aware of what you want the employees to do, it becomes easier to explain the same to them. This improves their understanding of what their job is and how they can help attain the business objectives along the way.

Sales Funnel vs. Customer Journey

There is a difference between a sales funnel and a customer journey. A sales funnel suggests that the top of the funnel consists of prospects who are mildly interested in your business and are merely looking at all that you offer. The lower they move along in the funnel, the more the event of conversion becomes a certainty. This is a rather simple way to look at the process of marketing and sales. The customer journey helps map out all the possible touchpoints a customer goes through while moving along the sales funnel. Here is an example of what a customer journey will look like in the digital world.

The prospect comes across a billboard of digital marketing or perhaps a display campaign on YouTube while going through something else online. It is quite likely that the prospect was targeted because of their usual behavior or even because of the demographic. For instance, a woman in her late twenties might be an ideal target for a campaign or ads for pregnancy tests and other fertility products based solely on her age and gender.

Once the prospect has visited the website of the business, it shows their interest. The prospect might have downloaded a brochure, surfed through a couple of pages, or even requested a quote. Then it is time for remarketing the content on other channels like any of the social media platforms and news websites.

Then comes the moment when the prospect will likely engage in content marketing of your business. For instance, the prospect might view videos about a specific product she wishes to purchase. This is the stage wherein a prospect will probably search for your business online and click on the ads displayed by the search engine.

When the prospect is prepped to buy, she will probably directly search for the brand online, locate the store, or even order the product online.

After the action is taken, it is time to leave a review for the product. A stage that was traditionally overlooked in a sales funnel is the post-action phase. This is the stage where the customer shares their experience of doing business with your brand and posts the same information on social media or even passes it on through word of mouth. This is an important stage because this stage has the power of generating referrals for your business.

Steps to Follow

Customer Persona

The first thing to do before you can start mapping out the customer journey is to understand your customers. The best way to understand your customers is by creating buyer personas. You need to step into the shoes of your potential customers and understand their behavior, along with their likes and dislikes as well as their wants and needs. Yes, all individuals are different, but a buyer persona gives you the insight you need to map out the customer journey. If you have not yet developed customer personas, then you must do that right away. Follow the steps given in the previous chapters to come up with detailed customer personas for your business.

While you do this, you must remember that you need to have several buyer personas ready. The prospects at different stages of the sales cycle will act, think, and interact differently with your business. So, it is prudent to differentiate between those prospects who have been doing their market research for a while and are keen on purchasing from someone who has recently become interested in your business.

Understanding the customer's goals

Once you have curated the buyer personas, you must start digging around a little and try to understand the goals each customer hopes to achieve through their journey. Take some time and think about the ultimate goal of the customer in each phase. For instance, the goal of a customer might be to analyze the different options available in the market, make sure that they aren't overspending, or even find reassurance that they are making the right decision.

A simple way to go about this is to identify the different paths your prospects might take on your business website. If your prospect is a pre-existing customer, it is quite likely that the first step is to log in to their member profile on the website. Other activities you can concentrate on include searching for products, browsing the menu, comparing the products, and so on. Once you make a complete list of all the activities a customer might perform, you must make a note of the different touchpoints and goals related to each of the touchpoints.

Once you have an idea of touchpoints, you must determine the different goals a customer has at each of those touchpoints. By mapping out the goals, it becomes easier to understand whether your business has been meeting such goals or not. Here are a couple of different things you can do to understand the goals of your customers.

- Survey or interview different groups of customers

- Go through the customer support transcripts and emails
- Identify the different customer questions in each of the phases
- Obtain feedback for user testing
- Talk to the customers

Mapping out the touchpoints

A touchpoint refers to all those times wherein a prospect comes into contact with your business before, during, or even after making the purchase. It also includes different instances that can take place online or offline, via marketing, in person, or even over the phone. Some touchpoints tend to have a greater impact than others. For instance, a poor check-in experience at a hotel can taint the way the customer views their entire stay. You must consider all the possible touchpoints which take place between your prospects and the business. By doing this, you can ensure that you don't miss out on any chances of listening to customer feedback and making the necessary changes that can improve the customer experience.

So, how can you identify the different touchpoints? Since there are several ways in which customers experience your business, the idea of making a list of all possible touchpoints can seem overwhelming. However, by placing yourself in your customer's shoes, it becomes easier to go along their journey.

Here is a simple exercise you can use while making a list of the touchpoints.

"Where can I go (and how can I get there) when..."

... I have an (issue with which your business or product remedies)?

... I find the product or business which solves my issues?

... I make up my mind about making a purchase?

... I come across the business after making the purchase?

By answering these questions, you will have a list of all the touchpoints. Another way to go about this is to simply ask the customers about their experience with your business or even include the questions mentioned above in the customer feedback or survey.

If you have set up Google Analytics for your website, then there are two reports which will come in handy. The first one is the behavior flow report, which shows the movement of a customer through your website, one step at a time. It helps you understand the way a customer behaves, the different paths they take while going through the website, and the different sources, mediums, or campaigns they come from. Apart from this, it also helps you make a note of any pain points on your website that the prospects struggle with. The second report is the goal flow report. This report shows the path your prospects take to complete your goal of conversion. It helps show how the prospects navigate the sales funnels and if there are any points which have a high drop-off rate that must be addressed.

Identify the pain points

At this stage, it is time to put all your qualitative and quantitative data together and try to look at the big picture. You essentially need to identify any potential roadblocks, or any pain points your customer experiences on their journey. You must also make a list of all those things you are doing well right now and must think of ways to take things up a notch. To do this, you must interview your customers as well as your employees who deal with customers. Here are certain questions you can include in the interview.

- Are the prospects able to achieve their goals on the business website?
- What are the main spots which seem to be causing frustration and friction?
- Are the prospects abandoning their purchase at any stage? If yes, then why?

Once you are aware of the different pain points and obstructions, make a note of them on the customer journey map.

Fix the roadblocks

Here are questions you can ask yourself while trying to fix the roadblocks: What are the changes to be made and what must be corrected? Do I need to do away with everything and start from scratch once again? Or can I make a couple of simple changes that can improve the overall customer experience?

For instance, if you notice that customers tend to complain that the signup process on your website is complicated, then it is probably a good idea to revamp it and make it simpler for your customers. Once you identify the roadblocks that exist, take a look at the big picture. Understand that the goal is to optimize each touchpoint, not for the sake of optimizing it, but because it will help move the customers further along the sales funnel and encourage them to convert. After all, your goal is to increase conversions. So, remember that all the changes that you make must help you attain your goal.

Time to update

Your job doesn't come to an end after you create the customer journey map. It is not a one-time activity. You need to keep updating it constantly to keep up with the constantly changing and ever-evolving customer behavior. You will need to keep testing, updating it, and improving it at least twice a year if you want it to be effective.

Things to Keep in Mind

There are different customer touchpoints you must concentrate on while mapping out the customer journey. The customer touchpoints are all the times when the customer comes in contact with your brand or business. There will be different touchpoints like the ads you publish or your website with which your customers will interact. Once you assume the customer mindset, you can start listing out the potential touchpoints like the reviews on social media, your business website, the customer service team, and even feedback and follow-up surveys. While analyzing the different stages and mapping out the customer journey, you must keep the following in mind.

- Once you figure out all the stages of the customer journey, you must think about what the customer does at each of these stages. You must think about the specific actions the customer takes along the way.

- What are the things which encourage or prevent the customer from moving onto the next stage? Are there any motivations or emotions which the customer experiences at each stage?

- Are there any points where the customers get stuck? Do the customers have any questions and do they find it difficult to find answers to such questions? Do they experience any uncertainties which prompt them to give up and go to your competitors? Are there any inherent complications in the products you offer, and can you do anything to remove such complications?

- Are there any obstacles the customers face in each of the stages of their journey? Is it related to the cost of the products or services involved? Are there any troubles with the return policy? Thinking about all these things will help you understand the possible reasons why a customer drops out of the sales cycle without making a purchase.

You can use diagrams to map out the customer journey or even create a list of different scenarios the customer goes through at each stage. You can create customer feedback surveys to understand what changes they would like. Please remember that the experience and the journey of customers tend to vary, and some might even skip a couple of stages altogether in their journey. This is precisely why you must walk through different scenarios and talk to your customers to get a better understanding of their journey.

By following the steps given in this section, you can easily map out the customer journey. Now, here is a small assignment for you: Keeping the information given in this section in mind, take some time and start mapping out the customer journey for your business.

Chapter 4: First Stop- The Awareness Phase

The first stage of the sales funnel is the awareness stage. In this stage, the prospect has a need or an issue that must be solved. They might not know what is required to solve their issues or satisfy their needs. They might not know much about the need, problem, or opportunity available at this stage. Their research for the solution at this stage consists of using phrases or words to describe their problem, the relief they are seeking, or the means to fulfill their needs. The fact that this stage represents an opportunity for your prospect is seldom spoken about. If you are a B2B company and your target customer has grown enough to reap the benefits of the solution you offer, then the said customer is displaying the symptoms. You must be able to identify and name them. If your prospect has witnessed business growth and your solution can help them grow further and give them a competitive advantage, then you must know the symptoms they experience to create content which will resonate with them at this stage.

When your prospects are in this first stage of the sales funnel, they usually search to understand the negative symptoms they experience. All of these prospects tend to have a problem that must be resolved. Your prospects are usually searching online for:

1. Any symptoms which match their own

2. A better understanding of their problem

3. The name of their problem

4. The different available solutions

So, what do the prospects look for at this stage? Before you can start creating content to attract your potential clients, you must understand what they look for at this stage. At this point, they are merely looking for a better understanding of their problem. They want information and are actively seeking knowledge about the same. The prospects aren't thinking about your business, brand, or even your products at the moment. Now is not the stage to start promoting your product to them.

The content which you must create for this stage of the sales funnel must be essentially educational. It needs to add value to the prospects' lives and must help them understand their needs better. The relationship you want to establish with your customers at this point purely depends on the quality and usefulness of the content you provide them. The better the content is, the more they will want to read about other posts, come back for more, and perhaps share your content. The purpose of the content at this stage is to ensure that your prospects stick around and go through more content. Navigating your website at this stage will help them move along their customer journey.

At this point, the call to action for any business must be to offer them good quality and helpful content to read. This is not the time to offer them any discounts. Don't place any trial offers at the end of the articles you publish. The prospect isn't ready to buy, not yet. Exposing the prospects to unnecessary sales pitches will ruin any chances of selling that you had. Instead, it is time to invite them to go through more of your content. By exposing the prospects to good content, you can easily keep them around.

It is quintessential to make a note of the different sources which generate prospects who are in the awareness stage. The different sources include results on search engines, social media networking sites like Facebook, Instagram, Twitter, and the like, online forums and groups, guest postings, and backlinks. Understanding where the traffic originates from is quite important since it helps you optimize your marketing strategies. Most of these channels are important in almost all the stages of the sales funnel, but optimizing them for the awareness stage is a good idea if you want to increase the number of prospects of your business.

The success of your marketing campaigns will depend on your understanding of buyer personas and your ability to leverage them. It is quintessential that you have well-thought-out buyer personas for all types of customers your business can expect. You cannot develop magnetizing and appealing content for the awareness phase of the sales funnel if you haven't developed the buyer personas yet. Once you have the buyer personas, then you can start defining the journey that they will take as they try to resolve their issues and make their way toward a buying decision. When you detail and define the buyer persona and map out the customer journey, you will effectively be taking all sorts of the guesswork out of the equation and can concentrate on developing effective content.

All prospects start in the awareness phase. However, it isn't necessary that every buyer who visits your website is present in the awareness stage. This is the stage wherein the buyer persona begins to attain a greater awareness of their issue. The prospect is experiencing pain, challenges, or maybe an opportunity they never had before. The prospects have realized that something is amiss or that they have attained such growth or success that it creates the need for an answer. The prospect's goal at this stage is to understand their problem and find a solution. If you are interested in marketing effectively to all those prospects who are in the awareness stage, then you need to understand their mindset. Try to understand the problem they are facing and the motivations or emotions which encourage them to solve their problem. By mapping out the customer journey of the buyer personas you have developed, you will be able to get some clarity and insight about the buyer's mindset.

What kind of content are the buyers in the awareness phase looking for? The kind of content prospects in this phase will be looking for can be divided into three categories- a list of different symptoms, a description of issues, and information that's specific to the industry. As mentioned, the buyers in the awareness phase know they are facing a problem. They are asking questions about the symptoms which are similar to the ones they are experiencing. What they don't understand is that the symptoms they are experiencing can affect other aspects of their business, too. So, you will need to draw these people to your website with content that lists their symptoms. You must help them and inspire trust as you are trying to help them understand their problems.

You must create content such that it provides details and gives a list of all the issues they are facing and the potential problems they will face in the future if the issue is left unresolved. It is quintessential that you create content which contains what they are aware of because most of their research will be based on what they know. They will be looking up their symptoms in the online search engines. Your click-through rates will increase if the content you provide is not just relevant and of good quality but is well-optimized, too. The content must provide them with insight into their problems.

You can also provide them with lists, white papers, eBooks, and also content which provide industry-specific data, research, and reports about their situation. The content you make available must not only address their pain and symptoms, but it must also include the different options others followed and how it helped eliminate their problems. By including the experiences of other clients or by providing customer testimonials, you can convince the prospects to move onto the next stage of the sales funnel. Buyers are actively seeking information which points them toward a solution.

What are the pages that the buyers in the awareness phase usually visit? The buyers are only seeking educational content instead of sales pitches. If you have a blog, then the buyers will thoroughly review it in this phase. Ensure that you also include links to any other industry-related articles and data in these blogs. Your goal at this stage is to try to establish yourself as an industry expert. Only if the prospects think that you are an industry expert will they want to learn more about your business and products in the next stages. They are actively looking for content with high integrity, which will enable them to diagnose their problems. So, you must provide them with informative and well-written articles that offer quality content and are easy to understand. They need to be able to draw accurate conclusions from the information you give them. Only when this is done will they be willing to move along their customer journey and enter the next step in the sales funnel you have designed. Different social media sites will help the prospects in the awareness phase identify with others who have the same concerns. This allows them to connect with others who can give them helpful advice. As an industry expert, you must always have your prospect's best interest in mind. Your content along with other advice they receive from you must convince them that you are an industry expert. You need to carefully nurture your leads in this phase and help them move on. You will notice that it gets easier to convert a visitor to a lead and then into a customer if you provide them with the necessary content.

Since the prospects are looking for content that's trustworthy and informative, the format of content you use must convey the same. The best formats for content in this stage include reports of research, analysis of research, white papers, eBooks, and educational webinars and blog posts.

The landing pages you create must have certain elements that need to appeal to your target audience. Remember that the content you are creating must appeal to the specific buyer personas you have created. The landing pages need to contain an offer, an explanatory paragraph, several bulleted statements, form fields, along with a call-to-action or CTA button. The offer you present must be in a format that will appeal to your target audience. Try to create aesthetically pleasing three-dimensional images and titles or subtitles that are compelling and interesting. The offer must be accompanied by an explanatory paragraph that gives a piece of succinct and value-laden information which will make it difficult for the viewer to refuse. The things you are offering or the solutions you propose must be presented in bulleted statements which give a brief overview of how the prospect's problems can be solved.

The call-to-action or CTA button you place on the landing page needs to be quite compelling. Design it such that it inspires the viewer to take the action you desire. You can include a compelling image showing the outcome to be delivered by the content below the CTA button. The text included in the CTA must be more than a generic word like "submit," and must include something specific like "Click here to resolve your issue immediately." You also need to place form fields for capturing the information about the leads who visit the landing page. In the awareness stage, you must not request a lot of information from the leads - try to limit it to their email address. If you feel that having their first name along with their email address is important to provide them useful content, only then should you ask for both.

Nurture Them

Once you have the prospects in the awareness stage, you are required to nurture them so that they move along the sales funnel. How can a business nurture their prospects? You must understand that most of the prospects at this stage are rather overwhelmed. So, you need to nurture them so that they proceed forward gently. If you do this well, your prospects will certainly appreciate the effort you've put into providing them with educational material. The way you nurture your leads in this stage can give you a competitive edge over others in the industry. Here are a couple of things you can do to nurture your buyers:

The first thing you must do is ensure that you create trust. You must assure the buyers that you will be with them throughout the buying process. Some prospects need a little reassurance from time to time. The best way to do this is by showing the prospects that you only have their best interests in mind and that you will help them answer their questions and solve their problems or issue.

You need to create a reputation for yourself as an expert in the industry. The simplest means to do this is by sending them research, case studies, or any other high-quality and high-value content you come across. The information that you provide them with can influence their decision to buy or do business with you.

You must ensure that there are necessary channels in place that will ensure that relevant communication takes place regardless of the stage the prospect is in the sales funnel. You can maintain a good customer relationship through regular emails and phone contact. Your prospect will feel more comfortable in doing business with you and will warm up to your business if you nurture them.

Content for This Stage

Now, this is the most exciting part of this stage. By now, you must have an idea of what your prospects are expecting. You are also aware of the fact that you must nurture their interest as well as expectations. There is one thing that is left to decide if you want to win them over, and that's selecting the right topics for the content you create. If you wish to stand apart from your competitors in your niche, you will need to select the right topics. You might have probably established an editorial calendar for the rest of the month. It might work for you. However, if you are interested in nurturing your prospects at this stage and encourage them to move ahead, then you need to work on the topics you wish to develop content on. There are three simple steps you must follow to ensure that you come up with the right content for this stage, and they are as follows.

1. The first thing you need to do is identify the problem or need your product or business is fulfilling. A lot of people tend to create unfocused or extremely broad content for the awareness phase, and that's a mistake you must avoid. The content you create must not only be valuable, interesting, and educational, but it must also be well-targeted. If you wish for your prospects to regard you as an authority, then you must refocus and learn to be specific. You must concentrate on creating content around the problem or need your business can help the prospects solve. Doing this will enable your business to seem like an expert in your chosen niche. Also, by creating content that's focused on the need you solve, it makes it easier for prospects to move along the sales funnel rather quickly. For instance, if a business is selling custom-made shoes for those with narrow feet, then the need they are solving is quite specific. So, the content that the business needs to create during the awareness phase will be based on the problems those with narrow feet face and how the same can be resolved. Take some time and make a list of all the core

issues your business is solving, and you can develop content for them.

2. The second thing you need to do is spend some time researching all the trending topics associated with that problem. You can use Google or a tool like Buzzsumo. It will help you understand all the different topics that your prospects find exciting. Not just that, it will help you shortlist all those topics that will click with your ideal audience. Try to identify the top-performing content for those topics and strive to create better content.

3. The final step is to conduct a keyword search using tools like Moz Keyword explorer or Google. It is quite important that you make a list of all the popular and trending keywords related to the issue. Doing this will give you an idea about what others are looking for while in the awareness stage. Keep these keywords and trending topics in mind when you start creating content. Also, you must ensure that the content you are creating is optimized for search engines and contains all the important keywords.

Use Social Media to Build Awareness

Using social media to build awareness is the best way in which you can nurture the prospects in the awareness phase. Here are certain techniques you can use to build your brand's awareness online.

- The first thing you can do is start encouraging social sharing. You must encourage your fans and followers on social media to share your posts. The way they share your posts will depend on the platform you use. A retweet, a shared post on Instagram, or even a repin on Pinterest can help spread awareness about your brand to a new audience.

- Everyone likes to win contests. So, leverage social media for creating contests that will spread awareness about your business. Creating a simple contest wherein the participants stand to win a free product for the best caption they come up with for your posts is a good idea. This is a good means to engage your audience and introduce your business to a newer audience.

- Creating fresh and valuable content will automatically increase your popularity with your followers. The content that you create needs to be humorous, informative, educational, and engaging. This is the best form of content to create to nurture your prospects in the awareness stage.

- Regardless of the social media sites you use, you must ensure that you are always social. To create a loyal audience, you need to engage and interact with them. This can be done by reposting their posts or even through a simple shoutout to acknowledge the support and love your followers show your business. Always reply to comments and the messages you receive. If you appreciate your audience, they will soon start to reciprocate this sentiment. Another simple means to boost engagement is by asking questions.

- You must not use social media platforms as a means to deliver sales pitches all the time. Instead of telling them about how wonderful your products are, you can work on showing them how the products work, and the different benefits they can gain by using those products. By posting customer testimonials and reviews, you can develop the necessary social proof about your business.

- Start using hashtags specific to your business or any trending hashtags in your niche to create awareness about your business. By using the right hashtags, you can increase the visibility of posts on social media.

- You can work with influencers in your niche to create ads for Facebook or Instagram. By collaborating with influencers, you can organically grow the number of followers on social media profiles. Not just that, it is a great way to market to the influencer's existing followers along with your own followers.

Chapter 5: Second Stop - The Discovery Phase

The second stage of the sales funnel is the discovery phase. At this point, the prospect is quite interested in your business or the product you are selling. Even if they are interested, the prospects aren't ready for a sales pitch or even a conversation with a salesperson, not yet. Your idea is to keep continuing the education process you started in the previous step. You must keep providing them with new and updated information about your products or services. At this stage, the content needs to be informative, educational, and engaging. The best formats for content creation are case studies, demo videos, and webinars.

At this stage, you can start collecting leads and identifying their actions, which can help move them along to the next stage. For instance, if you are hosting webinars to engage your audience at this stage, then your aim needs to be to gently nudge them into moving onto the third stage of the sales funnel. The likelihood of those viewers who attend your webinar converting into your customers is quite high. Remember that the prospects are already interested in your business, but they need more information. Don't try to push them for a hard sell at this point. You merely need to work on nurturing the relationship you establish with them in the previous stage.

A lot of sales professionals tend to think of the discovery stage of the sales cycle as a stage wherein they can learn more about their prospective clients. This is an incredibly important aspect of the discovery phase, but there is so much more to it. As a business owner, you must place yourself in the shoes of your prospective customer and try to understand the customer journey.

You must remember that the prospect's goal at this stage in the sales cycle is recognizing their own needs. The potential buyers tend to ask themselves the following questions in the second phase of the sales funnel.

- Do I really have a need right now?
- How is that affecting my organization on a personal level or me?
- What is not going to be affected if I leave my need unaddressed?

If the buyers are seeking this while interacting with your business, then your objectives as a seller become quite clear. Your primary objective is to help the customer get a better understanding of their needs and the consequences they stand to face if their need is left unaddressed. Therefore, the goal of the discovery phase of the sales funnel can mean the following.

- To identify any critical business issue the prospect faces at this stage.
- Try to surface and intensify the awareness of their need

or problem and the consequences of not solving the need or problem.

- Try to help the buyer solve their problem or help satisfy their needs.

If you or your business can help achieve these three steps, then it will help establish and deepen the trust the buyer places in your business. However, how can you successfully identify, intensify, and internalize the discovery stage? The simple answer to this question is by finding the optimum balance between gathering information and sharing insights with the customer. You must not riddle the customer with a lot of questions. This is not the time to grill the prospect about anything. You must merely help the prospect understand the importance of addressing their needs or problem immediately.

Pique Their Interest

You need to work on piquing the interest of your prospects in your business or products so that they stick around. It is rather easy to sell to those who are interested in your products. The prospects might have done the basic research and have concluded that their solution lies with your business. Now, all that you must do is answer some of their questions, make sure that you get in touch with them, and stop them from going over to your competitors. However, how do you ensure that the prospects stay interested in your products? You cannot start a relationship with someone who isn't actively looking for a solution or trying to fulfill a need. This might be rather challenging. However, it is not impossible to accomplish. Here are a couple of simple things you can do to increase the interest of your prospects in your business.

Don't sell the product

Not everybody that you try selling to will be interested in purchasing your products. However, there is one thing that everyone is interested in, and that is their own selves. You must try to create a vision of what is going to happen once they purchase your product. This is a simple yet great way of increasing the interest of your prospects in what you are selling. For instance, think about Nike's caption- "Just Do It," or Burger King's slogan - "Have it your way." These captions and slogans don't tell you what the brand offers, but they do tell you what you can do by using their products. You must keep in mind that the prospect is interested in your business, but it is time to pique their curiosity about what you offer. The harder you try to pitch selling to them, the sooner will they drop out of the sales funnel. Instead, it is about making them curious about what your product can do and how it will help add value to their lives, which will make them stick around. For instance, if you are a copywriting firm, then you can go through the prospect's website, look for any possible errors, and then email the prospect with certain corrections and add the line "as your copywriter, I am happy to say that now your website will be 100% typo-free, always."

The sales and marketing professional who comes across as reliable and trustworthy is the one who is likely to be able to convince prospects of the desirability of buying the product or service promoted by him. Nothing conveys that better than the ability to solve problems.

Say you are a furniture salesman who is trying to sell a dining table to a customer and the only thing that keeps you from convincing him to commit himself is the fact that he prefers the table in a different shade, which your store does not have in stock. If you solve his problem by promising him that you will organize to get it from the head-office warehouse in the next four days, he will seal the deal. What worked for you here is not any fancy sales talk or glib promotion of some other dining table he did not want, but your ability to solve his problem.

Rather than worrying about the fact that you may not be an extrovert, which is merely a personality trait, you should focus on your ability as a problem solver. If you earn the reputation of a salesperson who is also an ace problem solver, both employers and customers will place a premium on your services and prefer to work with you than anyone else.

You can be biased

A lot of salespersons tend to pretend like they are unbiased to sound more credible. However, you must remember that your prospects probably know that you will be biased toward your products and business. In fact, there isn't a thing you can do to convince the customer that your opinions are unbiased. So, it is better to drop the pretense and instead redirect these efforts toward moving them along the sales funnel. It is better that you simply embrace your excitement for your products. If you believe that your products are the best there are in the market, then it is your opinion to which you are entitled. You need to merely share your opinion with your prospects and show your commitment to that opinion. Doing this will make your opinion seem more genuine and natural. This, in turn, will make the prospect believe what you are saying.

Learn from your prospect

Another simple way to increase engagement and keep the prospects interested is by making sure that your prospect feels heard and respected. Everyone likes being heard and acknowledged. If your prospect has any questions, ensure that you answer them as quickly as you can. This is not only a sign of professionalism, but it will make the prospect feel like their queries are valid. If your prospect expresses their opinions, then you must ensure that you acknowledge the same.

Build Lasting Relationships

The focus of a lot of business owners happens to be gathering new customers. However, you cannot let gaining new customers to be your sole focus. If you want to increase your sales, then you need to build good relations with all those prospects who enter the sales funnel. If you don't establish good relations, then the chances of the prospects dropping out of the sales funnel increase.

Now that you have developed the customer personas for your business, it is time to use that information to build good customer relationships. The customer personas will help you understand what the prospects are looking for at different stages of the sales funnel and you can use this knowledge to provide them exactly what they need. In this section, you will learn about the different things you can do to build a relationship and establish trust.

Good communication

You need to ensure that timely and efficient communication is a priority for your business. It doesn't mean that communicating with a single prospect must encroach into your business's productivity. However, if you can demonstrate to the prospects that you are available when they need you, it does show that customer satisfaction is your priority. You must also make it a point to answer the queries your prospects have and address any of their concerns. If you do this in a timely fashion, it shows that you take their concerns seriously.

Tell a story

Customers like interacting with a company they feel is "real." They generally don't want to purchase from or develop a consumer relationship with a corporate drone that they can't identify with. Connect with your customers by showing them that you and all the people who work with you in the company are real people. While most businesses only include their story on their website's About Us page, it's important to keep the idea circulating. You don't have to push that you're down to earth and your company is all about helping people because that can start to feel insincere. Instead, use your marketing campaigns to tell a story.

The point is to let your potential customers feel like they're a part of something bigger. If their presence positively affects your business and they know that, they'll be more likely to stick around. It's a well-known fact that we like to do things that make us feel like we're good people, so make sure your customers know they're a part of your story. You can do this by posting customer testimonials and photos, describing how your product helped someone, or even share a behind the scenes look that reminds your customers that their purchases affect many lives, not just your company's bottom line. When potential customers see this kind of community building, they start to realize that they're not just buying a product - they're buying into a niche group.

Positive attitude

You must ensure that all the communications you have with your prospects are always positive. As a business owner, you must train all your employees who deal with prospects to stay positive at all times. Exuding energy and confidence makes the prospects trust you, and they will also feel like being involved with your business. Enthusiasm and zeal tend to be quite infectious. So, you can attract optimistic responses from your prospects if you stay positive.

Customer service

If you have a specific business channel or dedicated staff who respond to customers, then you must ensure that the channels are fully optimized. You can also switch to online customer assistance to make it easier for your customers to reach you. This is a simple yet brilliant means to add value to the customer journey and will make you stand apart from your competitors. It also helps in generating positive word-of-mouth publicity for your business. Prompt and efficient customer service is important to ensure a good customer journey experience.

Exceed their expectations

Your prospects will certainly have some expectations about the products or services you offer. The idea is to exceed their expectations. You must ensure that you deliver what you promise if you want to establish good customer relationships. A simple tactic used by businesses is to underpromise and overdeliver. When you can exceed the customer's expectations, it will certainly impress them and keep them coming back for more. It can be something as simple as delivering a product sooner than the promised date of delivery. For instance, you can promise to deliver a product within a week, knowing full well that it can be delivered within two days. So, when the delivery does reach the customer earlier than anticipated, it will make them feel like you are working hard to keep your promises.

Online presence

You can use your online social media accounts, blogs, and business website to engage your prospects. Promptly respond to their queries, provide them with useful information, and give them all the details they need about your products. By doing these simple things, you can ensure that your prospects stay interested in your business.

Having an online presence also shows that you can be trusted. By establishing trust with your prospects, you will be able to portray your business as an industry expert. Once the prospects begin to see that you not only talk the talk but can walk the walk too, they will start to think of your business as a trusted source of information.

Build Rapport with All Customers

If you want to build a relationship with a potential customer or customers, you should always investigate before the meeting. If you know something about your potential customer, you can always prepare a few questions or comments that will improve the discussion. For example, if you find that your potential client or customer breeds Golden Retriever puppies, it would be nice to learn more about dogs. This does not mean that you should become an expert. You should find enough information about Golden Retrievers and ask a potential customer some interesting questions. A potential customer would like to share this information with you and look forward to sharing with you something that interests him.

Many people do not use traditional methods to build mutual understanding because they believe that this is fake. You may not be interested in Golden Retrievers or other topics that may interest your potential client, but you need to spend some time listening to someone who talks about them. You do this because you have to make a sale. There is some truth in this objection, but it is important to establish a mutual understanding with the customer before concluding a sale.

People will never buy a product from people they do not trust, but they will almost always buy from someone they like. For the most part, they will buy from someone who looks like them. If you meet someone with similar tastes, you will feel comfortable in the presence of that person because you know what they are like. That's because you like the same things. In the above example, talking to a potential customer about retrievers shows that you have something in common with them. This gives a potential customer the opportunity to tell you about their dogs, and it is more convenient for them to talk to you. When the conversation goes on to the sale, he or she is ready to listen to you with an open heart.

You must be extremely careful if you want to use this kind of method to build understanding. This is because you need to bring a certain aspect of manipulation with you. It's perfectly acceptable to talk to someone about his or her hobbies, whether you're in the office or at a party. But, you should never go beyond the limit of deception. If you do not like the idea of exhibitions, you should never start a conversation and pretend that you agree. Not only is this wrong, but the potential customer will know that you are not as honest as you say. If you know that a potential customer has a hobby that you disapprove of, you should not discuss it at all. He or she may have many other interests that you can talk about, and there will be something that interests you and fits your perspective.

Even in sales situations, always be authentic. Most customers know when you're being dishonest in order to make a sale, and this will ruin any trust or rapport you had started to build.

Be friendly

A person who is cold to another person will receive the same reaction. You should always approach customers with warmth. You need to smile, make eye contact, give them a firm handshake, and engage them in conversation. Have a system in place to ensure your employees are friendly, too.

When customers feel that they are liked, appreciated, and they have a good experience with you and your business, they are more likely to turn into lasting customers.

Show real interest

This was mentioned earlier, but it shouldn't be surprising, as people often focus on themselves. This is a feature that will help you with sales, as you need to know more about your potential customers so that you can identify the best course of action. The buyer always wants to be able to communicate what he thinks, including his fears, problems, or wishes. They always want to feel that they are being heard. The more you show them that you listen to them, the more relaxed they become and the more willing they are to share information.

Find a common language

People often prefer people who are like them. This means that you can disclose some common interests that will help you build a better relationship with your prospective client. Maybe you went to the same school or you were born in the same city. You can also talk about your children if you want to. No matter what it is, you should find similarities that allow you to connect and communicate.

A new salesperson is often sensitive when it comes to the time he or she spends with a customer. They always think that they only have one hour or less to make an impression, and they feel they should use this time to convey all their points. They waste no time talking and dive into the commercial area without icebreakers. That is not a very good strategy. There are cases where there is too much talk and the customer wants to get to work, so always read the person you want to talk to and understand how much time you can spend talking.

You need to make sure that you are yourself, but you need to remember that you have to change your approach depending on the person or company you are selling to. You should never change who you are, just your tone or the way you communicate with people in your environment, depending on the culture.

Tools to Use

Once your prospects learn about your business and are interested in what you offer, you have pretty much gotten them hooked. Now, it is time to reel them in and help them move along the sales funnel so that they convert. Here are a couple of tools you can use to prevent any prospects from getting away.

- Once your prospects visit your website, the last thing you need from them is to drop out of the sales funnel completely. So, you need to be able to create a website that will keep your visitors around. A helpful tool you can use to create engaging and informative landing pages in Unbounce. By ensuring that the prospects stick around for longer, the chances of them converting into paying customers to increase.

- Do you ever think about how others use your site? If yes, then you should use CrazyEgg. This tool displays the different points at which most people click on your page. It essentially gives you heatmaps of all the links the customers click on when they visit your business webpage. You can use this data to optimize your webpages to ensure maximum conversions.

- If you are interested in learning about what each visitor does when they visit your site, then you must start using FullStory. This service essentially records the way prospects navigate your website and even shows the recorded data in the form of a video you can view later.

- If you are interested in collecting information from all those who visit your website, then you need HelloBar. This is a simple service that shows up in the form of a sticky bar on your website. The prospects are required to enter their email address in the sticky bars displayed on the screen so that they can be contacted later.

Additional Tips

There are a couple of simple tips you can follow to establish trust with your customers. The best option available at your disposal is to put up customer testimonials and product reviews of your business and products online. A potential customer would have done all the research they need about your products and business. By going through favorable reviews, it will convince them that choosing your business is in their best interest. You can ask your previous customers for their testimonials or reviews and can strategically place them on your business website and social media accounts.

Now that the customer is aware of the different products or services you offer, it is time to try and tip the scales in your favor. Everyone likes offers and discounts. So, it is time to leverage this fondness for discounts to increase your sales. You can offer discounts or offer higher-end products at a reduced price for a limited time. By creating a temporary sense of urgency, you can convince your prospects to move along the sales funnel.

If you have a brick and mortar store, then you must ensure that you place the address for it on your website and your social media profiles. You must ensure that your prospects can easily contact you. You need to provide viable contact information, including a phone number, address, and email address.

As you are engaging your social media accounts, please remember that you are trying to establish a good rapport with your prospects. The best way to do this is by engaging with them and promptly responding to their comments or queries. The longer you take to respond to the prospects, the less will they be interested in doing business with you.

Chapter 6: Stop Three - Evaluation Begins

If you want to create content which will appeal to your prospects, then you must ensure that you have a thorough understanding of the different phases a buyer goes through. In this chapter, you will learn about the third step in the sales funnel, and that's evaluation. In this section, you will learn about ways in which you can attract traffic, create content which is ideal for prospects in the evaluation phase, and certain tips for marketing yourself to enable conversion.

In this stage, your prospects are aware of their problem or need, are interested in the solution or products you offer and are now considering all the options available to them. These prospects are essentially evaluating the solution or products your business offers. Now that we have defined this stage, it is time to start decoding this stage of the customer journey.

So, what are the different thoughts that you might have at this stage? You might be wondering about how you can attract more customers. Or maybe you are thinking about ways in which you can increase the traffic to your site. Do you want to learn about techniques that can help in moving the customer to the final stage of the sales funnel from this stage? Are you wondering about how you can manage your social media accounts? It is normal to have all these thoughts, and you can answer them once you go through the information in this section.

Here are certain questions that you must ask yourself while deciding on the kind of content your prospects will need at this stage.

- What are the different types of solutions the prospects can investigate?
- How will the prospects educate themselves about the different options available?
- How do they analyze the pros and cons of each option?
- How do the buyers decide which solution is good for them?

By answering these questions, you will have the insights you need to create the ideal content along with the keywords you must use for leveraging your content.

What do the buyers usually look for in this stage of the sales funnel? Most of the prospects in this stage tend to compare the different solutions available to solve their problems. As a business owner, it is your duty to help answer their questions and provide them with helpful information, which in turn will encourage their conversion. A majority of buyers tend to search for information at this stage and haven't made up their mind about making a purchase, at least not yet. The world wide web offers a plethora of information to the prospects. When you are thinking about marketing to those in this stage of the sales funnel, you must not only understand what they are seeking, but what they are looking at, too. You must refocus your efforts on the content that your prospects view. A little research and you will be able to determine the kind of content which attracts response from the buyers.

What are the different pages the prospects will visit in this stage? Your prospects will be visiting those pages which include the keywords they are looking for. So, you must make it a point to include such keywords and phrases in the content you create, which will attract your prospect's attention. The different formats of content which will work well in this stage include blog posts, any downloadable content, and email marketing.

Prospects will want to decide based on their logic, even if it is known that you can persuade the buyers with emotion. So, this is your chance to appeal to the logic of your prospects, and you can use quantifiable data for compelling them emotionally to choose the solution you offer. You must be knowledgeable about and explain the best course of action to them and must give them examples or even case studies to show the outcomes they can expect. To do this, you can rely on the positive experiences other customers had in the past, like customer testimonials. You can use your knowledge about the industry as well as the understanding of their issue to offer them a solution.

Compelling, well thought out, and well-written content which addresses the specific needs of the prospects will help them understand the different challenges they are facing and the cost of solving the problem. As you have been trying to establish in the previous steps, you are an industry expert, and you must offer your expertise to your prospects. The information you are providing your prospects must be in sync with the wants and needs of the customer personas you have developed.

You need to earn the prospect's trust. So, you must help further their understanding of their problems. You need to examine your customer and the customer personas carefully. Here are some questions you must ask yourself at this stage.

- What is the customer's purchase behavior?
- What kind of research and information does the prospect need at this stage?
- Are there any essential keywords or relevant phrases that the prospect will use at this stage to facilitate their research?

To write content which is appealing, searchable, and conversion-inducing, you must use your in-depth understanding of the ways the prospects can use your products. The content needs to directly address the concerns as well as the goals of the prospects. Here are a couple of topics you can use to relate to the prospect.

- The prospect's approval process.
- Their specific environment and the different steps they must go through to implement your solution and optimize the returns.
- The usual challenges or obstacles that will come their

way while using the product.

- The different opportunities which will crop up while they are using your solution to satisfy their need or address their issues.
- The different unique experiences a specific customer's persona will experience from the stage of recognizing their needs, understanding their problem, finding the best solution, and making the purchase.

The best format to offer content to the prospects at this stage includes lists of pros and cons, comparisons, expert advice, and even live interaction.

If you have content already, you might be wondering if you can use it by repurposing or refreshing the older content in this stage. Well, you can repurpose old content if you do the following.

- Take stock of all the content available to you.
- You need to delete or edit it such that all the vague verbiage or any ambiguity present in it has been deleted.
- You need to update it with recent facts and data.
- You can use all the existing content and propose the information in the form of an attractive offer.
- You can modify or even create a new landing page for providing your new offer to the prospects.

A landing page is a web page your prospects will end up on after they click your business link. This is one of the best marketing tools you have at your disposal, and when you create effective landing pages, you can encourage your prospects to move onto the next phase of the sales funnel. You must understand that your prospect is willing to exchange some information if you provide them with an irresistible offer. The offer you propose must be such that it brings the prospects a step closer to solving their problem or need.

So, what are the different elements that must be included in the landing page at this stage? The first thing to be included is an attractive title for the offer. You must use certain keywords and phrases that your prospects might be looking for, like "tips to," "how-to," "what to," etc. You must not forget to use specific terms related to the products or services you offer like "fashion," "real estate," "marketing," or the like. You need to include a small paragraph describing all that you are offering your prospects. You need to explain how the prospects will benefit from your offer and how it will add value to their lives if they decide to accept it. You need to include bulleted impact statements which describe the key features you want prospects to focus on while going through the content you provide them. Apart from this, you must include a CTA button and form fields. The CTA button you design must encourage the prospects to take some action which will move them along the sales funnel.

Now that you have created a well-optimized landing page, the next thing you must be wondering about is how you can direct your leads to that page. Well, the answer is simple - you need to create content which will be relevant, helpful, and informative to the prospects.

Are there any specific key terms and phrases you must use in the content that you create for this stage? As mentioned earlier, the sole focus of prospects at this stage is to look for different options that will help them solve their issues. You must try to optimize and maximize your online traffic by including certain keywords and phrases. Here are a couple of examples of how you can design the content for this stage of the sales funnel.

You can include solution-specific terms in the content like "improve," "fix," or "redesign." The landing page will also be a part of the search results the prospects will search for, so it needs to offer them a concrete solution. You must call attention to your industry expertise along with the products or services you offer. Start thinking like your prospects or use your buyer personas to understand the different words and phrases you can incorporate in the content you create. All the key terms you make a note of need to be present in your offer title, the copy of the landing page, the CTA button, emails you send, the email subject line, post titles, and all the posts on social media.

Once you manage to attract your prospects, the next step is to guide and nurture them into the next stage of the sales funnel. Establishing a relationship based on trust with your prospect is quite important at this stage. If they are not prepared to move onto the next stage, then you need to stay in touch with them and slowly nudge them in the desired direction. You can send strategically planned emails to help them along. They might even need a little reassurance along with some hand-holding at this stage. Use the tips mentioned in the previous step to establish trust and your reputation as a problem-solver in the industry. You can send them information about other customer success stories, lists of product comparisons, any company-related news, and provide them all the research which will give them a better understanding of the solution you are proposing.

The continuous stream of interaction will ensure that your business or products are a part of your prospect's thought process. Once you do all this, it is time to pass on the lead to the marketing or the sales team. You must do this to ensure that they move along the sales funnel and close the deal instead of dropping out of sight. How will you determine when a prospect is ready to leap? You must start using sales tactics when you notice that the information being used by the prospect is no longer in the consideration phase, when the prospect starts looking at the pricing plans or pages, or when the prospect requests to talk with a sales rep.

Principles of Persuasion

There are certain principles of persuasion you can use in the evaluation phase of the sales funnel, and they are discussed in this section. Dr. Robert Cialdini described six principles of persuasion, which were explained in his famous book, "Influence." Three of those principles can be employed by you when you are trying to convert your prospects and move them toward the final stage of the sales funnel. For more than sixty years, researchers have been trying to understand the different factors which influence people to say "yes" to others. There is no doubt that persuasion is a subtle art by itself, but there is a surprising amount of science which is involved in this equation. Whenever someone needs to make a decision, it certainly sounds nice to think that they consider all the information available at their disposal, and this determines their thinking process. However, the truth is quite different. We all tend to lead extremely stressful lives. In this busy world that we live in, we constantly seek shortcuts to help guide our decision-making process and reduce the amount of thinking that one needs to undergo. There are six universal shortcuts that dictate human behavior, and they are reciprocity, authority, scarcity, liking, consistency, and consensus. The three principles of persuasion you will learn about in this section are reciprocity, scarcity, and authority. By understanding these principles and using them ethically, you can help in increasing your chances of persuading your prospects to convert into paying customers. Let us learn more about each of these principles.

Reciprocity

The first principle of influence, according to Cialdini, is that of reciprocity. It essentially states that people feel obligated to give back to others the form of service, gift, or even behavior that they have received from them. For instance, did you ever feel like you were obliged to invite someone to a party because they had invited you to a party in the past? If someone does you a favor, you automatically assume that you owe them a favor regardless of whether the same is stated or not. When it comes to social obligations, people are quite likely to say yes to those whom they owe something.

One of the best demos of the principle of reciprocity in action comes from a series of experiments conducted in a restaurant. Think about a situation where you go to a restaurant, and the waiter gives you a gift. Perhaps while bringing the bill to your table, the waiter gives you a free fortune cookie, a piece of cake, or maybe even a mint. So, the question is, will this gift you receive have any influence in determining the tip you leave the waiter? A lot of people might say that it will not have any effect. However, that simple mint which was offered can make a lot of difference. In a study that was conducted while researching the validity of this principle, it was noticed that the tips given by patrons who were given a free mint at the end of their meal increased by about 3%. It is interesting to note that when the patrons were offered two mints, the tips didn't double. The amount given as tips quadrupled, and it resulted in a 14% increase in tips given to the waiter. However, the most interesting thing about this experiment is that in one scenario the waiter walks away after giving a free mint, and then turns back and offers another mint to the patrons along with a compliment. The instances wherein this was done, a whopping 23% increase in tips was noted. It is not merely about trying to influence others that matters; it is also about the way you influence them. So, to use the principle of reciprocity, you must ensure that you are the first one to give something personalized and rather unexpected.

When you are trying to move the prospects along the sales funnel, you can use this simple principle. It is about doing something for someone without establishing a quid pro quo. You can use this principle while creating content. You can provide free access to certain content without asking visitors to register. When you send your prospects content or even give them free advice, it makes the prospects more susceptible to persuasion later.

Scarcity

The second principle of persuasion propounded by Cialdini is scarcity. It essentially states that the demand for those things is always higher when they are scarce. In 2003, British Airways announced that they would not be operating the

London to New York Concorde flight twice a day because it became uneconomical for the airlines to maintain. The day after this announcement was made, the sales for this flight service increased drastically. Observe that there was nothing that changed about Concorde itself. The flight time didn't decrease, there was no change in the service, and the airfare didn't decrease. The only difference was that it became a scarce resource. The result of this was that the demand for it increased.

So, when it comes to persuading others to act the way you want them to, the principle of scarcity wins. It is not sufficient to merely tell others the benefits they can gain if they choose the products or services you offer. You must also make it a point to tell them what makes your business unique. Tell your prospects about what they will lose if they don't consider your offer. This tends to create a sense of scarcity, which in turn prompts them to act quickly.

The human psyche is such that the chances of purchase increase if the prospects are informed that a special offer will expire soon or if they are told that it is the last product available. Essentially, people will come to believe that they will miss out on something they must have if they don't act quickly. This is a principle of persuasion that is commonly used by businesses to increase their rate of conversion. For instance, Orbitz.com included a line "Act fast! Only two tickets are left at this price!" in one of their ads. This tells the prospects that the supply of air tickets is limited and will not last long. By creating a sense of scarcity, Orbitz is trying to convince more prospects to convert. Scarcity can also be time-limited. For instance, if you include a blurb that says "this offer ends in two hours" while listing the products online, it creates a sense of time-bound scarcity. By adopting this principle, you will essentially be giving your prospects the nudge that they need to move in the direction you desire without seeming pushy.

Authority

The principle of authority is based on the idea that people tend to follow those who they perceive as being credible and experts. For instance, the ability of physiotherapists to persuade their patients to comply with their recommended exercise regime increases when they display their medical diplomas for others to see. Another everyday example is that people tend to pay a total stranger for the parking meter if the person requesting the payment is dressed in a uniform instead of casual clothes.

The science involved in this principle is quite simple. When you signal to others that you are a credible and knowledgeable authority, then the chances of them being persuaded to increase. Before you influence them to listen to you, you must first establish that you indeed are credible and knowledgeable. Of course, this can also cause certain problems - you cannot go around talking about your brilliance while interacting with your prospects. However, you can certainly make someone else do this for you. It doesn't matter if the person introducing you is connected to you or not. The only thing that matters is the introduction they give you to the prospects.

In a study, a set of real estate agents were able to increase their number of property appraisals and contracts when they arranged for their receptionists who answered customer inquiries first to mention the credentials and expertise of their colleagues. So, all those customers who were interested in letting out their properties were told something along the lines of, "Lettings? Well, let me connect you with XYZ, who has more than fifteen years of experience in dealing with letting out properties in this area." This led to an overall increase in the number of appointments along with signed contracts.

Take a moment and think about it - people tend to have an innate tendency to obey all authority figures. It is an inherent trait of the human mentality. Certain prefixes or job titles like that of a Dr. tend to make such people seem like authority figures and experts.

ShoeDazzle used this principle to increase their sales. It is an internet startup that sells accessories and shoes for women. It was founded in 2009, and Kim Kardashian is its co-founder. She also acts as one of the chief fashion stylists for this venture. Even though this company was founded by Brian Lee and Robert Shapiro, it didn't help increase conversions or attract more buyers. This happened when the company decided to bring Kim Kardashian on board as a co-founder. Regardless of what your personal feelings are about Kim, she is perceived to be a style icon by most of the young shoppers - the target demographic of ShoeDazzle. This helped in increasing the sales recorded by this venture.

Chapter 7: Final Stop - Seal the Deal

Well, the prospect has a need, has done all the necessary research, and has now decided to make the purchase - finally. All the stages which lead up to the conversion event have been completed. The prospect has come a long way, but this doesn't mean that things have come to an end. Marketing at the final stage of the sales funnel is as important as it was at all the other stages. If you don't take the necessary steps, you can still lose out on a customer. Marketing needs to be quite simple and straightforward at this stage. If you have an online website for sales, then ensure that you carefully test it to make sure that navigating it is easy and not complicated. Are there too many steps involved in this process? Does it take too long to process the requests? Is the website optimized for desktops as well as mobile devices? Ask all these important questions, and the answers to these questions will help determine whether the website is effective and efficient or not. If the purchase process seems too difficult or intimidating to the customer, then you can essentially lose out on a potential customer.

Once the prospect is certain of the solution which works best for them, the prospect enters the decision stage. In this stage, the prospect will be essentially compiling a list of all the different businesses and brands which offer the same solution as yours does. The prospects will them evaluate which option works out the best for them and go with it. Once the prospect has decided upon the product to choose, they enter the final stage of their customer journey. These individuals are no longer your prospective buyers; they are your customers now. They are in a stage where they need to decide whether they are delighted with their decision or not. They are looking forward to gaining all the benefits that the products offer. You must use good customer service at this stage to ensure lasting customer relationships.

Also, you must remember that just because the customer has made a purchase, this doesn't mean the process has ended yet. There is a post-purchase stage wherein you need to work on creating a loyal audience of brand advocates for your business. This stage matters because customer loyalty and advocacy help generate revenue for the business. After a purchase is made, it is an important part wherein the customer needs to decide whether they are happy with the purchase that they made or not. It is time for them to evaluate their decision.

If the customers feel like they made the wrong decision or took the wrong call, then they can easily return their purchase. You can mitigate this risk by ensuring that the customer's journey was a happy one and that they had a pleasant experience dealing with your brand. However, even if you have a satisfied customer, you must understand that the chances of repeat purchases in the future are still not guaranteed. So, to ensure that the customers stay loyal to your business and return in the future for more purchases, you can send them follow-up emails and surveys to understand whether they were satisfied with their experience or not.

The final stages of the sales funnel include evaluation and purchase. In the evaluation phase, the buyers are trying to make up their minds about whether to purchase something or not. Usually, the marketing and the sales teams both need to work closely to convince the prospect that their brand is the best solution for the buyer. Once this is done, the prospect will move onto the purchase stage. This is a chance for the business to leave a positive and lasting impression on the buyer.

Customer Experience Funnel

Here are the different stages of a customer experience funnel that your customers go through.

Repeat

Once the customer makes a purchase, the next thing you need to start concentrating on is to ensure that you transform them into a repeat customer. It means you need to work on customer retention and nurture the customer relations you create along the way. Repeat customers to ensure that you can generate revenue from the existing customer. You will need to work on marketing even after the purchase phase to ensure that the customers keep coming back for more.

Loyalty

In this stage, the customer develops a conscious liking for your business and starts to identify themselves with your brand and business. At this stage, engagement is quite important, and as a business owner, you need to work on nurturing the positive relations and connections you make with the customers.

Referral

Once you have managed to establish the loyalty of the customer for your business, the chances of them referring your business and products to others tend to increase.

Advocacy

You need to concentrate on transforming your loyal customers into advocates of your brand and business. This is the ultimate goal of a business owner for nurturing their existing customers. When your customers are happy with your products and business, they will want to share their positive experiences with others, too. By posting on social media about their positive experience and through word-of-mouth publicity, they tend to become self-appointed advocates of your brand. The publicity and marketing which comes organically from your existing customers is something that cannot be simulated by any other means.

The goal of all these steps is to increase your bottom line by increasing your sales and awareness.

What thoughts does the customer experience at this stage while evaluating the products and your business? The prospect will usually be thinking about the costs involved, the timeline for delivery, the results which are promised by you, and about the customer support they will need along the way. All of the prospects in this stage are trying to understand all the different aspects of their chosen solution fully. The prospects are trying to think about their future once they have their chosen solution ready. This is where content creation steps in. The aim is to understand what your prospects are looking for at this stage and making sure that you can create such content which proves to be relevant to them.

So, what are all the prospects looking for in this stage? In this stage, the prospects are certain that they want to purchase a product from you or pay for the solution you are offering. The prospects have compared the products you offer with those offered by your competitor and are now happy with their choice. However, for them to arrive here, they will need some content and information. As a business owner leading your prospects through the final stage of the sales funnel, it is time to deliver your sales pitch. You need to highlight to the customer the different reasons why they need to opt for your products. You need to explain how your business differs from your competitors and how you are better. Explain the reasons why they need to opt for your solution and explain all the value they stand to gain. While doing all this, you must also make it a point to include information to certain questions the customers might have. The customers might be wondering about how long it will take for your solution to solve their issues and create value as promised. The customers will be thinking about the costs involved and the results you promised.

At this stage, the prospects will be looking for information which will help them make the final call. The information they will be looking for at this stage is about whether the solution you are offering is the best one or not, about how competitive your prices are, and the quality of the products you offer. The two important web pages all the customers will refer to in this stage are the About Us page and the Products and Service page of your business.

The buyers will be paying close attention to your business's About Us page at this stage, and you must design this section such that it creates a professional first impression on the visitors. You must include information about the different services and products that you offer, your business objectives, and goals. You must understand that your buyers are looking for information which will give them the confirmation that your business is indeed the best option available for them. You can also include customer testimonials in this section. By providing case studies along with quantifiable facts, your business will look more trustworthy to potential customers.

The other page that your buyers will be keenly going through is the product and service description pages on your website. The buyers will want to know everything about the products and services you offer before sealing the deal and purchasing something. Keep in mind that the prospects in this stage are looking for certain reassurance to ensure that they are indeed making the right decision. They will carefully go through different pages like the one which displays information about your customer service team, the delivery policies, and the terms and conditions applicable to purchase.

The best forms of offers at this stage which can be made to your potential customers include free trials, live demos, consultations, and any discounted services, product discounts, or coupons.

Principles of Persuasion

Apart from the three principles of persuasion which were discussed in the previous chapter, there are three more that you must focus on. The other principles of persuasion enumerated in Robert Cialdini's book *Influence* are as follows.

Consistency

It is a basic human desire that people like to be consistent with the things they might have said or done in the past. Consistency is usually triggered by asking and seeking small forms of initial commitments that can be made. In a famous study, researchers noticed that very few individuals were willing to put up an unsightly wooden signboard on their front lawns to support the Drive Safely campaign started in their neighborhoods. However, in a similar neighborhood, about four times as many homeowners indicated that they would be happy to erect a similar signboard. Why is this? Well, ten days before this, all those homeowners had agreed to place a postcard on their front windows which signaled their support for the Drive Safely initiative. The small postcard they were required to put up acted as the small commitment, which led to the bigger change.

So, while trying to influence others, use the consistency principle propounded by Cialdini. The directive of this principle is to seek voluntary, public, and active commitments from others before getting them to do anything.

This principle states that humans have a deep-seated need to be seen as being consistent. As such, once someone has made a public commitment to do something, then the chances of them following through with their commitment increase tremendously. This is based on the psychological makeup of humans, which compels us to act according to the commitments we make. Most marketers use this principle for increasing their rates of conversion. Marketers employ this technique to increase their site visitors by offering them something free of costs like a sample or a guide. Copyblogger, a popular website, uses this principle of persuasion. Copyblogger is a popular blog, but it is essentially a training and software organization that sells content marketing software and tools via Copyblogger Media. On their homepage, you will notice a huge headline urging you to subscribe to the company's free course on online marketing. You merely need to enter your email ID to sign up. This process is seen as a form of public commitment the visitor to the site makes and will make the visitor view themselves as a customer of the company. By doing this, Copyblogger is essentially increasing the chances of its visitors purchasing the services they offer.

Liking

We all tend to prefer to agree with or say yes to those we like. However, what makes one person like someone else? The science of persuasion suggests that there are three important factors at play here. We like those who are similar to us, pay us compliments and cooperate with us. Since most of the interactions take place online these days, it is a good idea to think about how your business can use all these factors in online negotiations. In a series of studies based on negotiations performed between MBA students belonging to two famous B-schools, one group was told that "Time is money. It is time to get down to business immediately." This group recorded a 55% rate of agreement. The other group was told, "Before you can start negotiating, take some time and get to know one another. Identify all the similarities you share and then start the negotiation process." This group managed to have a 90% rate of agreement.

If you want to use the principle of liking, then you need to look for certain similarities you share with others before you can start conducting business. When you like someone, the chances of being influenced by them increase. It is based on sharing certain similar traits or qualities with others you like, and it can be based on something totally superficial like looks. You can increase your rates of conversion by concentrating on the About Us page of your business. Does this idea sound absurd to you? Before you write it off, here is a case study that will make you change your opinion.

A company known as PetRelocation.com assists pet owners globally by helping them relocate with their pets from one country to another. The "About Us" page of this company contains bios of all its staff, and each of the bios included not only show the staff's love for pets, but it also humanizes the qualities of the managers and employees by adding personal details like their hobbies. All of this helps humanize the entire company and increase its likeability, which in turn helps increase its rate of conversion.

Consensus

Especially in times of uncertainty, people tend to look at the actions or behaviors of others to determine their own behavior or action. You might have noticed that several hotels often place a tiny postcard or note in the bathrooms which try to persuade the guests to reuse their linens. Most tend to do this by directing the guest's attention to the different benefits reuse can have on protecting the environment. According to research, it shows that about 35% of guests would comply with such a request. However, is there any means of making this more effective? Well, it was noticed that around 75% of guests who checked into a hotel for over four nights or more tend to reuse their linens at some point during their stay. So, what will happen if you simply use the principle of consensus and place the information stating 75% of guests choose to reuse their linens during the stay and you must, too? Well, by doing this, it was noticed that over 25% of guests complied with this request of reusing linens.

Develop Customer Loyalty and Advocacy

The first thing you need to do is ensure that there is positivity. Positivity is quintessential for inspiring, persuading, and motivating the customers to stay loyal to the business. By opting for a positive approach while marketing, you can ensure that you win your customers over. For instance, by creating an engaging customer experience and providing good customer service, you can elicit positive emotions in your customers. Also, when you promote positivity, it helps improve your sales track record and helps develop customer loyalty. When you make the prospects feel good, they will automatically start to associate your business with positivity and will keep coming back for more.

You must ensure that the customer journey is not about you or your business and is instead all about the customer. When you are trying to influence the customer's thinking, you must shift your attention to the benefits your products can offer them and the way they can add value to their lives. While interacting with the customers, you must ensure that you use the words "you" and "your" instead of self-centric language like "me" or "I." The words "you" and "your" tend to be more persuasive since they directly refer to the listener.

There is always a stage in the sales process wherein a decision needs to be made. Depending on different factors, your prospect will either want to purchase something, or they will drop out of the sales funnel. You can use testers while trying to hold onto any uncertain customers. By giving out testers or free samples, you get a chance to connect with the customer and maybe even convert them into loyal customers of the business.

By establishing brand loyalty, you can easily secure future business. However, before you can reap the benefits it offers, the first step is to create brand loyalty. You can reward your customers with attractive offers or even discounts to motivate them to repeat their purchase. At this stage, you must use your business's message to relate to the customer. By doing this, you can establish loyalty and even form a helpful bond with the customers.

As a business owner, it is quintessential that you understand the importance of having a consistent voice. You must determine your target audience and then get started with marketing. You don't have to try all the different strategies for all your customers. There are some sales and marketing tactics that will work well for certain customers while something else might work for others. Regardless of the tactics you employ, you must ensure that your business can deliver a clear and consistent message across all the different customer touchpoints. If you know what you are offering, it becomes easier to persuade others to get on board.

The customer's awareness of your business along with the relationship they share with your brand are two important factors that influence their decisions. You must work on improving your brand image so that it reflects the values and objectives of your business. Not just that, a good brand image also helps in engaging your customers. Often customers tend to select brands the way they select their friends. They tend to look for certain traits that attract them. Your customers will decide according to the way you make them feel.

You must ensure that you always keep your customers informed about your business. Along with all your products and service offerings, you must also inform them about the different ways in which your products and services can help them. Make it a point to draft newsletters or even greeting cards that you can mail or email your customers at regular intervals. You must ensure that your business website consists of all the information that the customers will need to understand their problems and the ways to fix them.

Something as simple as a handwritten note showing your appreciation can go a long way when you are trying to establish customer loyalty. Your customers will certainly appreciate the fact that you took time out of your schedule to craft handwritten notes for them and have made an effort to get in touch with them. Often the simplest of gestures is all that's required for establishing brand loyalty.

You must ensure that you check in on your customers regularly. If you notice that it has been a while since a customer has made a purchase, you can get your sales team to contact them and find out why. When you make the customers feel valued and important, their chances of turning into loyal advocates of your business tend to increase. A simple phone call can make the customers feel like they are valued members of your business.

Whenever you deal with a customer, make it a point to collect some general information about them like their date of birth, any anniversaries, or dates of other happy occasions. Once you create a database of information about your customers and their information, ensure that you send personalized cards, e-mails, or messages to them on their special occasions. You can set reminders to help you remember all this. Doing this also opens up the door for follow-ups.

If you ever come across any content that you know your customers will value, even if your business does not compose it, make it a point to pass it along to them. By providing them with helpful and useful information, you show the customers that your business only has their best interests in mind.

Chapter 8: Time to Evaluate and Improve

Content Calendar

A content calendar is precisely what it sounds like - it is a calendar detailing the content you wish to publish. Creating a content calendar can help ensure that you are posting the right content at the right time and for the right audience. For instance, say you run a donut store, and one fine day a customer comes in and asks you about your plans for National Donut Day. Well, let us assume that you forgot all about it and this question caught you off guard. If you have a content calendar in place, then the chances of this happening will be quite low since it will give you a precise idea of the content that you must be posting. Here are all the steps you must follow to create a content calendar for your business.

The first thing you need to do is start taking stock of all the current social media marketing efforts you are making. You essentially need to perform a social media audit. The questions you must answer at this stage are as follows.

- What are the different social media platforms you are using?
- Which of these platforms is doing the best marketing work for you?

- Do you want to keep publishing on all these sites, or do you want to make any changes?
- Is there a possibility of limiting the social media platforms you are using?
- Are there any imposter accounts on these sites you must shut down?
- Do you have a list of all the passwords and usernames for each of your social media accounts?
- How often do you post on each of these accounts?
- Do you have any specific goals for every platform?
- Who maintains these channels for you?

You need to make a note of all this information that will be included in your social media calendar, especially if you are working in a team.

Once you do this, the next step is to perform a content audit. What sort of content do you usually post? Is there any content that seems to be outdated? If yes, then is there any scope to improve that content? Do you need to get rid of any content, or can you develop upon existing content? Also, what type of content usually performs well with your target audience? What sort of content do your competitors post? By answering these simple questions, you will have an idea of the kind of content you can work with and the content that needs to be scrapped.

Now, it is time to familiarize yourself with the network demographics. Every social media network tends to cater to a specific demographic and a specific audience. The kind of audience present on the network will help guide the type of content you need to create. Most people tend to have accounts on multiple social media channels these days. So, it is quite likely that your customers also follow you on multiple channels. For instance, the audience who follow you on Facebook or Instagram might be older when compared to the audience you have on Snapchat. So, you must make it a point to post content according to the demographics of the audience on a specific network. Understanding your audience is important for the success of a marketing strategy. The good news is that you can easily attain the demographic information of your target audience on any of the major networking sites like Facebook, Instagram, LinkedIn, Twitter, or Snapchat easily. Before you can start devising your content calendar, you must ensure that you understand your audience on those networks.

After you understand your audience, you need to determine the optimum frequency for posting on each of these platforms. Since you have already done your social media audit for your business, you will be aware of your frequency of posting on the existing social media accounts. Will you stick to the same frequency in the future, or do you need to make any changes? Either way, your frequency of posting will help in shaping up your social media content calendar. You need to decide the number of slots you will need per social network. So, the best time to make this decision is right now. You can always tweak it later according to how well your marketing strategies are performing.

The next step is to understand your content ratio. The social media content calendar you create for your business must have some system to categorize the content you want to post. Doing this will help you keep track of the kind of content that your audience seems to like. A common suggestion is to label the content that you create as self-promotional, user-generated and curated content categories. You can also distinguish the content you create according to its formats such as blog posts, announcements, or even videos. The way you want to label the content is entirely your decision. However, regardless of what you decide, you must ensure that the labels you are using are descriptive. It might seem like a time-consuming process at the moment, but it will help save time in the long run. Once you decide on the categories, the next step is to determine the amount of content you want to post in each category.

After this, it is time to establish a content repository. A content repository is a place wherein you can store all the content you want to use while planning your content calendar. Your content repository can be a simple spreadsheet or even an elaborate database. While creating the content repository, there are certain things each piece of content must include, and they are the title, the type of content, relevant links, its expiration date, and any related images or videos. You can also leave some space for any interesting excerpts from content which you can include in your final copy.

The next step is to identify your calendar needs. How detailed must the content calendar be? Do you need to create a separate database or spreadsheet for every type of network you use, or can it all fit in one? Do you need the assistance of your team members to help with this? Who gets to approve the content you want to post? It would be prudent to make the content calendar as detailed as you possibly can, at least during the initial stages. It is better to have more content to choose from instead of having to scramble at the last minute to find good content.

Now that you have gathered all the content you want, it is time to establish a process for posting the content. You need to be quite diligent about setting up a process since it will have a direct effect on the effectiveness of your marketing strategies. You must decide who will be responsible for updating the content calendar. After this, you get to decide who will be responsible for publishing and scheduling all the posts. Figure out if you will need any professional help for developing content. Also, decide where you will be sourcing the images from and if any approval is needed before you can start posting the content. The one final thing you need to determine is how you plan on scheduling the content. Apart from this, you must also make provisions for developing new content. These are certain basic questions you must have answers to before you can place any content in the content calendar. By going through all these steps, you can ensure that your content calendar is properly organized. When it is properly organized, then the chances of any mistakes happening also reduce drastically.

Now you have come to the final step of creating the content calendar, and that is scheduling the time for publishing the content. You have successfully made it through all the steps explained in this section, and now it is time to schedule the publishing time. You can use tools like Hootsuite for scheduling the time for publishing the content.

By creating a content calendar, you can easily automate the process of managing the content on your social media. It might take some time and effort to set it up initially, but once everything is on track, it will help reduce your efforts in the long run.

Measuring Social Media Success

The one thing which makes social media channels quite exciting to use also makes them tricky to measure. Social media platforms tend to undergo constant changes - they keep introducing new features, updating their policies, and making changes to the basic algorithm. All this means that a strategy that might have worked a couple of weeks ago might not make any sense right now. This is the main reason why it is incredibly important to measure the performance of your business on social media. By measuring your social media performance, you can determine whether you have allocated a sufficient social media marketing budget and whether you are using the right tactics or not.

The second problem which comes up is related to measuring the metrics on social media. The metrics are easy to measure, but they don't give you the correct projection of the return on investment. The important metrics like engagement rate, voice share, or even social media reach are tricky to calculate, and you will need online tools to help you calculate these metrics. To measure the success and performance of your social media campaigns, you must follow four steps, and they are given here.

The first step is to set your goals. Before you can start working on developing a marketing campaign, you must determine your goals for the same. What do you plan on achieving with the help of the marketing campaign? Do you wish to increase the traffic to your website or do you want to increase brand awareness? Do you want to reach a larger audience, or do you want to retarget your existing audience? There are various metrics you must use to assess all the results you obtain from the marketing campaign. Before you can measure the results, you must first set certain achievable goals for your business. An achievable goal for your business can be to increase the rate of engagement on Twitter by 20% in the upcoming quarter. That's a good goal because it is a SMART goal. SMART is the acronym you must use for setting goals. The goals you set need to be specific, measurable, actionable, relevant, and they need to be time-bound. So, to set a SMART goal for marketing, you must first determine the specific platform you want to work on. The next step is to ensure that the goal you set can be clearly defined using a metric that can be tracked. The goal must not be unrealistic and needs to be attainable. The goal must also be relevant to your business, and it must be attained within a specific time.

Once you do this, the next step is to select certain metrics to track. After this step, you need to measure the way these metrics are performing monthly. If the metrics seem favorable, then it means your campaign is going along smoothly. If they aren't performing as intended, then it is time to review the campaign and make necessary changes.

Social Media Fails to Avoid

Most marketers believe a marketing campaign cannot be successful without the use of all available channels of social networks. It may not be wrong, but it is not necessary. The social networking platforms you choose should be designed to fit your audience. It makes no sense to develop a brilliant marketing strategy for the platform if your target audience is not even active. Also, the various social networking platforms you use depends on your audience, budget, and campaign. If you have time and budget constraints, focus on one or two platforms instead of all platforms. If you try to use more than two platforms at the same time, it's likely that the content you created will not be personalized for each platform. It's simple:

If your audience is not using Twitter, you do not need a Twitter campaign. You do not have to spend your time, energy, and money to develop a campaign that does not generate interest. Use only platforms that are commonly used by your customers and subscribers.

Social networks are not limited to Facebook, LinkedIn, or Twitter. Facebook, Instagram, Twitter, and LinkedIn are popular social networking sites, but they only make up part of the social networking ecosystem. Web forums, email lists, user groups, various photo and video sharing services, podcasts, social bookmark sites, and online niche communities are all part of social networking. You need to remember that you need to make an effort to understand which platforms your customers are using for communication and start getting involved.

Social media is one of the most important marketing methods these days. This does not mean that it is the only marketing tool. There are several aspects of your business that you need to consider. For example, consider SEO, powerful marketing, and branding if you want to develop a comprehensive marketing strategy. For your campaign to succeed, you need to combine different elements. All elements of your campaign should be in complete harmony with each other. Social networks are just one element of your campaign, and you need all the other elements to work together. Traditional marketing methods should be used together with new ones. Instead of relying solely on social networks, you should consider all other aspects.

Some things never change. Yes, there was a complete paradigm shift in the way marketing practices have changed. However, the good old and basic rules of communication, PR, and marketing remain in place. These basics will never go out of style. Knowing the people you influence, the value your business has for their lives, and the ability to develop products and services that help meet their needs are paramount to any good marketing strategy. So, do not deviate from these values if you're considering the possibility of socializing.

Create Sales Funnel on Instagram or Facebook

Without the right marketing strategy, your business will eventually fail due to a lack of customers. Nobody will know about your business, what you offer, and where exactly your products are available. So, if you have not invested time and effort in this mission, now is the time. The easiest way to start is to use a sales funnel, which has been described in detail.

Put simply; the sales funnel shows the perfect way in which a potential customer becomes a customer. Even if you can sell your products or services to thousands of people, few will provide contact information and become leaders. Only a small proportion of these potential customers become customers.

Instagram advertising has proven to be incredibly useful to businesses and organizations of all types and sizes when it comes to marketing. Currently, Instagram Advertising is managed through the Facebook Ads Manager control panel. This makes it easy to sync with your paid efforts on Facebook and allows you to use a variety of targeting options. If you get it in an appropriate area where you can make a profit with every transaction, you can scale the campaign, increase your budget, and achieve greater success.

Start with your Profile Bio. This is your main property without much space to place what you want. You need to use the space by publishing only what your audience finds useful and what will draw them closer to yourself and your brand. If you're selling Instagram funnels, you'll need to use this section to create a compelling call to action. The application does not have much room for text or links throughout the user interface. That's why you need to be creative and use what you have to the best of your ability.

E-commerce products work especially well when managed by user-generated content. This includes using other customers to advertise to potential customers for your products. This can help you put an Instagram sales funnel into practice. So, persuade subscribers to post photos of the product you're using, add tags to your account, or use your corporate hashtag. If you have powerful people, you will kill it!

Custom content develops a culture around your brand, creates a true consumer, and helps raise awareness. With this tactic, you can build an online community that focuses on your business. This means that you have full customer support and benevolence. Resubmitting photos created by users will prompt your audience to participate and buy if they do not have a product. Ultimately, you need to develop constant interaction, increase brand awareness, and turn most of your subscribers into customers.

With the right strategy, your brand can count on a strategic partnership with a well-known, influential person. Make sure you get a high return on your investment in terms of conversion and brand awareness and evaluate it carefully. Working with influential people, you can leverage their network and brand to raise awareness of your e-commerce offerings. They will benefit from their success and popularity.

This method of disseminating your marketing message is not considered advertising because the message comes from the personal and real voice of an influential person. Followers continue to welcome the approval of trusted Instagram stars and influential people, even with stricter restrictions on the transparency of sponsored content.

Chapter 9: Additional Ideas for Automation

You can understand how important it is to start marketing or promoting your business. However, it is possible that part of you will continue to tell you that you can start after a while. This is basic human nature. We tend to postpone unpleasant things for a while. Marketing is not unpleasant by any means, but if you're trying it for the first time, you'll probably feel a little overwhelmed. The deferral begins, and the work is not completed. This can happen several times, and even if your intentions are good, the delay in getting to work can affect your bottom line. You can pause for a while, and at the end of the day, you have no energy left for the task. This behavior should be avoided. You cannot keep it on the back burner and you need to get cracking as soon as you can. You must have the right system that supports you. Do not say, "I'll do it later." This "later" will never come. Get started with your marketing tactics as soon as you possibly can. If you do not want to do daily marketing, you can schedule one day for it. On the agreed day, you should pay particular attention to promotions and nothing else. This avoids unnecessary distractions, and a timeline is always helpful. You will not feel overwhelmed, and you will know that you have enough time to get things done. There are several ways to automate this process. Here are some tools to help you with this process:

- There are several tools like GetDrip and other autoresponders that let you download a bunch of emails that need to be sent in a specific order to set up a simple drip campaign. You can easily add people to the list and then let the automator take over.
- There are several social media management tools such as Buffer, Hootsuite, and many others that allow you to pre-author all your posts on social networks and then strategically place them on multiple media platforms.
- You should also start planning your blog entries. Using various content management systems, such as WordPress, allows you to create multiple blog posts at once and set up their publishing at a specific time in the future.

Social Media Tools

There are different social media tools you can use, and the options available these days can be rather overwhelming. In this section, you will learn about the best social media tools you can use for improving your marketing efforts.

Mention

This tool is quite similar to Google alerts, but it is meant for social media. As the name suggests, this tool will help you monitor your online presence effectively. It also has certain features that allow you to respond to any mention of your business or brand name online. It also allows you to share any news you might have come across about your business in the industry.

Buffer

It is an analytical tool that includes social media publishing in it. It is quite a helpful social media tool that helps send your updates across various social networking sites like Facebook, Twitter, Google+, and LinkedIn. It comes with a prebuilt analytical system that not only helps you check why certain posts of yours seem to be doing better than others but also helps you understand the optimal time for posting content online. The features offered by Buffer also allow you to work along with your team for optimally maintaining your social media profiles.

Feedly

Feedly is a tool that helps with content discovery and helps you find helpful and useful content. It not only allows you to find good quality content, but it also enables you to share the content that you find with your target audience easily. You have the option to subscribe to the RSS feed so that you can stay updated about all the different updates in the industry that are being posted online. If you are interested in a specific topic, then you can use Feedly to track content that is similar to the kind of content that you like.

Twitter Counter

Well, the name of this tool is pretty self-explanatory. This is an online tool that will help you track all the changes associated with your followers, and it also enables you to make predictions and assumptions related to the growth of your followers over a certain period. After a point, it can become rather cumbersome to keep track of the way your Twitter account grows. This free tool comes in handy at such times. It will enable you to understand the growth rate of your followers. You can use these numbers to analyze whether the content you are posting is helping you attain new followers or not.

Bottlenose

This comes with an inbuilt search engine that can be used in real-time, and it helps in consolidating all your marketing efforts on different social media sites along with any other groups. The resultant data is displayed in the order of algorithmic importance. When you have all the information that you need in a logical manner, it becomes easier to analyze and share the results thus obtained. Another feature is that this tool can be integrated with Buffer. So, you can use a combination of these tools for scheduling your social media posts.

Paid Advertising

Paid advertising will help you reach out to your customers rather easily. According to a study that was conducted in 2014, over 80% of online customers tend to research before they purchase anything, and a majority of these customers start their search with a search engine. The best idea to advertise is to advertise on those platforms they use. Newspaper ads have become rather obsolete these days. In this age of digital marketing, the simplest means to start advertising about your business is to start using Pay Per Click or PPC ads like the ones that you will notice in Google's network. This option allows you to present your business as an answer to the customer's queries searched for in the search engine. If, for example, you try to search for "St. Louis, video agency" in Google, then you will notice The Storyteller Studios as one of the top results.

Although many businesses advertise on Google to reach a large global audience, you can also advertise on other networks. If you are aware of your target audience, then you can start using Facebook ads to promote your business on Facebook. However, before you do this, there is one thing you must do - you need to check for the platforms your target audience uses regularly. Once you have a list of all the platforms, you can use paid forms of advertisements on those platforms.

Paid advertising will help in increasing the credibility and awareness of your business. In the long run, a good quality product or quality service will strengthen the reputation of your business. In the short term, there is a component that improves the perception of your business in the eyes of potential customers, and that's advertising. In the short run, a fake it until you make it approach is often assumed by advertisers. When others can see an ad for your business (particularly good advertising), they automatically seem to assume that a business has money. If they think that a business has sufficient funds, then they also think that the business is doing well, which in turn implies that the business has customers. All these things help in establishing your social proof.

Paid advertising gives you the option to target your ads well. Different platforms like Google or Facebook tend to have access to vast amounts of data. It means that these platforms are capable of placing your ads in front of your desired audience. Google will not show you results for doctors in your area if you are searching for saloons online. Also, Facebook's algorithm is designed such that it will not show an insurance advertisement to an 18-year old student's profile. These platforms not only have the necessary data for proper placement of your ads, but they also have the incentive to help with proper placement of your ads. You will want other users to click on your ads, and since you will be paying for every click you receive, the ads will be placed strategically to increase the number of clicks you get. Also, they want those individuals who click ads to be the ones who are most likely to make a purchase. You will continue to advertise only if you see a return on your investment. You can easily obtain demographic data about your target audience online and then use the same for creating paid-for advertisement campaigns.

Paid advertising also allows you to access helpful analytical and monitoring tools. Google AdWords and Facebook Ads Manager measure the results and check how each campaign works. You can also easily view any demographic information that you need about the type of audience that is viewing your ads. You can then use this data to create well-targeted ad campaigns in the future. You can also see the devices that people use most often when interacting with your ad, make a note of the time when the ads get the most engagement, and even set up your profile such that it shows you only those metrics you want to collect.

As a small business owner, you might not have sufficient time to keep monitoring or reporting on your marketing campaign. Hiring a social media manager is an expensive move. You don't have to worry anymore about these things if you start using paid advertising options.

Perfect Your Sales Pitch

It's never easy to create the perfect sales pitch. This is because you need to identify your target customers and spend some time collecting customer information. Then you should invest enough time to analyze your customer information. It can be both expensive and time-consuming, the amount of time and money you spend changing the plan that benefits your business. If you are looking for your audience, follow these steps.

If you do not have a specific customer, it's difficult for you to get in touch with your potential customers. Therefore, you should consult your current customers and also look at the members of your target group. Then, you can figure out how to present a product or service to that audience and identify what's missing in the product or service you're currently offering. Then you should appeal to a broad audience to identify those customers who may be interested in your product or service. You should then use the collected data to design the brand or product to match the target audience. If you know who the audience is, you can write down your sales pitch and increase sales with this step.

When deciding what type of business value or strategy to use in the industry, you should watch what your competitors are doing. This is a cost-effective strategy that will give you some ideas for your commercial offer. You also have the opportunity to identify gaps in your competitor's approach. Then you can use your research to create a reliable sales strategy. When you enter a business, follow the audience of your competitors so you can use them as an example and improve your products and services to serve the customers better.

You should always make sure that you are present on social networks. You have to make a little more effort to keep your customers. This means that you need to make additional efforts on Twitter, Facebook, and Instagram to influence your target audience. Many companies use their accounts to promote their products and services. If you are a smart seller, you can always post some interesting articles or give interesting answers. This shows people that the person working with the site is not indifferent. Some companies are always helping their clients find new ways to use their products or services. They also help them to solve any problems.

Paul English, when he was the head of Kayak, always put a phone in the middle of the room. This phone was used to receive complaints from customers and had a loud and annoying tone. This phone guaranteed that everyone, including English, answered every complaint. Zappo's Tony Xie valued customer service and made sure every new employee was trained to serve customers no matter what they did. There was a time when they had to go to a competing store to buy the shoes the buyer wanted. The essence of these examples is that you should always look after your customers and potential customers and solve their problems as quickly as possible.

Affiliate marketing has been around since the origins of the Internet. Most people do not notice this, but this is a great way to increase your brand awareness. There are many affiliate networks through which you can promote your product. These networks use Pay Per Click or Pay Per Action methods to evaluate potential customers. Amazon, eBay, and some other marketing companies have their partner network, but you can always use other networks if you want.

When it comes to sales or marketing, the only task that takes most of the time is building potential customers. This includes analyzing customer data, their hobbies, professional activities, and social media activities, conducting online and offline surveys, and updating user data annually. Many companies are now in the market to help you do the same. One of the best ways to attract potential customers is to send them personalized emails or newsletters. You can also send them personalized products or services. You must use the data collected to optimize all your efforts and develop a better sales strategy. This may require a lot of work, but you can use companies like Lead Genius to develop and attract new prospects without wasting time.

Many new companies are joining markets that are overburdening the industry. Therefore, it is very difficult to highlight and collect the target group. If you want to create an audience, you need to make sure that you are trustworthy. Over 88% of consumers use online reviews before making a purchase. So, contact the people who wrote multiple reviews and send them something to write a review on. As your business grows in size, you should first place some internal content on the site. Always use your name if you want to gain trust, as this will allow the target audience to connect with the person rather than the company or product.

It's always helpful to interact with all the key players in your industry. This increases the target audience. If you can attract the attention of an influential person or an influential leader, you can also captivate their followers. This will help you build trust and confidence. You need to contact the right entrepreneurs and bloggers at conferences or in social networks. Send them interesting information that is relevant to you, your company, and the product you are selling.

You should always try to post relevant information on your company's website or blog so that your customers know your business well enough. You can always post information about where the company is and how it is developing. The content that you publish does not have to be self-promotion, but you should always talk about the meaning of the product you are offering or the service you offer. You can also talk about ways to solve industry issues or issues your audience faces every day. Try to share wisdom and inspire people who share your interests. If you do not have many people who can write, you can ask some online companies or platforms for help.

Mistakes to Avoid

There are certain mistakes you must avoid if you want to create a good sales funnel which will help improve your conversions. In this section, you will learn about the common mistakes you must avoid increasing the efficiency of your marketing efforts.

A common mistake that a lot of marketers make is that they don't track sufficient data. Most marketers tend to concentrate only on their major metrics like the number of views per page, the conversion rate of visitors, or even the bounce rates. They do this at the risk of ignoring other smaller but equally important metrics like return visitors, scroll patterns, or even the exit pages. This is one mistake you must not make. Even though the major metrics are certainly important, it doesn't mean you can ignore the other smaller metrics. The smaller metrics tend to provide actionable insight into how you can easily improve your sales funnel. For instance, say you notice that the overall conversion rate of traffic on your website is 1%. This is a major metric, and it suggests that one out of every one hundred visitors to your website will convert into a customer. Though this metric provides a broad overview of how conversion is taking place, it doesn't give any insights about the areas of marketing that you must improve upon. Now, let us assume that you go back to your sales funnel and go over it with a fine-tooth comb. When you do this, you notice that five out of every 100 visitors to the website tend to subscribe to your site using e-mails. However, only about 10% of these email subscribers tend to open the emails they receive from you. This percentage is rather low, and you must work on improving it. You can fix this by making sure that you are focusing on the major and minor metrics.

Another mistake is that a lot of business owners don't test multiple payment gateway options. An important yet tricky aspect of building a sales funnel is selecting the right payment gateway for your business. The ideal method of payment for a business in the real estate industry will be quite different from that ideal for a business in the e-commerce industry. Another hurdle you will need to deal with is choosing the right number of gateways you can use. If you select too few, then it can lead to congestion in the sales funnel, and you will not be able to accommodate all your prospects easily. If you have too many, then you might scare away any potential leads due to the excess choice you provide them with. The solution to this problem is to keep testing the different permissible payment gateway options regularly. You can try coming up with different combinations of payment gateways and select a combination that works well for your business. The most popular payment gateways available these days are PayPal, Google wallet, Stripe, WePay, and Braintree.

Conclusion

I want to thank you once again for choosing this book. I hope it proved to be a helpful and enjoyable read.

Developing a sales funnel is quintessential to ensure the success of your marketing campaigns. The sales funnel has certainly become a marketing buzzword these days, but seldom do people know what it essentially entails. A fully automated and well-curated sales funnel can help increase the rate of conversions while improving your customer relations. These are two key factors that directly influence your business's bottom line.

There are certain problems that prevent a business from performing optimally. As a business owner, you might be faced with the lack of time, the absence of a properly focused and targeted social media campaign, or even the lack of understanding of the simple fact that your sales depend on you. The good news is, you no longer have to worry about these problems holding you back from doing your best.

By implementing the simple steps and by following the suggestions given in this book, you will be able to successfully create, implement, and manage an automated sales funnel that will help increase your leads along with conversion rate. Follow the different steps given to thoroughly research and create a fully functional sales funnel that will push your potential customers toward fulfilling your goal: making a purchase. The examples, along with actionable steps given in this book, will help you along the way. Also, all the suggestions given in this book are cost-effective and quite practical.

So, all that's left for you to do is get started as soon as you possibly can and make the most of a good sales funnel!

Some further reading to consider for an expanded view of some of the topics discussed include two books also written by myself, see below links to amazon.

- <u>Facebook Marketing and Advertising for Small Business Owners in 2019</u>
- <u>Instagram Marketing and Advertising for Small Business Owners in 2019</u>

You will get practical, time and money-saving advice to set up your Sales Funnel on the specific Social Media Platforms.

Facebook Marketing and Advertising for Small Business Owners

Discover How to Optimize the Money You Spend on Facebook And Get Maximum Results By Using Proven ROI Methods

Introduction

Principles to Power Your Facebook Strategy

Marketing your business on Facebook can be very effective. If you are a small organization looking to expand your horizons, there is no better place for you to begin with than Facebook. It's a strong platform and with a little effort and the right persuasion skills, not only will you be able to market your business but also establish a brand that becomes popular in a short time span.

It is important to have an online presence if you want to stay in competition today and the best way for you to do this is to start marketing your business on social media platforms where most of the population spends its time. Facebook has over 1.7 billion people and that comprises almost 25% of the entire population of the earth. When it comes to marketing your business, not only is Facebook a great platform but it's also time-saving and helps you invest your money where you can get returns, thereby making it a profitable solution. However, if you want to make sure your marketing efforts do not go in vain you need the right Facebook strategy and principles to help you come up with a plan that accomplishes your goals and visions. Here are some interesting principles that you should base your Facebook marketing strategy that will help you create posts and content that's persuasive and helps increase your customer base.

Try Out Your Business First

Whether you are a service-based business or you are trying to sell products, always make sure you have complete knowledge of your business. It's important for you to first try your business out before you go out to the public and tell them to get involved with it. Once you know your business, it helps you to answer any questions that are thrown at you.

Apart from being able to identify the benefits and the USP of your business, you will also get to know any potential issues that may need to be rectified before it hits the audience. Marketing on a social media platform is great, but it comes at a price and if your business is not up to the mark, people are going to be vocal about it on the same platform. To put it in simple words, make sure you have all your corners covered and you start promoting your business on Facebook confidently, knowing that you are selling a strong brand to the audience.

Update Yourself with Information

Understand how social media interaction works so that you figure out a plan for your business and make the most out of each interaction in order for your marketing efforts to pay off. Learn more about Facebook analytics and the wide variety of different tools that Facebook offers to get data-driven results and figure out what strategies work best for your business.

Create A Personality for Your Brand

Instead of trying to blend in with the crowd, you need to focus on standing out and Facebook will be able to do this for you when you establish a brand that's different from the others. Do something unique and have your own identity that helps you differ from other businesses that are similar in nature to your business. If you do the same thing they are doing, you are not going to get different results. Your results are based on the effort you put into your marketing and the strategies you apply. You have to be a little persuasive, a little unique, and bold if you want to make a mark on Facebook.

Interaction Is Important

Most business owners think that Facebook is a one-way communication platform and post what they want to say to potential customers and wait for results to kick in. If you want people to show an interest in your business you have to interact with them and be available to answer queries or to give them solutions for problems they may be facing. Interacting with the audience makes it easy to increase your potential customers. You can always initiate an interaction by asking questions or creating a poll on your Facebook page to gather attention.

Creating A Community

Facebook allows you to express yourself and create a sense of community amongst your target audience. With Facebook, you are not limited to the number of characters you post, neither are you limited to sharing only certain images or certain posts. You can tell a story to your audience with the help of your Facebook posts and give them an idea of what your business is all about. This will help them connect with your business and become a brand. Share personal stories and involve the audience in your success. The way this can be done is by listening to your fans and respecting their opinions. You can start sharing success stories about people that your brand has helped. For example, if you are a shoe company, you can share stories where you have helped certain people with your products. There are various people out there that cannot afford expensive branded shoes. You can sponsor such a community with your shoes and share your story with the rest of the world. This will create a feel-good factor amongst your audience and it will also motivate them to do something good for others in society. Don't complicate your ideas too much. Just communicate from your heart and your audience will relate to you.

Be Kind to Your Audience

Facebook marketing is all about communicating with your audience for their benefit. You do not have to spam someone's news feed in order to get your brand name out there. You need to start sharing and interacting with people with a view to benefiting. When you start providing value, your audience will start paying attention. You should look to write for your potential customers rather than writing for yourself. Try to find out what your audience would love to hear and how you can benefit them through your brand. Show your audience that you are committed to their wellbeing and you will be able to connect with them emotionally.

If you are a local brand you should display fan stories on your Facebook page. These stories can highlight the heroes in your locality and show everyone the kindness that they have displayed. These could be local inspirations or heroic deeds that have helped the community. Help these heroes become an influencer within your community circle and start making a difference to the community. If you are a big national brand then you need to reach out to the people that communicate with you and thank them personally. How many times have you written to a brand and they have not bothered replying to you, apart from the standard auto-reply that you received? Start personalizing messages and see how much human interaction can help your brand go viral.

Be Transparent

Facebook marketing is all about transparency. A classic example is receiving a negative comment on any of your posts or your business page. The first reaction would be to lash out at this post or to delete it so that others will not be able to see it. However, the sensible thing to do would be to treat the comment with respect and respond immediately. If your business made a mistake you need to own up to it and apologize to your customers. You should also try to post about the mistake on your own rather than waiting for bad publicity to take its own course.

Make People Laugh

Yes, the world of marketing and branding is a very serious business but focusing on humor is extremely essential. You need to find the right balance between being serious and making people laugh every once in a while. If you only post about things that make people laugh, no one will take your brand seriously. But if you keep posting serious things on your Facebook page, your fans may shy away. One classic example is the ALS ice bucket challenge. This brand took a very serious issue such as a brain disease and communicated the seriousness with a fun challenge. Soon there were millions of people pouring ice water on their head and these are the kind of posts that you need to target.

Be Clear About What You Expect

While your Facebook page may get a lot of attention and you will get a lot of followers, you need to tell your customers what you are expecting from them. This means you need certain 'call to action' buttons around your fan page that will ask your fans to either visit your website or to read your blog post or to share your post or even purchase your product. You need to let your fans know that they have the power to make a difference and you need to empower them by giving them the ability to make your post go viral. As complicated as it sounds, it is a very smart way of convincing your reader that he or she can contribute towards an internet sensation.

Checklist for Creating & Optimizing Facebook Ads

A Guide On Performing The Basic Facebook Actions

It is important to create a Facebook ad in the right manner and there are a number of steps involved. You need to see if you are targeting the right audience, if your image meets the dimensions, or if you are selecting the right kind of ad. If you are doing all of this for the first time, it can get extremely confusing. There are over a billion people using Facebook and almost all of them visit it on a daily basis. This is what makes Facebook the perfect platform to market your business and become an overnight sensation. The flip side to this is that if something goes wrong or you are not creating the right kind of ads, there is very little that you can do to rectify it because of the number of people that would have seen the ad. You need to be accurate with regards to your ad creation and make sure that you keep the steps in mind before you publish your ad. Your Facebook ad can be broken down into three categories:

- **Campaign:** This will define your assets.
- **Ad sets:** If you want to target separate audiences across different geographies and other sectors, then you will want separate ad sets for each.
- **The actual ads:** Your ads are the actual images or posts that go out to the customers within each ad set.

Now let us look at how to create effective Facebook ads with tools that are provided by Facebook.

Choosing an Editor

There are two editors that are available to all Facebook users that will help create a paid ad. The first is the ads manager and the other is the power editor. You need to select an editor based on the number of words that you want to run as well as the size of your company. The ads manager is ideal for most of the companies out there while the power editor is ideal for large businesses that want control over their ad campaigns. Since this book deals with helping small businesses create a brand via Facebook, we will focus on the ads manager editor.

Choose Your Ad Objective

When you start with Facebook ads manager it will ask you for your objective for the campaign. There are 10 different objectives you could choose from. These include

- Sending people to your website
- Boost your posts
- Increase your website conversion
- Promoting your page
- Get users to download and install your app
- Increase app engagement
- Connect with people located close to your business
- Increased attendance for an event that you are organizing
- Get more people to claim any offers that you are offering
- To get video views

When you pick one of these objectives, Facebook will get a better idea of what you are trying to do and the best ad-options depending on your objective. Let us take an example. Assume you selected 'driving more traffic to your website' as your objective. Once you've selected this objective, Facebook will ask you to enter the URL you want to promote. Once you have entered the URL, Facebook will provide a list of the ad-options that will help achieve this objective.

Choose Your Audience

If you using Facebook Ads for the first time it will be difficult for you to select a target audience because you are not sure of how it will work. It's best to select different targeting options until you get the right mix and you find the audience that suits your requirements. Facebook also helps you narrow down your focus by providing you with filter options to help define your audience. When you select the criteria for your audience and you enter all the fields, you will be able to see your potential reach number.

You can play with the options available until you reach the ideal number and use 'select the right audience', keeping your objective in mind. If you just want people to get to your website you may want to target specific people that are interested in what you are offering. If you are looking to build brand awareness then you may want to target a general audience so that the outreach is not limited. Facebook has a number of built-in targeting options you can choose from. Some of the options include:

- Age
- Location
- Language
- Gender
- Education
- Relationship

- Finances
- Work
- Ethnicity
- Home
- Parents
- Life events
- Behavior
- Interests
- Connections

You can take a custom audience based on the kind of people you are targeting. You can build this custom audience with the help of your company database and get specific people to your business page. Once this is created on your Facebook page you may want to keep trying it with different groups until you find a group that is responding to your ads. You can create multiple groups and see which of them have responded to your ads better.

Setting Your Budget

Facebook allows you to select two kinds of budgets - setting a daily budget or setting a lifetime budget. The daily budget will make your ad run continuously during the day. When you select a daily budget Facebook will paste your ads on a daily basis, keeping your budget in mind. It allows Facebook to post your ads across a period of time rather than posting it daily. Once you pay for a specific period, Facebook will make sure that the ad runs uniformly across this period, keeping in mind peak hours as well as the audience.

Schedule

Once you select your budget and your campaign you then need to select whether you want the campaign to run right now or you want to customize the dates. You can select the parameters with regards to the times you want the campaign to run or specific days of the week.

Pricing

You can either choose to pay for your objective, your clicks, or your impressions. Based on the pricing model that you select, Facebook will decide when to display ads and to whom. Facebook will even provide you with a suggestion for the pricing based on behavior towards other advertisers.

Creating Your Ad

Your ad needs to match your objective. If you want to increase the number of clicks for your blog or your website then you will need to select a 'click to website' ad-option. There are two ad-options that you get. You can either pick a link or a carousel. Link a single image ad that will direct customers to your website. A carousel will be a multi-image ad that will also have a link to direct people to your website. There are design criteria that you need to adhere to for each of the two formats.

For a single image ad you need to keep the following criteria in mind:

- text no more than 90 characters.
- link title no more than 25 characters.
- image ratio needs to be 1.91:1.
- the image size needs to be 1200 pixels by 627 pixels.

For a carousel ad you need to keep the following criteria in mind:

- The image size needs to be 600 pixels by 600 pixels.
- the image ratio needs to be 1:1.
- text shall not exceed 90 characters.
- the headline should not be more than 40 characters.
- link description should not be more than 20 characters.
- the image cannot have more than 20% text.

These are only the options when you select the objective as 'send people to your website'. If you select a different objective you will get different ad-options. Each of these options has a different set of requirements and you need to explore all of them before picking the right advertising option. Once you select the type of ad, Facebook ads manager will help you with regards to the display of your ad. You can either from a desktop news feed, a mobile news feed, or a desktop right column.

If you have not created a Facebook page to associate with your ad you will only be able to create a desktop right ad column. If you want all three ad-options then you need to create a Facebook page for your business.

Ad Performance

Once your ad is live you will need to keep checking how it is performing and what the results look like. You will get the results in two places – one is your Facebook ad manager and the other would be your marketing software.

Facebook Ad Manager

The Facebook ad manager comes with a dashboard that will help you get an overview of all the campaigns running. The dashboard will show you how much you spend each day and you can filter your ads and customize the results too. You will get to see the reach, the frequency and the cost for each of the ads. You need to look at the performance of your ad and the engagement. If you have put up a video then you can see the percentage of people who viewed the full video and percentage of people who scrolled past. You can see the clicks to your website as well as the number of downloads for your mobile app. If you have created an event then you will be able to see the response for the event and the cost per response.

Marketing Software Ads

If you are not sure how to use Facebook ad manager then you can also use your marketing software to see the performance of your ads. Your marketing software will help you analyze the performance of an ad with the help of your URL. This will give you an idea of how many leads you have generated and how many of these leads are converted into customers. After reading this book, you will be able to put the following plans into action:

- Creating A Marketing Plan
- Picking The Right Social Media Script

Marketing Plan

There are over 2 billion monthly users on Facebook, making it the most popular social media platform you can use to market your business. However, the competition in this platform is fierce and if you want to make your business stand out amongst multiple other businesses marketing their products or services on Facebook you need a strategic marketing plan that works in your favor.

There are a number of small businesses on Facebook that looks to grow by using Facebook marketing to their advantage. If you are convinced Facebook marketing is the way you want to go then here are some effective marketing strategies to help your business become a visible brand online.

Goals

Before you pick any marketing strategy on Facebook, you need to set a realistic goal to achieve. Ask yourself why you want to market your business on Facebook and what you want to achieve by it. Some businesses look to create brand awareness, while others look to obtain leads that they can later convert into customers, while some people simply look to increase website traffic. Every business owner has a different goal and your marketing strategy should be based according to your goal.

You need to remember that there are no Facebook strategies that work well for all businesses and your goals need to be set in order for you to gain the most out of the activity that is specifically designed to benefit your business through Facebook marketing. When you plan to pick a goal you should always use the SMART goal strategy. This is easy to achieve and an effective way to transform your goal into reality. It focuses on the following

- Specific
- Measurable
- Achievable
- Realistic
- Timely

The reason the strategy is effective is that it helps you understand exactly what you want and it ensures that you take one step at a time to get where you want to be. It's specific because you can measure it and you know exactly how well you are doing with the plan in place. It also gives you a clear insight with regards to whether or not a strategy is actually working.

Your Target Audience

Yes, Facebook has over 2 billion users on a monthly basis, but all these people are not your target audience. When you are a small local business you need to focus on people who actually matter to your business and who can help you generate revenue. Whether it's geographical-bound or gender-bound it is always important you narrow down your target audience, applying as many filters as possible. Facebook ads manager gives you the option of figuring out what kind of audience you would like to choose and this helps you to market your business to the right people without spending unnecessary money on irrelevant customers that won't help your business grow.

Set a Budget

It is important for every business small or large to have a specific budget set aside for Facebook marketing so you don't go overboard with your marketing expenses and you manage to track whether or not the attempt was a profitable one or not. While it's good to invest money on Facebook marketing, it is important for you not to put all your eggs in one basket without knowing whether or not it's going to benefit you.

Create and Planning Engaging Content

It's not just about posting on Facebook but about what you post, which is why the content needs to be well planned, taking into consideration your goal, the budget, and the audience you plan on targeting.

It is important to keep pointers to help you create content that is highly engaging to the audience.

- Images with people's faces on them gain more attention
- A brighter and clearer image works well
- Stock photos never work for Facebook marketing
- Create videos that can be viewed with the sound off just as effectively as with the sound on. Only 15% of Facebook videos are watched with the sound turned on.
- People tend to get bored really fast so don't create a video that's so long, people end up losing interest in watching it completely. Post something that's fast, interactive, and intuitive.
- Post engagement advertisements

While it's important to create engaging content on your Facebook page you need to focus on the quality of the advertisements as well. Keep in mind the above information and use it for your Facebook advertisements to get better results. Remember, there are certain rules you have to follow when it comes to pictures on Facebook and so goes through them in detail before posting an image that might get rejected.

Monitor Your Progress

The only way you will be able to figure out whether or not your Facebook marketing strategies are paying off is when you monitor your progress on a regular basis. Doing it daily is highly recommended because you can change or spruce up your post depending on what you think may work better for the business, and this experimentation eventually leads to a foolproof Facebook marketing strategy that helps your business grow.

Split Testing

Always create two Facebook posts and label them as post-A and post-B. Measure the results for both posts to see how they perform and eliminate the one with the lower result. Continue repeating the split test using the higher result test against a new test until you figure out which Facebook strategy fits your business plan perfectly.

It's easy to measure progress because the Facebook ads manager provides you with complete statistics and reports that you can use to compare.

Social Media Script

Facebook is a large platform to market your business and, with the help of the right tools, not only will you be able to achieve your goals but you will also get closer to achieving business success. Most business owners use Facebook ads manager to effectively schedule and plan marketing strategies on Facebook. If you want to do something unique then a Facebook script add-on tool is something that not only helps you plan out of the box but makes it a little easier for you to deal with the various marketing campaigns you can share on Facebook regularly. Here are a few Facebook scripts you could give a try.

AdEspresso

Facebook ads manager could get a little difficult for some people and if you find it too complicated, AdEspresso is an amazing replacement that can help you to manage your campaigns on Facebook. The script allows you to optimize, analyze, and even execute your campaigns effectively. It also has the A/B testing capability that allows you to compare the various advertisements you post on Facebook to pick out the best ones.

AgoraPulse

This is a simple effective tool you can use that helps you to manage content and engage more people on Facebook. Right from scheduling your posts, to publishing them at a particular time, and monitoring the engagement for various posts AgoraPulse is a simple tool that can be used for your Facebook marketing plans. The highlight of this tool is that it has to keep tabs on your competition and get a fair idea of what strategies they are using on Facebook.

Buffer

Buffer is an interesting script you can integrate into your browser. It's really simple to use and it gives you complete analytics and insights on every post, helping you understand your marketing strategies in detail.

Driftrock

If lead generation is your main aim via Facebook marketing then the Driftrock FB script is something you should definitely give a try. Not only does it help you to create ads fast but it gives you various options to try out so that you can optimize your advertisement campaign and get better results.

DrumUp

Hashtags and emojis have gained a lot of popularity, and if you want to incorporate emojis in your Facebook post then

DrumUp is something that you must try. These different kinds, mostly emojis, are interesting and this unique feature helps to make your post stand out amongst the rest.

Fanpage Karma

If you want your business to grow, you need to understand your customers a little better. Fanpage Karma gives you insightful information about your fans and followers, helping you to understand them better and to service them more effectively. It also helps you to see what your competitors are doing and whether their advertisements are more successful than yours.

Heyo

Heyo is another interesting social media tool you can use if you are looking to generate leads. This marketing tool helps you to create various campaigns for your Facebook page and it also drives more engagement focusing on the right kind of users. Heyo is one of the few social media scripts that can help to create brand awareness as well as product awareness in the market.

Hootsuite

If you're looking for an analytical tool that can help you with Facebook marketing and optimize your campaign from time to time then Hootsuite is one of the most interesting Facebook scripts that you can use. Not only does it focus on lead generation but it also helps in better interaction and engagement because of the scheduling option it offers.

Likealyzer

It is important for you to get insights about your Facebook page so that you know how effective your marketing efforts are and what needs to be changed. Likealyzer not only helps you to get these insights but it gives you updates on your page, which determines whether your page is a good Facebook page or it needs improvement.

Meet Edgar

If you are looking for hassle-free and convenient management and scheduling tool then Meet Edgar is definitely something you should try. It helps you save a lot of time because it has an auto-fill feature that automatically fills using already entered information in the past.

Pagemodo

It's important for your Facebook page to stand out, and to be able to do this customization is vital. Pagemodo helps you customize your Facebook page with different impressive photo covers, tabs, as well as helps to organize contests to enhance the engagement.

Post Planner

Post Planner helps you to understand your publishing calendar and post-good-quality content until you reach maximum engagement for each post.

Facebook Facts

Facebook was only supposed to be a passing phase and a number of people didn't even register on Facebook when it first began. While this was something that only college students wanted to try out, it eventually expanded into something massive and today people cannot imagine their lives without Facebook. Apart from being a social media giant, Facebook also helps the number of communities across the world. Many small businesses have also turned to Facebook to build a brand name and go viral overnight.

Here is a look at the facts that make up Facebook and the mind-numbing numbers that many of you may not be aware of.

Facebook has over 1.3 billion users and these users are spread across the world. There are various family members and friends that live across borders and still manage to stay connected with the help of Facebook.

- it is said that almost 20000 people Login to Facebook every second. This means that 11 million users stay connected on FB every 18 minutes.

- every minute there are almost half a million users accessing Facebook on their smartphone.
- almost 80% of Facebook users access it from their phones.
- Facebook has the most mobile users across the globe and this number adds up to 740 million.
- Facebook messenger is one of the most used messengers and there are over 150,000 messages exchanged every minute.
- 49 million posts go up every 15 minutes. This boils down to 3 million posts every minute.
- there are close to 100,000 friend requests sent every 10 minutes.
- Facebook posts receive almost half a million likes every minute.
- in terms of generating revenue, Facebook helps to generate almost 1.4 million dollars every hour.
- most of the advertising revenue on Facebook comes from mobile ads.
- Facebook manages to earn 2.5 billion dollars through mobile advertising every quarter.
- over 350 million photos are uploaded on a daily basis on Facebook.
- almost 31% of the senior citizen population in the United States is on Facebook.
- the millennial (15 to 34 years) population accounts for

66% of Facebook users.

- The Asia Pacific has the largest number of Facebook users and they total up to over 450 million.
- Europe has the second largest number of users and this number is close to 300 million.
- USA and Canada have about 200 million users on Facebook while the rest of the world has about 400 million users.

How Facebook Helps Small Businesses

Small businesses have started realizing the potential with Facebook marketing and they have now started using it to their advantage. Almost 75% of all small businesses use social media to promote their brand as well as increase sales. Social media has become a necessity today and a number of small businesses are using these strategies to get a brand name and connect with their audience. When it comes to various social media channels, Facebook is number one followed by Instagram, YouTube, Twitter, LinkedIn, and Snapchat.

When it comes to gender, it is seen that women are more likely to use Facebook compared to men. This can be attributed to the fact that women are better at socializing and conversing with their customers than men. Women love expressing their emotions and female business owners are making the most of Facebook to promote their business.

When it comes to age groups, millennial businesses use Facebook more than any other age group out there. Almost half the businesses post on Facebook on a daily basis. Amongst these users, half of them use images and infographics while the others post about offers on promotions that are coming up.

What Users Are Looking for on Facebook

Once you understand what people look for on social media you will be able to provide them with posts that help in better engagement and benefit your business in the long run. If you were to figure out what people are looking for, you'll be able to provide it to them and create posts that make them engage with your business. Here are a few things that you should always try to incorporate in your posts for better engagement.

Information

Social media is a great way to share information about products, offers, and services and a great place to give people what they are looking for. You need to provide your users with as much information as possible in the least amount of words so that you don't take up too much of their time but give them what's important for them to know.

Inspiration

Everyone is looking for a little inspiration every day and when you can do that in the form of a motivational video or a beautiful quote with a certain call to action it will benefit your business greatly. When you tug on to the emotional strings of the heart of a person, the chances of that post being shared automatically increase.

Offers

This is a great way to market your business on Facebook because you don't really have to invest too much money to grab attention. Exciting offers and discounts are something everyone looks forward to, and not only does this help to engage more people, but it also establishes a strong relationship between the customer and the business. When you provide special offers from time to time it increases customer loyalty and you have a stronger chance of repeat business.

Educational

People love learning new things, and sharing informative or educational posts from time to time can work really well. A small DIY project using certain products from your business or tips and tricks on how the services of your business will come in handy are some exciting ways to share information that will grab the attention of people on Facebook.

Humor

Tickling the funny bone has never failed to impress people, and whether you share a funny video, a joke, or even a name it's sure to be popular on Facebook.

How To

How-To's are really interesting, especially when it comes to teaching people about a product because it gives them more information. Visualization of a product helps to increase the sales and how-to videos can definitely get you the kind of popularity you are seeking from a post.

When you share information on Facebook you need to make sure it's not monotonous because that makes people bored and they tend to lose interest. Always try to come up with interesting and innovative ideas that can engage more people and increase your fan following on Facebook.

Success Stories

Styleshare

Styleshare Is a Korean fashion brand that successfully used the Facebook marketing strategy to not only help them to get 15 times the amount they invested as returns but a 60% click-through rate to encourage people to install their applications.

They also had an increase in 25% of people who downloaded their applications in comparison to the previous year.

The business was established in 2011 and became an e-commerce business in 2016. As soon as Styleshare became an online brand they started marketing on Facebook. Their main goal was to increase the number of shoppers online to reduce physical storage and added expenses.

They targeted people between the age group of 18 and 37 and divided them into 4 groups

- Potential customers
- People using the application but not yet purchased from it
- People who added products to their cart but haven't completed the transaction
- Existing customers for their business

They planned their marketing strategy based on a carousel format that encouraged people to download the application. After they had a certain amount of people who successfully downloaded the application they then introduced app re-installation encouragement by telling people about special offers and discounts.

They came up with some creative advertisements from time to time to constantly engage the public, and not only did these advertisements include images but also contained videos.

They used the carousel method and displayed multiple images in one advertisement.

They displayed the collection of their products to lure people to download their app.

They used the dynamic app feature to personalize advertisement without too much effort.

They customized their audience preferences by filtering the ones that fit into their bracket the best.

They used a Facebook pixel to measure how effective the response was.

They even tested multiple social media platforms and marketing strategies but finally came to the realization that Facebook is a great place to persuade customers into purchasing and downloading the application, making the process a successful one.

Toyota Israel

Toyota Israel had one of the most successful Facebook ad campaigns when they planned to introduce advanced features on their popular car model. The campaign managed to boost their purchases by a staggering 48% and increased 33% in Agri fall, making it one of the most successful campaigns on Facebook. They also had an 80% brand lift in the automotive industry.

Toyota Israel focused on one particular car model - the Corolla and focused on the unique features and style of the car as its USP. People needed to know just what the car has in store, which is why they tried to incorporate as many video advertisements as possible. All of these videos were high-definition, bright, and spectacular in content, making them attractive in nature.

Unlike Styleshare, Toyota Israel chose to go a different route and they only introduced multiple video advertisements and focused on a wider audience to view the advertisements. In the end, they used the Facebook pixel to measure their activities and see how effective it was.

Chapter 1: How to Influence People?

Facebook helps a number of businesses grow and become successful with the right marketing strategies in place. It's important for you to persuade people to follow and like your Facebook business page, but it all begins with the right influence. If you want people to engage in your desired goal for your marketing plan you have got to influence them in that manner. Here are some interesting ways to influence people and benefit your business.

Start a Conversation

You need to let customers know how important they are to you and the best way to do it is to interact and converse. Communication is important and this doesn't just mean asking them to comment on your posts but rather interact with you and converse with them rather than having a one-sided communication with the posts you share. You should try to have a debate or a poll on your page from time to time or even ask questions and look forward to hearing from your customers or potential customers have to say because this will give you more insights on what they like and helps you to influence them better.

Motivate People

Motivation is really important if you want your business to grow, and in order for you to get the maximum benefit out of any marketing campaign, you have got to motivate people in a persuasive and subtle manner to carry out the call to action.

Make Customers Support Your Story

You have to tell people how happy your existing customers are with your business. Try asking customers to give you a testimonial or write a review for your business and share that on your social media page along with a tag to the customer. Not only does this increased reliability but it makes the brand more relatable and increases the value of your brand at the end of the day. Reviews and testimonials play a huge role in positively impacting your business so you need to make sure you use it in the right way to get the results you are seeking.

Provide Quality Content

Whatever your business is into, make sure you share quality content that is useful to the audience. When businesses know that you are the place to go to for quality content, you will automatically have more followers on your business page and people will start relying on your solutions. This makes it easy for you to promote your own brand without sounding too pushy.

Make Customer Service Your Regular Routine

If you want your business to double you need to service your customers effectively, and this doesn't stay limited to your website but it should be extended to your Facebook page as well. Not only should you be ready to reply to any queries but you should also resolve comments or issues that potential customers or existing customers have with a business. Whenever you are dealing with customers or potential customers, make sure to have a positive approach, no matter how negative the situation is.

Experiment with Videos

Videos are fairly new on Facebook and a lot of business owners are not very comfortable with the idea of investing money to show videos on their page. Statistically, videos are more likely to get engagement in comparison to posts, so the best way to start influencing the audience is to share videos that are of good quality.

Use the Insight

If you continue marketing your business without knowing whether or not your efforts are fruitful you will end up wasting a lot of money on something that might not necessarily be beneficial for you. You need to figure out whether or not you are influencing people in the right way and whether you need to change your marketing strategies to get more likes.

Target the Right Audience

This may sound too harsh but sometimes a small mistake with the filters you choose could end up getting you an irrelevant target audience that won't benefit your business in any way. Most small businesses are geographically-bound. Promoting your business on Facebook without selecting the right filters means you may end up getting audiences from different parts of the world. While this will help create awareness about your business, it will not help in terms of any revenue generation.

When you come up with a Facebook marketing strategy it doesn't only have to be one that works but it also needs to be one that manages to benefit your business, influencing it in the right way. Once you find the perfect balance between persuasion and influence, not only will you manage to increase your sales and online presence but it will help you to successfully establish and gain popularity even without monetary investment in the future.

Principles of Persuasion

The different forms of persuasion have been around for a while and based on the principles introduced by Dr. Robert Cialdini. It shows that these persuasion techniques and principles help people to say yes more often when you request something. Applying the principles of persuasion to your social marketing strategies on Facebook can benefit you a great deal and help you to get more responses to your business page. In order to guide human behavior, you need to follow the persuasion principles religiously if you are looking for positive results. Here we will discuss the six principles so you can apply them to your Facebook marketing strategies and achieve success.

Reciprocity

The nature of reciprocation is always handled well when you reciprocate good behavior with a service or a product. People start feeling good and there is an obligation they have towards you. If you go for a party empty-handed you start to feel out of place, which is why every time people invited to a party will turn up with a gift in their hand. Similarly, when you market your business on Facebook you are inviting people to like your Facebook page and interact with you and, in return, you need to reciprocate with small gestures. This could include anything from an offer to a discount. It doesn't need to be something big. Even small gestures can go a long way.

Scarcity

Another great way to persuade people into choosing your business products or services is to create scarcity. This means you need to announce that it's a limited period offer and more people are ordering it, which is why they start thinking it's a great product and this is why everyone wants it. Psychologically, scarcity of products automatically increases the demand, which is why using terms like the last few pieces left in stock or limited offer is something that attracts more people to an advertisement. When using scarcity you have to play with your words wisely to ensure that you don't promote the same product over and over again because that will create doubts in people's minds and they will think that this is a marketing gimmick.

Authority

The next principle of persuasion is an authority and it may sound a bit harsh but it actually works very well to persuade people into doing what you want them to do. However, if you want to make authority work in your favor you have got to have a thorough knowledge of your business and answer any possible questions. It's like giving somebody more information than required that will let them know how credible your business is.

Consistency

This is the fourth principle of persistence and it is one that makes a lot of sense. People always look for consistency when it comes to marketing campaigns. When you achieve consistency in your marketing campaigns you will be able to make sure that you convince people with regards to your business as well as your ideas. There are a number of businesses that look to persuade people without being consistent. Let's say for example you are trying to build your business brand name on Facebook. If you are a business that sells health products and you claim that there are no side-effects, your customer feedback cannot contradict your claims. You need to make sure that your product is consistent with your claims. If you sell products based on a lie, sooner or later your bluff will be caught. You need to make sure that you deliver your campaigns with consistency and you make claims that will hold true even when somebody purchases your product. When you start pursuing people with consistency and you follow up with your claims, you will become a reputable brand in the market because of positive word of mouth publicity.

Liking

This is the fifth principle of appreciation. People will always say yes to something that they like. Not only does this hold true in terms of business but it also holds true in terms of the people that we surround ourselves with. You will always be friends with people that you like and not because you are forced to be with somebody. This is also the case with business. Nobody is going to purchase your product if they do not like you as a brand. This means that your Facebook campaign needs to create a general feeling of liking among people. This is why you need to focus on campaigns that have a feel-good factor and people should be able to connect with the work that you are doing. You will see a number of businesses that go out of their way to help certain communities and give back to society when needed. This is how the principle of liking works. You should know that liking always equals brand loyalty as well as sales.

Consensus

The last principle is the consensus. The consensus is when a group of people look at each other's behavior and then decide upon their own behavior. The principle of consensus simply shows the buyer that the majority of people out there are also doing it. Whether that is true or not is another question altogether. You will see a number of ad campaigns that will claim that 80% of people purchased this product or 50% of people are using a certain product these days. This is enough to convince most of the customers out there that the general consensus is good. This is what is known as going with the flow. When a majority of your customers agree with you, they will try to mimic what the others are doing. If you are a company that sells products that are made of paper and you are trying to convince people to recycle the paper once they have used the product then you need to show that consensus is on your side. The small print on your product stating 75% of your customers recycle this paper when they are done using it goes a long way in convincing others to do it as well. The principle of consensus is extremely powerful and you need to use it to your advantage in order to build a brand name and convince people.

Chapter 2: The Foundation

The Important Buyer Persona Questions That You Need To Ask

Buyer personas play a huge role in determining the success of a marketing strategy because at the end of the day it is important for you to know as much about your potential buyers as possible so that you can market your products to them more effectively and in a personalized manner. If you are a little bit confused with regards to how you should determine a buyer persona and what filters need to be added in order for the campaign to be a successful one, you need to continue reading. There is so much information out there that it could become intimidating just thinking about what you should and shouldn't include. If you are a small business and you are looking to market on Facebook effectively, here are a few persona questions you should ask in order to identify the audience

Understand Personal Demographics

Demographic information is a great place to begin with because it helps you to narrow down your buyers in an effective way to see whether they fit into the criteria you are looking for. There are many demographics you can include and, apart from location and age, you can also check for demographics that will help you to find the gender, household income, and whether or not they have children or are single or dating.

Educational Background

Understanding the level of education of potential buyers can also help you to figure out whether or not they are ideal buyers for your product. If you are omitting people from a particular University or college, you simply need to ask them the name of their university or college to identify the buyer persona.

Career Path

Some businesses need to target people who hold a certain designation or belong to a certain industry and using this particular buyer persona can help you to narrow down the selection quite easily.

Identifying the Industry of the Buyer Persona

It makes a lot of sense for you to look for people from a certain industry because they may be in a particular employment role that scatters across various industries, and if you want to talk with those people it's difficult to do it by selecting the industry and then narrowing it down to the kind of people you want to talk to. For example, if you are looking for products to sell to a hospital you can't just get in touch with any Human Resource

Department. You need to narrow down your industry selection to the hospital and Medical Services only.

The Size of the Company

It is also important for you to know your buyer persona's company. Apart from the Industry, you need details such as the size of the company and the number of employees working for it. If you want to target the entire organization you should always know how many people there are so that you can switch your product accordingly. If you are a B2B business and you are looking to target small and large organizations to sell your product you can always fix the price based on the number of products you would sell and the only way you will be able to determine the number of potential buyers is by the size of the company.

Job Title or Role

Sometimes, someone may be into professional sales and you may or may not be able to determine whether they are the right people or not for the job, and figuring out the job title or role can help you decide whether they are in a position to make a decision or not.

Who Do They Report To?

It's important for you to know who your buyer persona's report to because if they are not the point of contact to go ahead with your business idea, then there will be somebody above them, and unless you identify that person this will be your dead end.

Information about Their Daily Routine On A Work Day

This question is not relevant to a buyer persona question, but when you know what a particular day looks like, you know exactly when to talk with them or when to place a call where they are less likely to be busy and you will be able to get in touch with them and discuss the business opportunity.

What Tools Do You Use And What Knowledge To You Have?

This question will help you understand what kind of tools your customers use on a daily basis in their job and what level of technical knowledge they have. You need to understand if they use any applications such as Photoshop or a CRM, and how often they use it. This will also give you an idea of the kind of products that they like using and the products that they stay away from. You should try to draw parallels between the products they like and products that you are selling, and this will help you pitch your product appropriately.

What Are Your Challenges?

When you are in a business you need to understand the kind of challenges that people are facing and how you can solve them. With this question, you will try to understand what kind of problems people are facing daily. This will help you to pitch your product accordingly, based on the challenges. For example, you are a company that makes earphones. If your customer is a transcriber and he or she states that they are not able to hear their audio very well because of the background noise, you can pitch your product stating that you have noise-cancellation software that can help them focus on your audio and transcribe better. This is just a small example and there are other parallels that you can draw based on the customer's problems and the solution that you are offering.

What Kind Of Work Are You Responsible For?

This question will help you to understand the persona of your potential buyers and see the level of stress that they are under. You can also try to help your customers achieve their goals or overcome the challenges based on this question. If you sell electronic appliances and a customer states that they get late when they are trying to get things done in the morning, you can then pitch your products, such as a toaster that is quicker than others or an alarm clock that is really effective in waking you up.

Where Do You Get Your Information From/Which Websites Of Blogs Do You Frequently Visit?

In order to understand your buyer, you need to make sure that you look at their internet usage and how they use the internet to their advantage. This question will help you understand their social network usage, as well as their usage of search engines. You will also understand which sources they trust and how often they read blogs online. If you find that most of your customers refer to blogs for information then you can start your own business blog and get them to subscribe to it. Blogs are the best way to gain the confidence of customers and build a brand name without being too obvious about it.

Where Do You Purchase Your Products From?

This will help you understand what kind of online shopping activities your customers do. If most of your customers are comfortable shopping online then you need to create the ideal sales experience for them. You need to get into their comfort zone so that you can reciprocate their sales experience and help build your brand name.

A Basic Buy Persona Template Example

Age	
Location	
Language	
Job title	
Average income	
Buying behavior	

Interests & activities	
Life stage	

Pain Points and Goals

Customer pain point	Customer goal	How you can help?
[**Example**: We have trouble keeping our fans on social media engagement because we only have so much time to dedicate to each network.]	[**Example**: We want to be able to engage our social media audience <u>and</u> save time.]	[**Example**: Your business allows you to schedule posts and messages across networks from a single dashboard.]

Pain point #2	Goal #2	Your solution #2
Pain point #3	Goal #3	Your solution #3
Pain point #4	Goal #4	Your solution #4

Real Estate Example

Age	30 Years

Location	New York
Language	English
Job title	Software Engineer
Average income	$150000
Buying behavior	First Time Buyer
Interests & activities	Computers, Swimming, Music
Life stage	Single

Pain Points and Goals

Customer pain point	Customer goal	How your product/business can help?
No time to go house hunting	Find the ideal house and close on escrow	Give a virtual tour
Budget constraints	Find house within budget with wiggle room for renovations / minor interior changes	Look for a smaller, cozy home - or ready to move in home that requires no additional expenses.

Restaurant Example

Age	45 years

Location	Dallas
Language	English
Job title	Homemaker
Average income	$50000
Buying behavior	Return customer
Interests & activities	Socializing, partying, kid-friendly activities
Life stage	Married, with two kids.

Pain Points and Goals

Customer pain point	Customer goal	How your business/product can help?
Looking to celebrate the kid's birthday party	Needs a place big enough to accommodate 100 guests (Budget constraints)	Offer package deals with mini-meals and fun kid activities and a parent area to socialize

Chapter 3: Start Growing Your Business with Facebook

Although Facebook was under the scanner in 2018 for not maintaining data transparency, it still happens to be the number one platform for people to socialize on a regular basis. This is a considerable amount of people who like keeping themselves updated with what's happening in and around them but scrolling through what was initially called the Facebook wall. If you are a small business owner there is no denying that Facebook is the best way for you to market your business and help it to grow fast.

What Content Can You Create On Facebook

Facebook has a wide range of different tools that small businesses can benefit from. Whether you choose to use it organically or through various methods, you can definitely benefit by creating a Facebook page and using it to your advantage. Organic content that you share on your Facebook page starts gaining more and more popularity if you combine it with ad campaigns that you plan strategically.

There are various campaigns you can conduct on Facebook, and whether you choose pictures, carousel, or video format, you can increase the online presence of your business to a great extent. You can also consider using blogs and video content to initiate conversation or follow it at a later stage.

How to Effectively Market With Facebook

If you choose a Facebook business manager to begin your campaign, you can use multiple filters to set your goal and create awareness or increase the sales of your product effectively. Facebook has some interesting tools that not only help you to target people more practically but also in a more systematic manner, which means you will not spend money on unnecessary lead generation. Genetic exposure is not effective because this is not going to get you any revenue or help your business grow. If you want your business to succeed you need Facebook marketing to work in your favor. You need to use it to target the right customers and that's where your buyer persona and the effective tools that Facebook have to help segregate the audience come in handy.

Facebook Marketing Advantages

While Facebook may look very simple from the onset, it does provide a lot of creative support and helps small businesses grow their brand name. Facebook provides you with a lot of tools that will help you create content for your desktop as well as mobile devices. Even if you have no designing skills, you will be able to create content for your small business with the help of Facebook. Some of the content that you can create on Facebook includes:

Images

There are a number of images that you can create on Facebook with the help of the creator support that is available behind the scenes. It has been seen that any post that has images will get more engagement than a text-only post. There are a number of resources that will help you to create images using clipart as well as photo resources. You will be able to brand your image and put your point across with the help of this resource.

Video Content

Video content has a massive reach, however, very few businesses use video to their advantage. A video could be anything related to your business such as an advertisement or even a campaign that shows your business in a good light. There are a number of video creation options that Facebook has and you should use this to your advantage in order to help your business prosper.

Live Facebook

This is another great tool that Facebook provides to all of its users. As a small business, it is very beneficial to use Facebook live and interact with your customers in real-time. You will be able to get an instant reaction and you will see your business prosper.

Facebook also offers targeting opportunities for small businesses. You will be able to target specific customers based on their behavior. Behavioral targeting not only helps you reach the right audience, but it will also help create an impact in no time. This targeting feature helps you target local communities as well as large geographical areas. This feature is extremely important because in today's world, targeting random people for promoting a business is not going to work in your favor.

Paid Content Vs Organic Content

Over the years Facebook has been known to encourage organic content, however, that trend changed a couple of years ago. Facebook started paid advertising and started downgrading organic content. This caused a number of businesses opting in for paid content because organic content reached very few potential customers. Facebook was no longer happy with just regular posts and updates in the organic news feed. Going with the paid option was one of the best things to do if you wanted to get noticed on Facebook.

However, recently Facebook changed its approach and began returning to its roots. In 2018 it started favoring personal content over promotional content. Facebook has also started appreciating content that is shareable, valuable, and community-based. You no longer need to rely on corporate methods of promotion. You only need to create content that will fit into your customer's newsfeed. Facebook customers now have the option of marking certain advertisements as spam and if you do not want your ads to be listed as spam you need to start getting organic with your content and get more personal with your customers.

Creating A Facebook Business Account

Setting up a business page is extremely important to make sure that your business has some kind of identity on Facebook. Facebook offers a number of tools to small businesses to promote their products and services and this can be done with the help of the business manager. The business manager allows you to create your Facebook page, identify your audience, and list down your product catalog. You can even set up permissions for your account and give the user access to various employees on your page as well as your apps. The business manager will even allow you to track your advertisements and see the kind of impressions you are making and how much you are spending on your ads.

Creating Your Account

When creating your account you need to go to business.Facebook.com/create and click on the option to create an account. Then you need to enter your name and enter your Facebook login credentials. You will then get several prompts that you need to follow in order to create your business account. Once you have entered all the information you then need to go ahead and select the settings and assign permissions to your Facebook account. You can assign up to two people as your administrator and these are the people that will approve posts and they will be responsible for maintaining the page. You don't need to add a new ad account. This account will help manage all your advertisements and make sure that you tweak the ads based on your requirements.

Assigning Levels

Once you have created your business account and you have given permissions, you then need to assign levels to the people that are on your team. You need to decide roles for your employees and these rules will hold true across all accounts, the business app, as well as the ad account.

Add a Payment Method

When you set up your business account you also need to add a payment method. This payment method will allow you to pay for Facebook ads and also receive a line of credit whenever you are eligible. You will need to define a payment method before you create your ad account.

Creating a Facebook Company Fan Page

Every business needs a fan page in order to grow their business and get the word out there. Just creating a Facebook account is not sufficient. You need a fan page to interact with your fans and make sure that you generate sufficient leads and increase sales for your business. Here are a few simple steps that will show you how to create your business fan page and generate leads and interact with your potential customers.

You need to first go to Facebook.com/pages. Once you are on the website then you need to click on the 'create a page' button that appears on the upper right-hand side of the page. Then you will be asked to select the category for your business. This could be a local business, an organization, a company, an artist, a brand, a public figure, a community, or entertainment. If you are not sure which category your business falls under then you could either select company, organization, or institution.

Once you have decided which category your business belongs to, you will then be asked to fill out information regarding the business. Depending on the category that you selected you will be given subcategories to choose from and then you will need to enter your company name. You will then need to select that you agree with the Facebook page terms and click the 'get started' button.

Enter Basic Information

The next stage is entering the information for your business and uploading a profile picture. You will also be asked to select a Facebook web address and fill in the 'about' section. When you are uploading the profile picture for your business you should pick an image that is 180 pixels by 180 pixels. When you have uploaded this image it will show on your fan page. After you upload the picture you need to click on the button that says 'save photo' and then click next. If you do not have a picture ready to upload you can even skip this step for now.

When filling out the basic information for your business you need to enter information that is clear and accurate. You should also include keywords that are relevant to your business as this will help with the SEO of the business page. You then need to type in your website URL and set up your Facebook link. You need to make this link short as well as memorable because this is the link that your potential customers will use to find you. If your business name is very difficult to remember you need to consider using something shorter that will be easy to recollect.

Use the Admin Panel

When you become a fan page administrator you will be able to see the admin panel. This admin panel will give you information regarding your pages, such as new people that have recently liked your page, notifications regarding your page post, and information regarding how your fan page is performing. You can use the control panel to add new administrators and you can even edit the information on your fan page. You can invite people to like your page and follow it, however, you need to be careful about using this option because if your pages are empty people may not want to follow your page. Put relevant information regarding your business and add content to make people interested in following you.

Tell Stories

People do not like random posts that are put up on fan pages. Your content will decide how successful your fan page is and this is what you need to focus on. It is important to share regular status updates, milestones, and images along with videos that will tell a story to the audience. All your updates on your fan page should revolve around your brand as this will help create an impact amongst your fans.

Build Tabs to Generate Sales

You need to then build tabs on your fan page that will help connect with your leads and increase traffic to your website. You can create one tab that will help you get email ids while another tab will help sell your products. Facebook even allows you to accept payments through its integrated payment gateway. Your fan page can promote and sell your business on its own as long as the content is relevant and interesting.

Facebook Marketing Tips for Small Businesses

Facebook is focusing on delivering content that is useful to users and, in most cases, organic content is declining. If you are spending to advertise on Facebook for your small business, it is necessary for you to make the right decision in order for the marketing efforts to pay off.

It's common for small businesses to lower marketing expenses on Facebook because of not being too sure whether or not they will be able to choose the right path. There's nothing to worry about because no matter how limited your budget is, a little persuasion and the right influencer will manage to get more customers for your business.

Post with Intent

You have to think about what you want to share on Facebook and how you would like to interact with your audience. Reciprocation is necessary which is why you have got to focus on content that establishes two-way communication rather than just being a platform for you to share without knowing whether or not it's actually interesting to your customers. The more people reciprocate, the higher the chances of the content going viral, and you will benefit from it.

Try To Blend In

Your Facebook marketing tactics don't have to stand out in your campaigns. It needs to be subtle but clear, so people know what you're talking about but they also enjoy the content you share. Whether it's a humorous post something informative to make sure that anyone who checks your post benefits from it even if you don't benefit from them.

Don't Forget Your Content Calendar

A content calendar helps you to effectively plan your posts and schedule them even on days you won't be accessing your computer, and this helps regular interaction and posting, which is vital for your Facebook page and your marketing efforts to work.

Optimize Your Profile Page

Your Facebook business page is the face of your business and has to be complete. Make sure all the information is updated on the page; that will make it easy for the customer to get in touch with you. Whether it is providing the timings of your business operations or giving them the official website to visit always make sure information on your Facebook business page is updated.

Clear the Community Page

A smart way to use persuasion principles in Facebook marketing is by creating a community page. You can not only manage to make people feel special and reciprocate but you can also create an illusion of scarcity of products or services that they automatically want to invest in.

Create a Facebook Group

It's difficult to handle so many Facebook accounts. You need to make sure you share the right kind of information on the right pages. The benefit of creating a group is that you can invite people to like it, and this is a subtle persuasion principle that you can put to use and benefit from. One of the best things about creating a Facebook group is that you can automatically increase your likes without spending money by simply inviting your circle of friends and family members to join in.

Strategically Choose Your Name

Sometimes your business name might already be taken up by another Facebook page and this may get you extremely disappointed. If you are a local business, try using your business name and local city name to let people know the difference between your Facebook page and the other one.

Use the Facebook story to your advantage

People are always curious to watch your Facebook story because it goes away after 24 hours. This will give people the curiosity to see what's happening and it helps you increase visibility on Facebook.

Start With One Advertisement At A Time On A Limited Budget

When you start advertising on Facebook, always begin with a small budget. Even if you fail, you know for a fact that you didn't invest too much money and it gives you the motivation to start over.

Consider Boosting Posts

When you share something organically and you realize it is doing really well, consider boosting the post to get more exposure. This can be done with a small budget and it can give you the kind of revenue returns you were seeking.

You can also try to use Facebook pixel and other add-on tools to your benefit one at a time to see which works well for you. Most Facebook marketing strategies can be applied to other social media platforms as well, as long as you use them effectively. While it's good to have a social media presence across all platforms, it is important for you to focus on one at a time so that you create a strong influence on one platform before you move to the other.

Biggest mistakes you make on Your Facebook Profile & Fan Page

It is important for you to understand the various mistakes people usually make when it comes to promoting their business on Facebook. This helps to avoid making these silly mistakes that will cost you the right kind of exposure and limit your marketing efforts.

Posting too many times on Facebook

Whether it's sharing on your private business page or fan page, you need to make sure that you limit the number of posts to a maximum of 5 posts a day for businesses. Posting irrelevant information too many times is not going to help your Facebook page. Some business owners are in the habit of sharing too much information from other pages thinking that it will benefit them and help them to get more exposure. This is not beneficial for your business in any way, so make sure you focus on sharing information relevant to your business at the right time.

Not Engaging In Comments

It is vital for business owners to have two-way communication and reciprocate with potential customers and existing customers if you want persuasion to continue. The best way to do this is to engage in the comments whether good, bad, or ugly and reply to your customers regularly.

Arguing

One of the worst things you can do is arguing with people on your Facebook page because this will create a negative impact and hamper the reputation of your business. Always leave positive feedback, irrespective of how hurtful comment is.

Deleting negative comments

It's not recommended to delete comments unless they have pornographic or graphic content. If something is said to you or your business, try dealing with it but do not delete a negative comment against your business; rather, show a brave face to prove credibility.

Running competitions against the rules

Running a competition on Facebook and trying to lure customers by promising them a gift when you don't actually provide them with one is something you should avoid doing. Facebook does not share information directly with business owners and if a business owner wants to get in touch with the customer they need to do it directly.

Posting similar content

Maintaining a business page is extremely difficult if you are not sure what you need to update on it. Some businesses update just one type of content on a daily basis. This content is usually in the form of images that give out a social message or promote the brand name. While posting images is fine, doing the same thing multiple times a day can get monotonous, and your fans will lose interest in your page. You need to post things that add value to your business page and also show your fans that you are interested in communicating with them. Try to make some interactions by asking for the opinions by inviting them to certain sales. This will make fans want to look forward to your next post and it will also help improve your brand value. You can always mix things up by putting up a joke or putting a funny message, but these are the things that should not dominate your fan page. Your fan page should be about your fans and your business and nothing else.

Not using applications properly

There are a number of built-in applications on Facebook that help you create campaigns and drive more traffic to your business. Most fan pages do not use this to their advantage and they end up hoping fans will turn up to their business website and get converted into a sale. You cannot live on hope in the world of business. You need to take the initiative and use the applications as well as the tabs to your advantage. Introduce competitions amongst the fans and create various campaigns that will help promote your business. When fans start showing interest in your business and they stand to gain something out of it, it will work wonders for your popularity.

Not responding

Social media is all about interaction with fans and when the interaction stops, you will end up losing a lot of followers. Most fans usually comment positively on your posts and you should make it a point to reply to these comments. If there are too many comments you can always thank them in your next post rather thanking them individually. If there is a negative comment or if somebody is asking a specific question, make sure you individually respond to such comments because this will put you in good light and it will show the fans that you are interested in communicating with them. The key to responding is doing it fast. Replying after two days to a comment is not going to be helpful.

Generating traffic to your website

The purpose of a fan page should be to increase traffic to your website. This can be done in a number of ways and with various calls to action. You need to mix up your call to action and persuade your audience by using the six principles of persuasion. These principles are proven and you should be able to increase traffic to your website in no time. Mix up your content and make sure that the fans do not get bored with what you are offering. Asking your fans to visit your website through each and every post is not going to do the trick because fans eventually realize that your intention is wrong.

The Most Common Persuasion Mistakes

Using the rules of persuasion to lure people into showing interest in your business is a common habit most small business owners adapt to. Principles work really well in helping your business get the kind of exposure that it needs. It's important to understand how to avoid the common mistakes people make when they try to use these principles for marketing.

Validating undesirable

Too many times people share stuff on social media that may not necessarily be accepted. With a view to reciprocate to that post a lot of business owners go to validate the behavior. You need to understand that you have got to stay away from such posts, even though you may want to reciprocate because it's not healthy to confuse contacts with reciprocity.

Just because somebody purchases a product from you doesn't necessarily mean you have to return the favor by doing something in addition to providing them with the product. When it comes to marketing business your reciprocation is in the form of quality products or services you provide and you need to focus on that rather than giving an additional service or product that has no value or meaning in the life of the customer. Sometimes it's always better to stay away and be a silent spectator. If these comments are on your Facebook page you can always reciprocate in a healthy manner without validating the behavior.

Highlight gain instead of the loss

Many times business owners tend to spend more money on promoting their business than they actually get a profit out of. One of the major reasons we need to start with small marketing efforts is because it helps to understand just how profitable the entire strategy or plan is. When it doesn't work out you can always change the strategy to something more effective but when you invest too much time and money in one particular plan and focus on the few profits instead of focusing on the major losses your business does not grow.

Misusing your authority

The principle of authority is one principle that a lot of businesses misuse. People usually look at influencers in social media when they make their decisions. These influencers help customers make decisions based on their personal experiences as well as the facts. Some of these influencers end up misusing the authority and give wrong information to the customers. You need to make sure you do not repeat these mistakes because when you misuse the principle of authority and the trust is broken, customers will not hesitate before they speak out. Rather than convincing somebody that your product is good, even though it has flaws, you need to make sure that you work on the flaws and improve your product before asking customers to opt for it.

The principle of liking

You need to build your relationship based on this principle. Most businesses are very happy with a few likes on your Facebook and are content without following up on those likes. If a follower likes any of your content, you need to make sure that you connect further with them and make sure that they converted into a customer. If you do not see too many likes coming on your Facebook fan page then you should try to make customers like you rather than forcing them to like your posts. Posting over and over again is not going to gain you any additional customers. You need to speak about your brand and make people like you because the principle of liking is very strong. Once customers start liking you they will always look forward to your posts and they will stay loyal to your business.

Enforcing the principle of consistency

Most businesses fall flat with this principle because they are not sure how to bring about consistency in their behavior. Changing a few statements and posts can bring about a change as long as it stays consistent with your brand image. If you are promoting ethical behavior then your post should also reflect that behavior. When you start contradicting this principle, you will see your number of followers backing down.

Not giving a reason

When you do not provide a reason for a certain kind of behavior you will not gain the trust of your customers. If the pricing for any of your products has increased you need to explain to your customers through your fan page for the reason in the increase. Doing things without reason will not work in your favor because customers want to know why they are being affected because of a change in your policies.

Proven Ways to Boost Organic (Non-Paid) Facebook Posts

Facebook uses an algorithm to determine which posts of yours are popular and which are not. Posts that have the potential to go viral can always be boosted and these posts can not only manage to help you get more exposure but they can market your business without any expense. Here are some smart ways to boost your Facebook marketing efforts without spending any money.

Analyze Your Top 10

One of the best ways to post on Facebook and know it will get exposure is to check in on your Facebook marketing efforts and see the most popular posts that you shared in the form of advertisements. Select those posts and use them in a persuasive manner to promote it again but in an organic way.

Post amazing content

In order for a business to post healthy content, they need to make sure that they follow the Persuasion principles because this method pretty much guarantees more followers and it's important for you to have responsive posts if you want your business to stay popular on Facebook. Take time to create the content or hire a specialist to do this, but make sure that all the content you post is good quality and the kind of sentences people look forward to seeing.

Optimize targeting

You can filter the kind of people you want to target on Facebook, so do that by applying a variety of filters to the post that can help you get better exposure to people that matter most.

Don't cross-post

The posters on Twitter have no relevance on Facebook and hashtags are not trending right now, so you need to make sure that you design posts specifically for each platform and share it on those platforms only.

Learn the best times to post

There's a lot of information out there with regards to which is the best for you to share on Facebook, but the best way to figure that out is to see what time your previous posts got the best response and mimic those steps taken to posting at that time.

Share on weekends as well

It's important for you to share information on weekends, and in case you not planning to go to your office, you can always use scheduling tools like Hootsuite to automatically send outposts on weekends to engage customers and potential customers.

Make the most of Facebook live

Facebook live is an amazing feature that will allow you to communicate directly with your customers. You can stream any events you're hosting or even celebrations within your organization. A number of small businesses provide updates to their customers through the Facebook live feature. If you are a real estate business, you can provide live views to a new listing in your portfolio. Not only does this get you more outreach, but it will also help customers communicate and connect with you in a better manner.

Use your blog posts to your advantage

A number of businesses run blog posts simultaneously and this is something that you should also get into the habit of doing. Your blog posts are a great way to communicate with your customers, and getting customers to your blog is not an easy task. You can start embedding your blog URL into your Facebook content, which helps redirect customers to your blog when they click on your images or posts to increase views on your blog. If you have an onsite blog, this automatically increases traffic to your website which contributes to SEO efforts in the long run.

Use events to your advantage

Creating an event on Facebook does not cost you anything and it can give you the outreach that you desire. When you announce a sale or an upcoming launch via an event, people will start showing interest because they have nothing to lose. Even if you get a 10% conversion from the number of people that attend your event, your event can be termed as successful.

Make use of webinars

A number of businesses use webinars to communicate with customers as well as employees across the world. You can now use Facebook as a webinar discussion board and invite people to join the discussion. When a lot of people start joining a webinar it will automatically boost your Facebook page and you will reach more customers.

Email marketing

You need to use your Facebook fan page to collect emails from potential customers. You need to then use these email ids and utilize them in your email marketing campaigns. Since most of the recipients will know your business they will not mark emails as spam and they may end up liking your business and promote your business to their family members and friends. Email marketing has a lot of scopes and you can use it in collaboration with Facebook marketing to get good results.

Using Pinterest

If your products or services are appealing to women you need to make sure that you use Pinterest to your advantage as well. Most small businesses upload the Facebook images on Pinterest as well and backlink it to the fan page. This strategy has worked tremendously and a number of businesses have seen an increase in their followers.

Ask your fans to enable notifications

While you may have over a million followers on your Facebook page, not all of them will know if you have posted something new. This could be because they are not following you and your updates will not appear in their news feed. You can ask people to follow your notifications as well so that they get an update and your followers on your fan page will convert into potential customers.

Facebook Engagement Tactics for Your Business Page

The first principle of persuasion is reciprocating, which means it's important for you to interact with your potential customers and customers if you want your business to grow and get the kind of exposure you believe it deserves. There are different things you can do on Facebook if you want to engage with your customers but you have to come up with effective ways you can convince people to reciprocate.

Collect questions in comments

Always encourage your audience to reply to questions about your business, asking for suggestions, put them in the spotlight and tell them to give you certain tips and tricks on how you can either improve what they are looking forward to from your business. Not only does this help you to interact with your potential customers and customers, it lets you know what they are looking for and you to strive to be a more customer-oriented business.

Share offers about products to anyone who pings you on messenger

This is a unique and smart way to get people to reciprocate. All you need to do is have a small code ready that you can share with them on messenger every time they ping you. This will also help give you an idea of how many people are actually watching your business and what kind of reaction they have to the posts that you shared.

Use emojis to your advantage

People love looking at emojis and it shows that you have a friendly and casual approach in your business, which makes it easier for people to communicate with you. These emojis are easy to use and they help spread a more sentimental message that helps you connect with the people.

Shout out to customers

When someone purchases something from your business or you have a new customer that you are proud of, have a shout out and let them know that you are feeling appreciated and loved. However, when you plan on doing this make sure that you ask the customer for permission prior to creating the post just to make sure you don't make the customer feel embarrassed or out of place.

Run a contest!

Post a riddle on Facebook and ask people to answer it. Give them a gift voucher or a chance to win something big if they reply with the right answer. This is a lot of potential reaches and many customers love engaging, not just because of the prize but because they want to test their intellectual skills.

Ask for feedback

Customers usually love when they are included in any decision-making, and this is what you should be doing with your Facebook posts. A number of businesses have to interact with the customers in this manner and have tried to get their views on certain business decisions. Not only does this help with increased engagement, but it also ensures that fans look forward to contributing to your business success. This can be done in the form of a survey or asking a question on a Facebook fan page and noting down the answers. You should also reply to the feedback on your fan page and let people know you appreciate their suggestions.

Share relevant information

Most of the time you do not need to share information regarding your business. You need to make sure that you share information that will be helpful to customers because this will create a positive impact on their minds. If you are in the health business then you can share information regarding an outbreak of a virus that people need to be careful about. This does not necessarily promote your brand but it will show people that you care about them even if they are not your customers yet.

Ask open-ended questions

Try to have a bit of fun with your audience and ask them questions that they will love answering and will be beneficial to your business as well. For example, if you are in the hotel business you can ask questions such as 'how much are you willing to pay for a fancy meal with your significant better half?'. People will love answering this question and they will even give you vital information with regards to what people's budget is. Once you have collated all the information, make sure that you launch an event or offer something to the customers in return that will connect back with your question. In this example, you can offer a one-time-only dinner for two for $200, if that is the amount that most people have said they would pay for a romantic dinner date.

Start Joining Conversations That Are Relevant

Look at the world around you and create the content that will be relevant to what's happening across borders. You need to start aligning your posts with news and give information to people because world news will affect them. Try being a friend to your audience rather than a salesperson. You will see the level of interaction increasing when you start posting relevant information on your fan page.

Speak About Your Community Involvement

People love it when businesses give back to society and you need to make sure that you do that as well. While most people would not know what you have done to help society, you could provide information to the people proactively and show them that you care and are giving back when it's needed the most. If your local area has been hit by a flood, you can give out free food to all the people that are homeless or are struggling. This gesture will definitely pay off and your fans will be grateful when you do something for others.

Don't be serious all the time

Add a bit of humor to your posts every now and then because everyone needs a laugh occasionally. Do not try to put others down with your jokes and also try to stay away from political statements or religious statements. Generic humor will be accepted by a majority of your audience and you will not have to regret putting any of this up.

Examples of Interactive Facebook Posts

Type Of Posts	Example 1 (Realtor	Example	2

	- Local Business)	(Restaurant - Local Business)
Contest	Tell us what you think about the latest bridge construction in one word	Give us your famous 3-Ingredient recipe!
Run A Poll Or A Survey	What's better? Oceanview or Gardenview? Share your opinion with us now	Have you tried out our new desserts yet? Tell us which one you'd like to continue seeing on the menu!
Facebook Live	New open house today for all via Facebook Live. Get a virtual tour! Click on the link to book your slot.	Watch our cook live in action as he prepares his famous Chilli Chicken recipe! Watch and learn!
Create Events	Ten new open houses scheduled	We're finally opened for

	in the Dallas area next week. Click if you are interested and invite your friends along as well.	wedding bookings! Booking from Monday - Check the listing on our fan page!
Share Inspirational Stories	See how this 24-year old built an ultimate dream home for his parents! Get those tissues out!	Watch this war veteran propose to his fiancee over a romantic dinner! There is nothing better that you'll see on the internet today!

Scroll Stopping Content

When you market on Facebook you need to make sure that you create content that stops people from scrolling and make them want to take a look at whatever you have to share. You have a very small window to influence people to do that before they scroll past your post, so you need to make sure you include bright vibrant pictures and catchy phrases that don't take too long for a person to read. Video content works really well as long as there is a catchy tagline to it.

A major mistake people make when sharing video content is not adding a tagline. People are not going to guess the video content and they will not watch it unless there's something that makes them curious or tugs on an emotional string. When you put the principles of persuasion along with the right tactics Facebook marketing, you manage to come up with a scroll-stopping post that will benefit your business.

Why do people share content?

A Facebook advertisement is usually a place to share information. People are not really sure what they need to share and what they should stay away from. Most people will share when it elicits a positive response in their mind. Happy posts are something that a lot of people will openly share. Another post people usually tend to share is information regarding health or maybe a post that has gone viral. The trick to making people want to share a post is to engage with them. The more engaging or interesting your posts, the more people will want to share it and make others aware of it. As a business owner, you need to keep the following points in mind when it comes to sharing habits.

- almost 60% of people share a post when they find it interesting and relevant to their daily lives.
- 40% of the posts are shared are because people found

that the content was funny.

- 30% of posts were shared because it was a social message and people believed in that message.
- 35% of people share posts when they found that it was regarding a sales recommendation. For example posts regarding the 10 best smartphones that cost less than $100.
- 25% of posts were shared when they were promoting a social cause or promoting a local business.

You need to understand the psychology of your readers in order to make your post shareable.

Targeting on Facebook

Sharing information without a target audience on Facebook is not going to benefit your business in any way because unless you talk with customers who are relevant to your business you are not going to make any money. If you are a local business and somebody who is not local sees your advertisement, it's not going to do much for you as a business owner. It's important for you to understand the various ways you can target customers by using filters on Facebook to narrow down people who are most likely potential customers or will be interested in your business.

Targeting on Facebook can be done in a number of ways. You need to look at all the criteria which could be relevant to your customers and target based on these criteria. Some of the criteria include:

Location

If you want your business to grow locally then you should target customers that are local. If you do not have the capacity to scale at the national or international level then there is no point selecting customers from different geographic areas.

Demographics

You need to get the demographics right when it comes to targeting the right audience. Most products and services would be relevant to a certain age group or even certain sex. You need to also target specific demographics such as marital status as well as yearly earnings.

Interest

Most customers update their interest on their Facebook page. You need to use this to your advantage and target people based on the interests they have mentioned. If you are a company that promotes music then you can sell jazz music to people who love that genre.

Look for partner connections

Partner connections are important because you will be able to target an audience before anyone else as targets them. For example, if you are looking to sell a new smartphone, look for customers that have contacted a local repair shop. If a customer's phone is not working, there is a 50% chance that they may look for a new smartphone in the near future.

Chapter 4: How to Set up Facebook Business Manager

A lot of people tend to avoid using Facebook business manager because they believe that it is a complicated setup that will consume a lot of their time. One of the best things about the Facebook business manager is it actually helps you to save on a lot of time and, while the initial setup may seem complicated, once you've gone through it, you will be able to benefit from it long-term. Here is a detailed break-up of how you can set up your Facebook business manager by following the simple steps.

Create Your Facebook Business Manager Account

In order for you to create your Facebook business manager, you need to first create an account. In order for you to do this, you have got to go to business.Facebook.com and click on the create account big blue button which is at the left of the top of the screen. You then need to fill out all your information in the popup box and continue. Make sure that you enter your business email address to manage your business account and click finish once all these details are completed.

Add Your Business Page

This is really simple, and if you already have an existing Facebook page, you can automatically integrate it into your Facebook business page with a few steps. If you are trying to replicate your pages, you will need to grant access from your Facebook account to the business manager account in order for this to happen.

In order for you to do this, you need to go to the dashboard, click on the add page, and click add page in the popup box again. If you have more than one account then make sure that you select the right one.

Add Your Facebook Ad Account

Once you get access to the existing Facebook page you can then request access to your Facebook ad account as well, which means if you have existing advertisements, you can control them using the business manager. On the business manager dashboard, once you click on add ad account you will also manage to get access to your ads manager. If you don't have an ad account on Facebook you can then create one in the business manager. In order for you to set up an ad account, you have got to go back to the dashboard, click on the add ad account, and start creating your ad account. You need to enter all your details including an email address, payment method, and a little more information before the account is successfully set up.

Add People to Help Manage the Facebook Business Page

Marketing on Facebook is quite difficult, and if you are a large organization and have multiple tasks at hand you can always hire a business manager to handle the page for you. You can add team members and also limit or restrict the amount of accessibility you want to give to them. There is a people and assets column in the business setting that you need to go to where you can assign assets to certain people and also grant how much access you would like them to have on the manager page itself.

Assign People to Manage Your Facebook Page

There are a number of assets that you would have on Facebook, and you need to be on top of your marketing efforts in order to be successful. In order to be in control of your Facebook marketing efforts, you need to add team members that can help take care of your Facebook business page and control your Facebook ad campaigns. This can be done through the business manager dashboard. When you are on the dashboard you need to click on business settings at the top of the page and then click on the people and assets tab. Under this tab, you need to select people and this will show you a list of people that can access your Facebook business manager. If you have not added anybody then you will only see your name and the address list. You can then start adding team members and assign privileges to each of the team members. You can add a number of people depending on their responsibility. This includes freelance writers, employees, and business partners. This step only involves adding individuals to your Facebook business account. Once you have set the privileges for each of the team members, you then need to click on add people and move to the next section.

Next, you need to decide which of your team members have access to which part of the business page. Some people would have access only to the advertising page while others will have complete control as a moderator. Once you have assigned responsibilities to them, each of your team members will receive an email regarding the same. They need to accept the invitation in order to become a part of the Facebook business page. You need to inform your team members in advance that they could receive an email and they should accept the invitation immediately.

Link to Your Instagram Account

Instagram is an important social media channel and linking it to your Facebook account will give you more outreach. This can be done again under the people and assets tab and then you need to click on add Instagram account. You will then be asked to enter the credentials for your Instagram account. Once you enter that information you need to click next. The next steps will ask you if you have more than one account for your business and you can enter that account information as well.

Now that you have your business manager running, you need to access your dashboard where you can control all the activities for your Facebook business page. Apart from doing the above you also need to go ahead and set up Facebook pixels that will allow you to take your Facebook advertisement to the next level.

Setting Up Facebook Pixels

Facebook pixels is coding that Facebook will help generate for you. When you enter this code on your website it will give access to information such as optimizing Facebook ads and tracking conversion through your website. Facebook pixels is very helpful and it should be set up even before you start your first ad campaign. Under the people and assets tab, you need to select pixels and then click on add. You don't need to give a name for your Facebook pixel account and click on create. On the next page, you have the option of setting up your pixel now and once you click on next, your pixel will be generated. You can create up to 10 pixels for your account and you can use this to your advantage.

Placing Your Ad

When you are on the Facebook business manager dashboard you need to click on business manager that is at the top left-hand side. When you click that, you need to click on create and manage and click on the create button. If you are doing this for the first time, you can select guided creation which will help you set up your campaign objective as well as select your target audience and your budget. Here you will be able to select your schedule for your ads and, when you click on save, you are ready for your first ad to go live. When you follow all the steps correctly you will be set to start your Facebook marketing campaign today.

Reasons You Should Be Advertising on Facebook

There is no denying that social media is definitely ruling the market when it comes to promoting your business online which is why it is very important for you to select the right platform for your business to grow. Facebook is still the best social media platform you can select because it has the highest number of active users and people tend to check Facebook on a regular basis. If you decide that you want to go with social media marketing but you are not too sure why Facebook is the best then here are some things about Facebook advertising you should know about.

Your Audience Is On Facebook

There is no denying that the people who you want to target are available on Facebook and it's easy for you to touch base with them because you are able to easily filter out unnecessary people and limit your budget effectively.

Facebook Advertisements Are Cheaper

There is no denying that Facebook advertising is relatively cheaper in comparison to the other advertising platforms on social media. You can also use organic boosts to increase your fan base and customer reach, which helps you to generate customers without spending any money.

Facebook Targeting Capabilities

There are a number of advertising channels that you can target, however, Facebook targeting is definitely the best. Facebook has a number of targeting capabilities and it includes demographics, interests, behavior, age range, connections, and locations. Each of these capabilities can be further expanded and you will be able to target a specific group with the help of Facebook.

Facebook Helps Convert Leads

Facebook is perfect when it comes to targeting customers that have already visited your website in the past. Irrespective of whether or not these leads became customers in the past, Facebook will keep remarketing to them based on their behavior online. A number of businesses have called this the social stalker. Facebook is capable of stalking all your potential leads and targeting them based on what they currently require. For example, if a customer has been searching for laptops, Facebook will know about this and will promote your business if you are in the laptop business. Facebook will never promote your ad to a customer that has been looking for products that do not fall within your niche.

Get New Leads Easily

Facebook is the perfect platform where you will be able to generate new leads almost on a daily basis. Apart from being able to generate new leads, you can even clone these leads with a lookalike audience feature that Facebook has. This feature enables Facebook to target an audience that is similar to your current target audience but may vary on a couple of parameters. The likelihood of these people also being interested in your business is very high and this is something that only Facebook can do for you. Facebook's target lookalike audience is based on people that have downloaded apps similar to your business app.

248

Benefits of the Facebook Pixel

Facebook pixel is one of the most interesting add-on tools that Facebook gives you. It's essential to help you create an interesting and successful marketing strategy that works in your favor. If you haven't already started using Facebook pixel then here are a few reasons why it needs to be integrated into your advertisement today.

Understanding Your Audience Better

Facebook pixel provides you with detailed insight that helps you to determine who your existing customers are as well as who are the potential customers. It provides you with analytics that not only identifies the browsing activity of people but also their purchasing activity.

Relevant Engagement

If you are in the e-commerce business and you are looking to talk with people who are relevant to your business using pixel is highly recommended. It uses behavioral targeting to identify people who are looking for services or businesses like yours so that you can get in touch with them faster or they can get in touch with you after they see your advertisement.

Identify Shopping Journeys

The Facebook pixel will help you understand shoppers that take a long time when they are browsing through products. Pixel data will help you understand what each of the customers looks for when they are selecting a product and what is the one aspect that appeals to them before they make the purchase. For example, for customers shopping for a new pair of jeans, there are a number of things that he or she could look for. Your pixel data will give you all this information and it will show you what features the customer is looking for in their pair of jeans. Once you know the kind of features that attract a customer, you will be able to customize your ads based on that.

Quick Shoppers

Similar to shoppers that take a long time to purchase things, the Facebook pixel will also help you identify shoppers that are very quick in their decision-making. Such customers are very specific with their requirements and they make a decision within a matter of minutes. Based on your pixel data you will be able to customize ads for these customers and help them purchase very quickly. These customers are driven by a call to action and you need to make sure that your ad features that.

Shopping In-Store

There are a number of customers that still prefer walking into a store and purchasing things rather than purchasing online. If you are a business that also has stores across a city or a country, you can use your Facebook ads to promote the stores. You can provide the store location as well as your operating hours along with all the pricing information that will help your audience make a decision.

Chapter 5: Choose The Best Advertising Option For Your Business on Facebook

Facebook advertising comes in a number of forms and you need to make sure that you pick the right advertising method based on your business. Irrespective of what product or service you deal in there is a Facebook option available for you. Here are a few Facebook ad templates that you can use along with some successful examples.

Video Ad

As the name suggests this is an ad that features a video and it will appear in the news feed for your potential users. You need to get as creative as possible with your video because it can help create a very positive impact on the audience. If you are into the food industry then you can show a video of a recipe being made and how it can benefit the users. You can also show gadgets that are featured in your video that can help make life easier in the kitchen. There are various kitchen hacks that you can share with your users in the form of a video and this is something that will definitely create a positive impact. Your audience will know that you care about their comfort rather than trying to sell your own business product. Take a look at this example of a successful video ad.

Photo Ad

Photo ads are generally useful for businesses that deal with products that can be seen. Photo ads are more effective in selling products rather than selling services. For example, if you are in the fashion industry then you can showcase pictures of your products worn by various models and this will help you create a positive outreach. Here is a classic example of a successful photo ad.

Reach Ad

A reach ad helps with promoting a particular shop or a product in a local area. For example, if you are having a sale in your local store, you can give information to customers based in that area and also provide details regarding the store. This ad will not show up to people that do not live in that area and this is how your ad can reach the maximum number of people. Reach ads can have a lot of impacts, however, there is a very limited scope because it is only specific to a particular segment. Here is an example of a successful reach advertisement.

Offer Ad

An offer advertisement helps promote certain offers that your business is bringing up. This will help get more customers interested in your business and you will be able to reach a wider audience irrespective of whether they have been your customers or not in the past. This advertisement will be shown only two people that have shown an interest in a similar product or service as yours. A classic example is if you are a local business that caters to pest control and if a customer has searched for pest control via a search engine, your Facebook ad will show up in the news feed of that particular customer. When you combine this targeting along with an offer ad, there is a very good chance that you will be able to convert a lead into a customer. Here is a very good example of an offer advertisement.

http://bit.ly/2IHNuVE

Event Ad

An event ad is very useful when it comes to promoting events in certain localities or even in certain cities. The event ad will give information regarding the event along with the timings. The event ad also ensures that you reach maximum people and you gain maximum participation for your event. Event ads will only be shown to people that have shown an interest in similar events in the past. Here is a look at a classic event ad.

http://bit.ly/2TjPmb7

Retargeting Ad

Retargeting ad is a generic ad that will help target customers that have shown an interest in your business or are currently contemplating purchasing a product similar to your product. If a customer looks for restaurant listings in his or her area and you are a local restaurant that has newly opened, your ad will appear to this customer and you will be able to get them to eat in your restaurant. In order for your ad to be successful, you need to have certain offers that may interest the customer. You will need to do proper research and prepare your ad based on what customers are looking for. Here is how a retargeting ad should look.

http://bit.ly/2EB3rbR

Targeting Based On The Audience

Facebook is available across multiple platforms and multiple operating systems. This means that every gadget that you have can be used to access Facebook and this makes it easier for you to reach a wider audience. However, you need to make sure that the format is correct irrespective of how the customer is viewing your ad.

Desktop / Laptop

If a customer is accessing Facebook from his or her desktop or laptop, then you will need to showcase your ads in a more traditional format. There are two ways it can showcase your ad to customers. You can choose to display ads on the right side of the screen. This ad will not interfere with the customer's newsfeed and it will be visible to the customer even if he or she keeps scrolling. The other way that you can display your ad on a laptop or a desktop is in the middle of the news feed. While this ad can grab attention, it can also get annoying if the customer keeps seeing your ad again and again. You need to make sure that you are selecting the right criteria for displaying your ads otherwise your ad may be marked as spam if it is being shown to the wrong user.

Mobile User

Almost 90% of all Facebook users access Facebook from their mobile phones. This means that you need to focus on creating the right mobile format for your ads so that the customer does not miss out on the ad and the visual experience is not hampered as well. When a customer is accessing Facebook through their mobile phone the ad will appear in the news feed and you need to make sure that you create the right ad because mobile phone users generally scroll by very quickly. If something does not catch their eye, they will not stop scrolling and you lose your chance of impressing and gaining a customer.

Chapter 6: Ideas And Tips For Ads Using The Persuasion Principles

We've already spoken about the persuasion principles and how they can help create better ads for you. The principles of Dr. Robert Cialdini have been very useful for a number of businesses and his research and training have helped people understand the psychology of influence and how to link it with their marketing efforts. The principles of persuasion will help you get better outreach, drive more customers to your website, increase subscriptions to your newsletters and get more downloads for your app.

Here we will look at the principles of persuasion and how you can use them to create effective Facebook ads.

Reciprocity

Reciprocity is nothing but responding to favor by doing another favor. When someone does not reciprocate, it is considered to be ungrateful. A number of businesses use the principle of reciprocation by offering discounts as well as free samples. The principle of reciprocity can be used in a number of ways to gain more customers, and here is a look at a few examples.

Going with an example of a realtor, you can offer a substantial discount to one of your listings in an area if somebody purchases within X number of days. You can also offer a free consultation or no brokerage if somebody refers to a customer to you within the next month. If you are running a restaurant, then you can offer discounts to your regular customers in order for them to come back to you in the future. You can even offer a membership program where customers would get a fixed discount each time they visit your restaurant.

Consistency and Commitment

This principle is all about retargeting your audience. There are two advantages of retargeting. One is you will always be the number one choice for a customer because you want them to come back to you. Customers like it when a business makes them feel important and want them to return as customers. The second advantage is customers start trusting you because they have availed of your services in the past. The principle of commitment and consistency will hold true when you keep delivering the best products to your customers over and over again. This shows the ability to commit and deliver quality products and the consistency to deliver this product over a period of time.

Here we again look at an example of a realtor. If you are in the business of real estate and you have various open houses coming up, you should contact customers that have purchased from you in the past. No one said that you cannot purchase more than one house at a time. Your customers will also feel honored that you consider retargeting them when it comes to a new house being sold. A restaurant can also retarget its customers by offering discounts from time to time or reminding customers of important dates coming up in their life. Wishing customers happy birthday on their birthday or offering discounts in the birthday month are a few of the things that will hold true to this principle.

Social Proof

The principle of social proof is based on your online reviews as well as endorsements by influencers or celebrities. When there is collective approval for your product your customers will not hesitate choosing you over a competitor. In the case of a realtor, if you have successfully sold in the past and your customers leave positive reviews online there is no reason new buyers would not approach you. Online reviews are a great way to ensure that you keep getting new customers and it is the greatest form of publicity. When it comes to picking a restaurant most customers would read reviews online before they choose any particular restaurant. If you are a local business and there is a lot of competition you can request the local influencer to leave a positive review online that will help other customers come to your restaurant.

The Principle of Liking

The principle of liking is very similar to social proof. If customers see a particular product or service being promoted by a celebrity that they like, there is a very good chance that they will pick that product over other products. As a realtor, you may want to get somebody to promote your page. This person could be an influencer or it could also be a celebrity that a lot of people like. The same can be done for a restaurant. Promoting your restaurant page online through an influencer or a celebrity is something that works in your favor and many people will queue up to make reservations because they believe in your product.

Authority

The principle of authority is also based on the principle of liking. People will usually opt for a product that is promoted by an authority that they believe in. If you are promoting a particular product or service you can have a social figure or an authority promoting your business. In the example of a real estate business, you can get local celebrities to give a seminar on the changing face of real estate and why it is good to invest today. You could even hire real estate authority figures that people trust. When it comes to a restaurant, people are very particular about the kind of food that they eat. With the help of an authority figure in the culinary world, you will be able to get more people to pick your restaurant over a competitor.

Scarcity

Scarcity is a very common persuasion principle that is used by businesses all over the world. Scarcity usually creates urgency and this helps in selling products and services quicker. In the example of a realtor, you need to offer a limited time discount as well as free open houses that will attract more buyers towards your business. In a restaurant business, it is very easy to implement the principle of scarcity. All you need to do is offer a free meal or a buy-one-get-one-free offer depending on what festivities are coming up or if there is any occasion that is approaching. Giving a limited time offer will make sure that your restaurant will do more business than any other restaurant in your area.

Now that you understood the principles of persuasion in detail and you have seen the kind of ads that can be created based on each of the principles, you can go ahead and create an ad based on each of the principles. Make sure that your ad takes into account what the concept of each principle is and how it can convince the user to pick your product or service over anyone else. You need to be subtle while applying the principle because customers usually do not prefer an ad that is too pushy or direct to the point.

Chapter 7: When It All Comes Together: The Plan

Now that you understood what Facebook marketing is all about you will need to come up with ways to bring all the learnings together and implement it properly. One of the first things that you need to do is create a content calendar. A content calendar helps you to create engaging content and create brand awareness. This calendar will help you improve customer engagement and will also help with your SEO efforts. A calendar will help you plan your content across various platforms. You can either create this content calendar for a month or the next couple of weeks. It does not have to be an extravagant calendar that is very detailed. It could be a simple spreadsheet that will help you note down the dates along with the content that needs to be published. This will not only help you maintain consistency with your content, but it will also help you stay organized. Here are the benefits of maintaining a content calendar.

Implement an organized Content Strategy

A content calendar will help you stay organized across platforms for the duration that you created the calendar. When it comes to content on Facebook you need to make sure that it is consistent and regular. When you do not have a content calendar in place, you will usually panic and end up creating posts just for the heck of it. This is bound to create no impact and you will end up losing a lot of your followers that you already have. When your audience sees that you are putting no efforts towards your posts, they will lose interest in your business as well, and this will not be great for your development. When you know that you have to post content later on in the day, you will keep the content ready well in advance. A content calendar will help you stay organized by pushing you towards publishing content and creating quality content for important dates that could be coming up. For example, creating content for Valentine's Day or remembrance day or the fourth of July.

Save On Time

With the content calendar in place, you will be able to save on a lot of time because most of your content would be organized and ready to publish. When you are not spending too much time stressing about your Facebook marketing, you will be able to focus on other important aspects of your business and this will help your business grow along with creating brand awareness through Facebook. A content calendar will also help you pre-schedule posts so that you can ensure your Facebook marketing is happening even if you do not physically log in to Facebook and check the same.

Create Content Well In Advance

When you do not have a content calendar, you will suddenly realize that you need to post regarding a certain event today. Imagine you are on your way to the airport for a business trip and on the way you realize that today is memorial day. If you do not post on Memorial Day there is a very good chance that people will get offended because your business did not care about an important holiday. You will then be forced to create content while you are on the go and this is something that is not recommended. When content is created on the go, it looks rushed and it will not be very creative, as well. A content calendar will help you create your content at least a couple of days in advance. This will ensure that the content that you publish is timely and top quality.

You Can Create A Strategy

When you run a Facebook marketing campaign you will need a strategy in place. Publishing random posts on your Facebook page will not really get you anywhere because the audience will not see the connection between your posts. Most big brands will have a strategy as far as their posts are concerned and you will see that most of the posts are consistent towards a certain strategy. With the help of the content calendar, you will be able to create a strategy and implement it properly.

When you are marketing on Facebook there are a number of ways to get carried away and you will end up wasting a lot of time as well as money. There are certain things that you should not do when you are focusing on Facebook marketing. Here are a few tips that will help you save time and money.

Stop Building Facebook Apps

There are a number of ideas that are floating out there and they tend to suggest that this could be the next big Facebook app. You will end up spending a lot of time and effort in building the app because most of the concepts are never successful. The Facebook experts that suggest building these apps also claim that the app will bring in a lot of new customers as well as new fans. That is far from the truth. The best thing to do is to pick up an app that has already been built by a developer. This will help you save on a lot of time and money and you will also be able to target the right audience with the money that you saved.

Picking the Wrong Prize For Your Contest

Facebook comes down very firmly on clickbaits and it often bans ads that hide content from users until they share certain posts on Facebook. If you want to hold a contest you should ask a simple question and give away a price that is relevant to your business. If you are in the restaurant business you could give away a gift voucher that will gift a dinner for two or you could even offer lifetime membership to the customer to a gym that you may be running in the local area.

Post Educational Content

If you want people to start liking your post and you want organic followers on Facebook then you need to start posting content that is relevant to the audience and will add value. You need to make sure that you are posting information that will be useful and not just promoting your business. You should also try to personalize your posts and make sure that you connect with your audience in the right manner.

Stop Wasting Time on Facebook

A number of business owners end up wasting days on end trying to figure out what kind of ads to post and at what time to post them. As a business owner, you need to invest in post managers that will help you understand what kind of posts would be relevant to your business and when you should post them. These post managers will help you understand the right kind of audience and they will also help you post the right kind of content.

Don't Purchase Fans

Purchasing fans to increase your followers on Facebook is like getting mannequins to come and stand at your live event.

These fans are not relevant and will never add value to Facebook. Try to attract organic fans by posting interesting information regularly.

Get More Out Of Your Ad Results

Not every business has unlimited resources as well as a limited budget that will help towards Facebook marketing. While every business wants to succeed, you need to make sure that you use your resources properly so that you make the most of your Facebook advertisements. In order to use Facebook advertisements effectively here are a few tips that you need to keep in mind. These steps will ensure that you spend minimum time on Facebook and get the maximum benefit out of it.

Choose Your Tools Wisely

Facebook has a number of inbuilt tools that will help you with your ad management but you need to make sure that you are selecting the right tools. There are many changes that Facebook makes on a daily basis. Using the right tool will help you promote your product in a better manner and save on a lot of money. For example, if you are selling only one product, there is no point in using the Facebook carousel ad. This format is used to display different products from a single brand. When you are looking to sell one product then you should select the single image ad.

Choose Quality Over Quantity

Login into Facebook 10 times a day and posting 10 irrelevant posts is not going to make much of a difference if the posts do not have a positive impact. Rather than spending the entire day on Facebook and publishing a lot of posts, you need to select two or three posts that will make an impact and use the rest of your time improving your business.

Targeting The Right Audience

You need to use Facebook targeting tools to your advantage. Rather than promoting your ad to millions of users across Facebook and getting no results, you need to target the right audience and get maximum outreach. You need to also target the right geographic areas so that your business can grow within the budget constraints that you have.

Chapter 8: Email and Email marketing

Targeting your customers through email marketing is a very important aspect that you need to focus on. While Facebook marketing is important, you should use it to your advantage and collect as many email leads as possible. These emails will help you connect with your leads through your email marketing efforts and it will ensure that you continue connecting with them even after they have converted to a customer. Facebook keeps changing on a daily basis and there are various algorithms that could be introduced that may block access to your Facebook page. In such a scenario it will be very difficult for you to build a customer base overnight if you have no information about who your followers were and what their contact information was. This is where your email list will come very handy. You need to keep collecting emails on a daily basis to ensure that you promote your business to potential leads in the right manner.

Facebook Marketing Versus Email Marketing

Business owners usually offer Facebook marketing over email marketing because they believe that most of their audience is on Facebook. They are not wrong because Facebook marketing is definitely trending these days and going with the trend generally works in your favor. The one thing that you should remember is you should never stop your email marketing campaigns because it has its own benefits. There are a number of differences between email marketing and Facebook marketing and this section will let you know what the differences are and what benefits you gain from each of these marketing campaigns.

The Difference

The big difference between Facebook followers versus email subscribers is your email subscriber list is usually your current customer base and your Facebook followers are potential leads. You will have complete control over your email subscription list whereas you do not control your Facebook followers. Most of your current customers will always opt-in for your email marketing campaigns because they have used your services in the past and they know that you can be trusted. Facebook followers are not necessarily your current customers and they may never be. You will need to put in more effort towards converting your Facebook followers into customers while that is not the case with your email subscribers.

If you compare the people that use email on a daily basis versus Facebook on a daily basis, you will realize that the numbers almost double up. Almost 90% of people will use their email on a daily basis because that is a way of communicating with other businesses as well as their family members and friends. Facebook is a casual activity and almost 60% of users use it on a daily basis. Facebook is used primarily to check in with family members and friends and see what is happening around the world. If you have to communicate with someone professionally then you will come to your email rather than Facebook. The click-through rate for emails is higher than the click-through rate for Facebook marketing.

The Reach

The one question you need to ask as a business owner is how many people check their mailbox before they check Facebook on a daily basis? Once you get the answer to this question you will know which of the marketing campaigns are more effective. Most of your serious customers will always check their mailbox before they check Facebook because they expect important emails from different people in their lives. This could be emails from other businesses or even from their loved ones, and in some cases from their boss. Most people would turn to Facebook only when they have nothing much to do during the day.

Getting Traffic to Your Facebook Ads

The main purpose of Facebook marketing should be to get more people to your website. When people start clicking on your website or visiting your blog you can ask them to subscribe to your notifications and this will help you get the email IDs regularly. with is where Facebook marketing can help you tremendously. When you are selecting the purpose of your marketing campaign, you should make sure that you specify promoting a website and enter the URL of your website. You can use a single image ad for this promotion and get maximum people to your website through your Facebook marketing campaigns. The more people that come to your website, the more subscriptions you get and the more email IDs you collect.

Create a Landing Page within Your Facebook Ad

Apart from having a call to action, you also need to have a landing page on your Facebook ad. This landing page will usually divert all traffic to your website and it will help you generate more leads. All the leads that you get through the landing page would be potential customers because these are people that are interested in your product and that is the reason they clicked on the link. The landing page needs to be strong and should capture the attention of the audience. There are various landing page builders that you can opt-in for and these builders will help you create a very professional-looking and effective landing page.

Create the Right Campaign For Your Email Ids

When you have collated your email IDs, you need to have a strategy in place that will help nurture the leads. It is important to make people feel welcome and not spam them with emails 4 to 5 times a day. You need to send a welcome email as soon as somebody subscribes to your mailing list and you need to follow up on your leads effectively. With the help of a welcome email, you will be able to connect personally with subscribers. You can even send out birthday wishes or anniversary wishes based on the information that you have regarding the leads.

Ways to Collect Leads From Your Facebook Campaign

There are a few effective tools that you can use to your advantage and collect email IDs through your Facebook marketing campaign. The steps are very useful and it will help you get maximum fans to subscribe to your email list. Here are the best ways to collect email IDs from your Facebook fans.

Create A Signup Form

This is a very effective method of collecting emails and a number of businesses use this basic method of getting people to subscribe to their mailing list. There are a number of email service providers that will help create a signup form and you can integrate this with your Facebook tab. You can also try and promote your subscriber list on your Facebook page.

Offering Incentives

Another way of getting email IDs is by offering something in return. This can be seen with the example of the restaurant. If you want to start running email marketing campaigns for your restaurant then you will need people to subscribe to your mailing list. As a restaurant owner, you need to make sure that you are offering something in return so that people give you their email IDs. The best way to do this is by offering people a flat discount when they arrive at your restaurant. All you need to do is offer the customers a survey form that they can fill out and receive a 5% discount in return.

Organize A Contest

Most fans get very excited with the prospect of winning something out of a contest. People would enter any survey form just so they can receive rewards. If we take the example of the realtor, you can offer exclusive open houses to people that have subscribed to your email list. Most people love exclusivity and they will do just about anything to get their hands on a top property before anyone else.

The habit of browsing through Facebook is usually done while traveling or when you are sitting for lunch or maybe when you take a quick 5-minute break. The seriousness associated with email marketing is a lot more compared to Facebook marketing. Most of the ads that you will see on Facebook prove to be clickbaits and this is what diminishes the trust factor for Facebook marketing. While the same can be said about emails, the percentage of clickbaits is a lot lower and most email clients have a built-in spam filter that will keep unwanted emails away.

Chapter 9: Improve, Test, Grow, and Monetize

Your content is extremely important when it comes to attracting customers on Facebook. While there are a number of content tips that we have spoken about, you should always focus on creating content that will keep your audience engaged. Here are a few tips that you need to keep in mind when generating content for Facebook marketing.

Mix Up Your Content

Irrespective of what kind of business you are into, you need to make sure that you make new posts and publish content in different formats. Facebook allows you to create ads in different formats and you should use that to your advantage. You can choose to publish a blog post every week that will help customers understand what your business is up to and what has happened in the past. You can even get people to subscribe to your blog post by inserting a call to action at the end. Another way of sharing content is with the help of photos. Rather than downloading images from search engines you need to take live snapshots of your workers as well as customers and post them on your Facebook page. You should even post pictures from events that you have hosted or any of the marketing strategies that you have tried. You should also keep publishing press releases every now and then. Press releases are a professional way of communicating with your customers and informing them about any updates that are coming up. This is also a great way of informing people of any new store openings or a new sale that may be coming up by the end of the month.

Encourage Posts from Your Fans

As the name suggests, you run a fan page and not a business page. This means you will need to give fans the opportunity to voice their opinion. You should not be scared of negative comments because that is going to happen irrespective of whether your fans can post on your page or not. Encourage fans to post success stories on your wall and tell the world how Facebook has made a difference in their life. The success stories will encourage other potential leads to become customers because they know that this content has not been created by the business but it has been created by a live customer. This is like a Facebook review but in the form of a post on a wall.

Use Contest in Moderation

While it is advisable to announce contests every now and then, you should not overdo the contests because it takes away the excitement. Most of the fans will end up following your business page just because you are running contests regularly and not because they are interested in your product.

Create Interesting Content

While you are a professional business and you want to have serious information posted on your fan page, there is no point being serious all the time. You need to inject a bit of humor in your posts because this will help your fan page to stand out and get more followers.

Define your USP

Every business needs to have a unique selling point that will help them stand out from the crowd. You need to make sure that your USP is very different and you offer something that no one else does. This does not necessarily have to be a product, it can even be a service that you are offering. There are a number of brands that promote their customer service rather than promoting their product. This is because there are millions of products out there but very few brands that offer brilliant customer service. You need to come up with a USP based on what your customers think your strong point is and the feedback that you received. Your USP also depends on your target audience and what you are offering them. For example, your audience could be looking for a product that helps them save on time or a product that is trustworthy. If your brand is offering these value additions to the customer, then you will be able to claim that as your USP.

Your USP can change depending on the kind of business you are in and the target customers that you have. You need to deliver on what you promise and based on that you can claim your selling point. When you know what your USP is, all your communication should focus on this USP and your company vision should also be based around it. Always communicate your USP clearly and make sure that you are providing it in every offering as well. Don't try changing a USP too often because it will take away the identity of the business. Here are a few things you need to keep in mind when you are creating a USP:

- make sure you know who your target audience is.
- try to note down all the ways that your product or service could help people. This will help become a very strong selling point for your business.
- compare your selling point with your competitor and see what they are proposing. Make sure that your proposition is unique and it will help you capture a majority share in the market.
- conduct surveys with your potential customers as well as your current customers and see what they feel your USP is.
- monitor the current trends and see how your customers are being affected and whether you will be able to

provide a solution.

Targeting Current Customers

Most businesses make the mistake of ignoring their current customers and focusing on new leads. This is because business owners feel that if a customer has purchased once from their business, they will always rely on their business in the future as well. The fact remains that every business still needs to compete with other businesses for their current customers as well. Brand loyalty is built over a number of years and not just over a couple of purchases. The example of a restaurant or a soft drink is more relevant. If a customer has been going to a restaurant to eat for the past decade along with his family members it would be very difficult for any other restaurant to convince him otherwise. However, if someone had a single meal at a pizza joint, it doesn't mean that the customer will be loyal to the pizza joint. As a business owner, you need to make sure that you are looking to improve your brand in order to retain your current customers. While email marketing is very effective in retargeting customers, you also need to make the most of Facebook marketing and get more customers to do repeat business with you.

When you are running a business you need to make sure that you use Facebook marketing to your advantage and see what the current customers feel about your products or services. You need to make sure that you live up to the expectations of your customers because their brand loyalty and their views are going to be vital in you acquiring new customers. You need to test and see what your customers like and what they are not happy with. If you feel that your product could solve another problem that your customers are facing, you need to communicate with the customer and make them aware of the solution that you are offering.

It is important that your business keeps evolving as time goes by. Let us take the example of a real estate business. If you have sold properties to various customers in the past decade, you need to look at those customers once again and see if they want to move into a bigger apartment or if their current apartment is giving them some problems. The one area where most realtors fail is not following up with their current customers because they feel that they cannot get any more business out of them. However, that is far from the truth. If you have sold the wrong house to a customer you need to make up for that mistake because word of mouth publicity can put you down in no time. There is no shortage of realtors in the market today and if your potential buyers learn about the way you do business, they will avoid you. You should always look for the benefit of your current customers before you move to generate new leads. This is where Facebook marketing can help you. You can target your current customers by checking how they feel about the last purchase that they made. Try conducting a survey to see if any of your current customers are unhappy and communicate with them if you feel that there is something that you can do better for them.

The Ladder of Engagement

The ladder of engagement has been created to improve engagement between a business and its potential customers. Most business owners are not able to relate to their customers because they are not sure what it takes to encourage more engagement from the customer. This is where a ladder of engagement helps. This ladder encourages you to take one step at a time and this will gradually help build a strong relationship with your customer base.

Start Easy

When you build your Facebook page you need to start slowly and ask your audience to do small tasks for you. These tasks could involve sharing your fan page with their family members, and friends, clicking on your website link or subscribing to your email list. None of these tasks require too much time investment from the customer's end and they will be more than happy to do it. Once your customers have completed these tasks they will be ready to perform even bigger tasks for your business.

Collect Key Data

As the engagement level between the customer and the business increases, the collection of data should also increase. You need to collect information such as email ID, name of the customer, location, along with interests. This will help you customize your communication with the customer in the future and it will help build on the initial engagement.

Don't Demand Too Much

Let us again take the example of the restaurant. If you want more people to come and become a customer at your restaurant you should not directly ask for it. Instead, you need to put it in the form of suggestions made by your current customers. You are allowed to rope in big-name celebrities or local influencers that will help create a positive impact.

Expand the Ladder of Engagement

Once you have reached a level where you are communicating effectively with your customers, you need to make sure that you expand the ladder further. This can be done in the form of asking people to help your business grow in your local area. If you are struggling, you can go ahead and ask local investors to come in and take over a percentage of your business in return for an investment. Since the level of engagement is so high, many people will come forward and it will help your business survive even in an aggressive market.

Tell Stories as Part of Your Facebook Campaign

Storytelling is extremely important and you will be able to connect to the audience in a better manner. A number of brands tell stories to reach a high level of connection with their customers and you need to do the same as well. There are a number of advantages that storytelling has to offer and it will help with your marketing efforts tremendously. If you target your Facebook campaigns based on the emotional response of the customer, you will end up reaching a wider audience. People usually connect with a story a lot more than a marketing campaign. There are various kinds of stories that can help your business get its point across. Here is how you can tell the stories effectively.

Focus On the Issues At Hand

As a business owner, you always need to look at the trends that are happening and how they are affecting your customers. There are a number of issues that need to be taken care of and this can be done through your Facebook marketing campaign. If you feel that racism is on the rise, then you can create a video celebrating different ethnicities and showing that unity is what prevails. You need to come up with a story that will touch the heart of your audience and they will be compelled to share the story forward. There are a number of big brands that are using storytelling to their advantage and it is working.

Connect With the Audience

Try and relate to the problems that your customers are facing and put forward your product as a solution to the problems. You will see the biggest cosmetic brands touching on the most sensitive issues that are happening around the world today and telling a story around that. In most cultures color is usually a problem and most big guns will point out that this is wrong. Acceptability in society is something that everyone is entitled to and when you tell a story around such a sensitive issue people that are affected by this will relate to your brand.

Try and Relate With the Problems That the Customer Is Facing

There are different segments of people that face different kinds of problems on a daily basis. Some parents facing an issue with their children not respecting them while others face a problem with their children not even visiting them when they are old. Some children face neglect in life while others are harassed in school and college. If you can create awareness as a business owner around these issues, you will be able to get the right message across and create an impact in society. Most people are not even aware of what's happening around them and releasing a short video on the realities of society can be an eye-opener for many people.

Storytelling is very powerful and you need to make sure that you use it in the right manner. Promoting the wrong stories or giving false information is not going to hold you in good stead. Apart from helping you grow your business, the story should also make a difference in society and that is what you should be aiming for.

How To Stop People From Scrolling Past Your Post?

Facebook marketing is extremely important and you need to create the right kind of posts in order to get people's attention. Spending hundreds and thousands of dollars on Facebook advertising will not really be helpful if your ad campaigns are not powerful enough. You should never be satisfied with the number of followers that you have and look to acquire some new followers on a daily basis. The only way this can be done is when your posts are reaching more people. There are various reasons why a post may not be going viral and you need to figure out what can be done in order to attract more attention. Here are a few tips that you can keep in mind in order to create engaging posts on Facebook.

Understand the Platform

Facebook business pages are not very complicated and you need to understand how to use it in order to come across as a professional outfit. Sharing random images or putting up a random text on your fan page will get you nowhere. You need to make sure that you understand how the advertisements work and how to create content that will be engaging.

Understanding Your Audience

You should always be aware of what your audience needs when you are posting content online. If your ideal age group is above the age of 40 then there is no point posting information regarding the latest trends in hairstyles. You need to make sure that you're posting information that will be useful to your audience and not something that may offend them.

Use Pictures Relevant To Your Business

Downloading images from the internet and posting them on your business page is not going to benefit anybody. You need to start posting images that are relevant to your business and unique. If ten businesses use the same image, they will not have an identity of their own and their fans will stop relating to them. Also if you use an image of another business post then fans may scroll past the post thinking that the post is from that same business and not yours. You need to create an identity for yourself and make sure that you are posting images that are only unique to you.

Ask Question through Your Post

As a business owner, you need to realize what will make people stop and look at your post. When people are presented with a question or a riddle they will stop and think about it for a couple of seconds before they scroll past. Those few seconds are all you need to create an impact and make people click on your post. You need to make sure that you are catching the imagination of your audience in a matter of seconds. Posting generic content without an interesting headline is not going to be beneficial and 99% of your audience will scroll past your post.

Create Engaging Video Content

Publishing posts and blogs on your Facebook page can be relatively easy, however, creating and posting videos is not that straightforward. You need to keep a lot of tips in mind in order to create a video that will catch the attention of your audience.

Create a Sharp Video

Most videos start off with a boring introduction and this is where the audience loses interest. Make a video that gets straight to the point and does not waste the time of the user.

The best way to do this is by eliminating unnecessary content from the video and choosing a thumbnail image that will make the user click on the video.

Use Captions Effectively

Not many people play videos with the sound enabled on it. This could be because they are at work or they would be traveling and they do not want to disturb others around them. When creating a video you should make sure that you caption it properly so that people would be able to understand the video even if the sound is off. This will keep the user engaged because without proper captions or sound, your video may seem confusing and you will lose the user.

Choose the Right Title

The title plays a huge part in capturing the imagination of the audience. You need to make sure that you are choosing your title wisely and you need to use appropriate keywords that will help increase the visibility of the video as well.

Create a Short Description

Facebook allows you to post a short description of your video. This description will help your audience understand what is in the video and why they should click on it. This is extremely important because the thumbnail may not interest them but the content of the video may be interesting.

Always Include a Call to Action

No Facebook ad is complete if you do not add a call to action in it. This holds true for a video as well. You need to make sure that you are adding a call to action, either during the video or at the end of it. This will help the audience engage with you and you will be able to make full use of the effectiveness of the video with the help of the call to action.

Understanding Content Marketing

Content marketing is extremely crucial in today's date and you need to focus on having the right strategy in order to be successful. A number of business owners go to great lengths in getting the right content for their campaigns. Apart from having engaging content, you also need to look at strategies to get more content from various sources. You need to look at effective ways of content marketing and how it can be useful to your business. You could market your content through various methods on Facebook. However, you should know what the strong points for your business are and whether it will be useful to you or not. Here is a look at the various content types that are available on Facebook and how it can prove to be beneficial to your business.

Video Streaming

The concept of video streaming has caught on in the past year or so and it is one of the biggest trends on Facebook right now. A number of celebrities use live video streaming to connect with their audience and a number of businesses also use this method to promote or launch new products. The problem with a live video feed is that almost every business is doing the same thing and the audience will eventually get bored of it. While it is an effective way of promoting your business, you need to make sure that you are not creating a live video for every ad that you post on Facebook.

Engage With Your Audience

No matter what business you are in, you need to make sure that you are soliciting some kind of response from your audience through your Facebook marketing campaign. Most businesses try and introduce a poll that will help the audience get involved with your business. Some businesses also publish maps or quizzes in order to capture the attention of the audience.

Online Webinars or Courses

The internet has made the world smaller and a number of businesses are offering their services online as opposed to offering it physically. Education is one such field that is constantly evolving. If you are in the field of education, you no longer need to conduct physical classes around the city. You can offer online courses and cover twice as many students as you did when you conducted classes in local areas. The reason students prefer online courses is that it offers the flexibility of timings and it also allows students to takes up more than one course at a time.

Influencer marketing

Influencer marketing is another trend that is growing by the day and a number of large businesses as well as small businesses are turning to influencers in order to increase their fanbase. Depending on the budget for your business, you can choose a local influencer or a national influencer. The best part about having an influencer is they will help create an impact instantly and their fanbase will automatically convert into a fanbase for your business.

Look For Inspiration

There are a number of places where you can find inspiration for your Facebook posts. Your audience wants to see something new on a daily basis and the only way you will be able to give them something new is by being inspired. Looking at unorthodox places for inspiration can prove to be beneficial for you.

Online Galleries

There are a number of online galleries that will give you ideas for your visual ads. These galleries will also help you find inspiration for your text posts as well as headlines. If you are in the publishing business then you can find inspiration for your book covers as well as poster designs.

Product Descriptions

Most of the inspiration for your post comes from your previous work. If you are stuck with a particular post on Facebook, you can go back and see the work that you've done. There always comes a time when a business is very proud of the way it handles itself in the marketing world. You should always look back on these moments and see the product descriptions that you had created at that time. These product descriptions will provide you with amazing ideas and it will help you create engaging content once again.

Go for A Walk

This may sound cliché, but it is very effective. Going out for a walk and clearing your head is an excellent way to get new ideas for your latest content. When you have no distractions around you, your mind will be a lot sharper and you will be able to get ideas almost instantly. If you are looking to get inspiration, you can even take a walk by the beach or a calm lake.

Check Out Customer Surveys

Customer surveys are a great way of getting more information and new ideas. If you have already conducted a survey in the past then it's a great time to take it out and see what your customers think about your product. If you have never conducted a survey then there is no harm doing one right now. You need to find out a few things from your survey. You need to get feedback regarding the products and services that you are offering, you need to understand what people's expectations are from your brand and you need to understand where you are going wrong. Once you get the answer to these questions you will be able to get ideas and promote your business in a more effective manner.

Fashion Magazines

Believe it or not, fashion magazines have a lot of well-written content that can provide inspiration for your next Facebook post. Most fashion magazines approach the top writers for their content because it is a very competitive field. If the top magazines do not deliver content that is relevant or up to the mark, they will lose their readership in no time.

Quotes

Quotes are highly motivational and they can help you get some interesting ideas on what you can post to Facebook. Try looking for relevant posts that describe the kind of work you do or your business in any way and use them to your advantage. Whenever you quote someone remember to give them credit by mentioning the name in the post. You can do something creative with a quote by creating an image and using some sort of picture in the background, or even a simple text that can blend in with a relevant link or product your business offers.

Trending News

Keeping an eye on the news and checking out what's trending is definitely a great way to design your posts. Seasonal posts and posts around the time of a festival definitely need to be customized and more in sync with the flavor of the season. Incorporate posts in a manner that reflects a current trend because that's would people look out for. During Christmas, try having the entire holiday festive season theme posts because these do really well around that time.

See What Your Competition Is Up To

One of the best ways to get inspiration is by looking around you. This does not only include looking at the things that you love but you can also look at your competition. Sometimes your direct competitors may have better ideas and there is no harm in getting inspiration from their posts. If you look at the biggest advertising wars for the past decade, you will see that competitors have been swiping ideas from each other and taking a dig at them in the process. While you do not need to go ahead and make things ugly, ensuring that you look to them for inspiration is a very sensible thing to do. There is no harm in admitting that your competition is better than you in terms of ideas and the only way you can get better is by getting inspired.

Conclusion

Facebook marketing is perfect for small businesses and there are a number of entities that are still not sure of how it can work to their benefit. With the help of this guide, you can now understand how a business owner can take his business forward without having to spend too much money on marketing efforts. The reason Facebook marketing is so effective is that it has a wide outreach and there are a number of tools that are available for the business to use. A number of business owners have turned to social media marketing in the last decade and this trend will keep continuing because of the marketing tools that social media channels provide. Without the right social media interaction, business owners would not be able to make an impact in the market.

If you look at the most successful businesses, you will realize that Facebook marketing has been an integral part of their journey. While some businesses move forward and choose other channels of marketing, their initial base would have been created with the help of Facebook marketing and this is something that cannot be replicated. Since Facebook provides a large variety of posts, you will be able to make the right decision and choose the right tools to help your business move forward. Facebook is also very helpful when it comes to interacting with your current client base as well as your new potential customers.

You can combine Facebook marketing along with the principles of persuasion and have the perfect marketing strategy to help your business grow. Facebook is a continuous marketing effort and it never stops showcasing your business to your intended targets. All you need to do is make sure that you engage your audience with the right kind of content and tell stories that will help you connect with society. Establishing a brand with the help of Facebook marketing is not that easy. You just need to look at a few successful examples out there and try and replicate their marketing strategies to help your business grow. Apart from providing you with effective solutions, Facebook will also contribute towards making your business bigger than it currently is. If you follow the steps correctly you will realize that Facebook marketing is all about the right content and the right strategy.

If you are looking to run a successful business you need to make sure that your time management, as well as money-management skills, are up to the mark. There is no such thing as a perfect solution and you need to work towards building the right brand for your business. You need to work towards defining a business strategy and this book will help you achieve this.

Instagram promotions are limited to images and videos, hence you can't experiment too much. There's a limited audience on Instagram and if you're looking for a crowd that is serious and professional, then Instagram won't work as well. Instagram may not be as effective as you want it to be and this is the reason a number of businesses prefer choosing Facebook over other social media channels. With Facebook, you will even be able to experiment with your target audience and find out their likes and dislikes. Instagram would not give you much of an option as far as understanding your buyer profile is concerned. Another advantage of Facebook over Instagram is you will no longer have to spend time finding the right audience because Facebook tools do that for you. You will no longer have to worry about how you will find potential buyers for your business. Using the Facebook tools correctly will ensure you build your brand name in no time.

It's important to focus on a method that works and helps you generate potential customers and leads for your business. Converting these leads into actual customers is the next phase of marketing which involves the use of an effective sales funnel. Sign up for my newsletter and I'll let you in on an extra chapter about how you can use the sales funnel to step up your efforts on social media and get more customers to your business. It's time to begin your journey from a small business to an established brand with the key persuasion principles and the right knowledge of marketing & online sales.

Instagram Marketing and Advertising for Small Business Owners in 2019

The 5 Step Insta-Profit Formula to Create a Winning Social Media Strategy, Grow Your Brand and Get Real-World Results

Chapter 1: Instagram for Your Business

As a small business owner, you have a lot of work on your plate. You have to manage the business, handle clients, solve problems, all the while managing the marketing side of your company. These are complex areas and for the most part, will take up a lot of your time. The last thing most business owners want to do is create *more* work for themselves. And oftentimes, the idea of getting involved with a new social media app seems like just that: more work.

However, marketing is still a major responsibility of the small business owner. Like it or not, you're going to be spending a large chunk of your time working to market and advertise for your products or services. But what if there was a way to streamline your marketing process? What if there were a series of simple steps that could be taken that would increase your profits, build stronger relationships with your customers and promote your brand?

The purpose of this book is to teach you five steps for using Instagram for business success. While Instagram might appear at first glance as a little more than a social media tool for taking pictures of food, the truth is that Instagram is a powerful engine for direct marketing. By learning how to use it properly, you will be able to greatly increase your income while simultaneously decreasing the amount of time you need to spend on marketing.

The Insta-Profit Formula is based on two underlying principles:

1. The key to successful marketing is by creating relationships and telling stories.
2. Your time is extremely valuable.

We won't waste your time with endless amounts of theoretical and hypotheticals. Rather, we're here to show you have proven methods that will get real-world results. By following and holding to these five steps, you'll be able to achieve tremendous success using Instagram. And best of all, you won't have to commit hours upon hours a week to achieve these results. You'll learn all the best ways to maximize your marketing results!

So, let's break down exactly what Instagram is and how it's relevant for today's small businesses. Instagram is a social media app owned by Facebook. It primarily focuses on visual mediums, i.e. photographs instead of plain text. Over 500 million Instagram accounts are active on a daily basis worldwide. Who are these users? For the most part, Instagram users tend to be young. 64% of users are between the ages of 18-34. On top of that, those under the age of 25 tend to spend upwards to an hour and a half using Instagram *every day!*

Instagram is also a highly global platform. 80% of its total userbase is located outside of the United States. But don't let that number fool you into thinking the U.S. has a small number of users. It's estimated that there are 105 million Instagram users in America alone! It's a busy platform with plenty of traffic.

In terms of gender demographics, more women use Instagram than men, however, when it comes to daily active users, they are fairly close together, with 50.3% of the userbase being female. The fact that there is little difference in gender makeup means the platform is essentially unisex, making it appropriate for any product regardless of gender demographic.

So, there are quite a bit of people who use Instagram regularly. The question then is, what type of content are they interested in? And does a small business have the ability to reach those users? As for content, it really goes across the board. Users enjoy following a wide variety of different types of accounts and generally move towards accounts that post related to their interests. After all, Instagram is a form of social media. This means that people will aggregate towards their chosen niches and look for a steady stream of content that is related to that niche.

On the business end, however, the numbers are quite impressive. There are currently over 8 million business accounts set up on Instagram. 80% of users follow at least one business account. And on top of that, 60% of Instagram users report that they first heard about a product or service on Instagram. 30% of users even make purchasing decisions based on Instagram posts that they've come across featuring a product.

These numbers show that there is a big market of people who are readily engaging with the platform on a daily basis *and* are willing to engage with business accounts. Ad revenue is staggeringly high on Instagram, in fact, in 2018, they sold over 6.8 billion in ads. This means that advertisers have clearly seen value in using Instagram as a marketing tool and have put out quite a bit of money in order to get their ads in front of the relevant audience.

As you can see, Instagram is a big field, ripe for those who are looking to market their products and services. Let's move on to the first step, where we will learn how to create a customer persona to better help with targeted marketing.

Chapter 2: Step 1: It's all about them

The customer is the most important part of Instagram marketing. If you want to find financial success, then you're going to have to develop a customer-first mindset. In everything that you do on Instagram, you must be thinking purely about the benefit of the customer. In other words, it's all about them!

A lot of times, social media marketing can tend to come off as self-serving. A marketer will spend a significant amount of time promoting and talking about their brands and products in the hopes of making sales. However, in reality, marketing efforts that are entirely self-focused fail to capture the interest of potential customers. Most of the time, people are turned off by this behavior. Why? Because self-focus in marketing doesn't provide any *value* to the customer.

At the end of the day, everyone is concerned with what brings value to their lives. People engage with the things that they find valuable and ignore the things that they don't. It's as simple as that. When people engage on Instagram, liking, following and commenting, it's because they find value in those posts. They find enough value that they are motivated to engage, follow and pay attention to.

So, the trick to learning how to capture the interests of people effectively is to learn what they value. Then, once you've learned what they value, you simply provide those things to them. In turn, they will begin to pay attention to your marketing efforts and over time, will begin to value your business or your products. This creates a bond that will ultimately lead to your customers making more purchases and being more receptive to your marketing efforts.

So, what do people value? On a consumer level, people value *solutions* to their problems. Ultimately, a customer makes a purchasing decision because they perceive that the product will be successful in fixing whatever problem they are currently facing. All products solve problems. The core of good marketing is identifying what problems your target customers are having, then proposing solutions to those problems. This is what captures the attention of a potential customer.

One of the most important steps to Instagram marketing is to develop a proper customer persona, so you can exactly know what problems they are currently facing. When you have a clear profile of their problems, you can then begin to develop solutions to those problems. Let's take a look at a step by step method of developing the Customer Persona.

Customer Persona

The Customer Persona is a collection of thoughts, concerns, and interests that your ideal customer would have. By defining a customer persona, you'll be able to develop a concrete Instagram marketing strategy. You'll be able to determine what kind of content would be the best to share as well as what your customers are going to be looking for.

Developing a Customer Persona is fairly simple to do. All you need is to do is use a series of questions to create a "profile." Then, you'll want to keep that profile in mind whenever you're developing your marketing material. And it's important to know that you can have multiple customer personas. Most products appeal to more than one type of group. By developing multiple personas, you'll be able to develop content strategies to reach each group with specific marketing methods.

The questions below should get you thinking about the customer persona. Your ideal customer is going to be primarily based on the product that you are selling, so you'll most likely need to do a bit of market research to determine things like age and gender demographics.

Question One: What are my customer's age and gender?
Getting age and gender profile is fairly simple, but a necessary component. Age is extremely important when it comes to different types of marketing methods, or even if Instagram is actually for your product. Gender is important because it will influence how you are marketing the product.

Question Two: What are my customer's interests and hobbies?

The key to developing a good relationship with your customers through Instagram is learning what their interests and hobbies are. The more you know about their interests, the more relevant content you'll be able to create. Try to spend time going into as much detail as you can and create a wide pool of interests and hobbies to choose from. This will help you much more when it comes to planning out a content schedule later on.

Question Three: What are my customer's problems?
Your customer will most likely have more than one problem. Your job is to come up with a concrete definition of what those problems are. Once you are able to describe what those problems are adequate, you'll be able to work on developing methods of communicating with your customers about that problem.

Question Four: What solutions are available to my customer?
While your product or services are the most obvious solution, this question is more about determining the competition that is working to vie for your customer's attention. Spend some time looking at the different solutions that are available, so that you can get a pulse on the competition.

Question Five: How would my product benefit my customers?

Here is where you'll work to put together benefits that solve your specific customer's problems. Don't generalize in this section, write answers that only apply to this current customer persona. For example, if you're selling a product that would appeal to three different customer personas, each persona may look at the product in a different light. What would motivate Customer Persona A to make a purchase might not motivate Customer Persona B.

These five questions will help you to develop a great customer persona. But what do you do with this information once you have it? Well, first and foremost, think of the customer persona as a style guide. Whenever you're working on a marketing effort, you will want to be working to impress that customer persona. Try to think of the persona as a concrete person, an individual who would be looking at your marketing efforts.

This type of thinking helps you work on creating content that is valuable to your ideal customer. With the Customer Persona fully developed, you will be on point every single time you develop an ad, create a post or even when commenting. By keeping the Customer Persona in mind, you will be able to create the kind of value that will attract real-life people who are quite similar to your ideal customer. And unlike your Customer Persona, these real people are actually capable of making purchases!

Summary

To summarize this chapter, one of the most important things that you can focus on is your customer relationship. Rather than worry about your own business' needs or desires, you need to pay attention instead of what your customers want and then give it to them.

You must also know exactly who your customer is before you can effectively market to them. Without a clear idea of the customer persona, you won't have a clear idea of what kind of content they are going to enjoy. You won't know what motivates them to buy what you are selling.

Creating a customer persona isn't hard to do, but it does take time and effort. You'll need to sit down and answer some key questions in order to create the right kind of persona. You also need to make multiple personas, one for each possible group that your business or products will appeal to. Try to be as specific as you can when defining a persona.

Chapter 3: Step 2: Set Up For the Long Term

Once you have a clear understanding of who your ideal customer is, it's time to begin working on the more practical side of Instagram marketing: Setting up your Business Profile! While it might seem relatively straightforward, there are a few things that you should keep in mind when developing an Instagram profile.

How to Set Up An Instagram Bio

First and foremost, you'll need to make sure that you are creating a separate account from your personal account. It's all well and good to have your own Instagram profile for personal uses, but you will want to keep your professional and personal accounts separate. This is for a few key reasons. The first is that the personal Instagram page is a reflection of you as an individual. A business profile, on the other hand, is a reflection of your company values. If there are people who are interested in the product but can't seem to find the company profile on Instagram, they may end up not getting further involved. They most likely aren't going to be searching for you by your personal name.

The second reason you'll want to set up a business account is that business accounts have access to extremely important metrics for data analysis. This will help you understand how many people are looking at and engaging with your content.

Step One: Download the App

Instagram is an app for your phone, so the first thing you'll need to do is download it if you haven't already. You can find the app from either the Apple Store or the Google Play Store.

Step Two: Sign Up

When signing up, make sure that you use your business email, not your personal one. This will be helpful just for the purposes of organizing any incoming messages you get later on from Instagram.

Step Three: Convert to a Business Account

Once you're inside the app, you'll need to go to the settings section and convert your newly made account to a Business Account. To do that, you just need to go to the settings by tapping on the gear, then go to Account. Then, select the *Switch to Business Account* option. This will prompt an invitation for you to link your Instagram directly to your Facebook Business Page. It will be helpful to link the two because it's easier to move people from Instagram to Facebook and vice versa.

Step Four: Add Relevant Information

Once you have set up your Business Account, you'll need to add relevant information. This means filling out your profile, adding the right kind of profile picture and then selecting the right link.

Staying on Brand

Your brand is one of the most precious things when it comes to online marketing. Your entire company is built around the brand identity that you have created for yourself. A brand identity is composed primarily of a combination of messages, visuals and specific colors. You must work diligently to make sure that your brand is highly visible on your profile page.

When an Instagram user lands on your page, there is only a short amount of time to make an impression on them. One of the first images that you'll want them to see is your logo. In general, the logo should always be the profile pic. It's where most users tend to look at first and it will stick with them. This will help develop "brand recognition," meaning that the visitors might end up seeing a product of yours later on and will recall having seen the brand before. On top of that, customers who are visiting your Instagram profile so that they can follow you are expecting to see your logo somewhere, as a means of confirming your identity.

The language you use in your profile description should also accurately reflect your own brand. Feel free to use a slogan as a profile descriptor, but make sure that you are clearly conveying your company's identity in the description. A visitor will see the picture first but will then quickly read the profile. Don't be verbose, either. Be quick and punchy with what you have to say about your company. Use humor if it fits your brand.

What Not to Include in A Bio

Generally, you want your bio to provide a quick "snapshot" of your company, its values and what it offers to the consumer. That being said, there are quite a few things that you will want to avoid when creating a bio. The biggest is the unprofessionalism. At the end of the day, you are still a company, even if you are the only running the business. People expect businesses to behave just like a business. This means that you should keep your bio professional as possible. Don't ramble, rant or write offensive content. Don't get political and avoid making any kind of inflammatory statements.

What Not to Use as a Profile Pic

When it comes to using a profile pic, you really have two options. The first is using your logo, which is highly recommended. If for some reason, you don't want to use a logo, then we would suggest that you use a professional photograph of yourself. The photo should be of high quality.

The list of acceptable phototypes is fairly short, but the list of things you shouldn't use as a profile is exceptionally long. In general, you shouldn't use anything unprofessional in your profile pic. This includes poorly lit photographs, images that are blurry, offensive or tasteless images and certain images that are unrelated to your business. The key is professionalism. There are plenty of ways to appear approachable to your customer, but the first impression that they'll want to get is that your business is legitimate. Don't undermine your great company and product with a poorly lit photo of you on a summer vacation. Keep it tight and professional.

Your Link

You'll notice that Instagram gives you the opportunity to create one and only one link on your profile page. This link is extremely important. Unlike other types of social media platforms, Instagram doesn't allow you to create links inside of your posts. This means that while you will be able to post pictures and all sorts of content, you can't create links that will direct consumers to your website. This is extremely limiting, as it means all traffic will essentially remain on Instagram.

You are provided with one link in your profile and that's it. This means that in order for an Instagram post to move a visitor from Instagram to your website, they'll need to visit your profile. And, since you get only the one link, you'll need to choose very carefully what you link your customers to. In general, you'll want to send them to the most relevant place for your business. For the most part, this would be your main website. However, in some cases, if you're pushing one and only one type of product, you may want to direct them straight to a landing page instead.

Don't make the mistake of simply linking the customer to another social media site. While you might have a more active account somewhere else, you're not actively helping your cause by shuffling the customer around from social media to social media. Instead, try to bring them to your main website where they can begin to evaluate your product for the purpose of making a purchase. Remember, all social media sites are tools meant to help sell products. The last thing you want to do is create a maze for your consumers, redirecting them from site to site until *finally,* they are able to find what they are looking for.

Summary

One of the most important things to remember about using Instagram for Business is that you aren't representing yourself anymore. Rather, you are going to be representing your entire company. Even if you are the only employee in your company, you will want people to look at your profile and see an upstanding business that is both professional and good looking.

You need to make sure that you have a good brand profile on your customer page, allowing people to know immediately what your business is about when they land on it. Your link should be taking customers to the most important part of your website and you should have all the contact information present so that customers are able to get in touch with you quickly and easily.

Finally, you should also take care to avoid posting personal matters or opinions on your social media account. The Instagram profile should be solely for the purpose of conveying company opinions, brand messages and photos. Leave all of the personal stuff to your personal account and never mix the two up!

Chapter 4: Step 3: Relationship Building

This chapter will be broken up into two sections. The first will be mostly outlining the nature of how relationship building works in broad terms. The second section will be more focused on nuts and bolts, actionable steps that can be taken to increase your Instagram following. But before we can get into the specifics, it's good to take a step back and look at the whole of what it means to use Instagram for the purpose of marketing.

As mentioned before, everything that you do should be about the customer. The goal isn't to gain as many sales as possible, because a sale is a simple transaction. Once a sale is made, it's done. As a marketer, you'll want to be able to go past sales and create a follower, someone who is passionate about your brand and your products.

A customer buys and goes on with their life, but a follower rants and raves about you. A follower engages with you and with others. Followers are enthusiastic about what they love and become mini-representatives. Best of all, you don't have to pay a follower, because their passion comes from a place of love and enthusiasm for your products.

Instagram is unique in that it allows businesses to connect with their customers on a closer level. A business owner gets the opportunity to get to know their customers intimately, learn what their interests are, what their hopes and dreams compose of. They get to see aspects of their customer's lives through windows. And in turn, your customers can see what your business is about. The things you post, the content you create, can have a profound impact on the way customers view your company.

If the customer perceives that your business' motive is purely for the sake of profit, that you are just interested in generating as many sales as possible, they will most likely keep you at arm's length. Sure, they may be interested in your product, but that's simply because of the problems that your product solves. If it's a really good product, it will most likely speak for itself.

However, just because a customer is satisfied with the product doesn't mean that they will become excited enough to engage with you. If they view your relationship as a primarily transactional thing, then they will simply buy your products when it suits them, but never engage past that. And honestly, if your focus is purely on generating sales, why should they engage? Once they have made the purchase, there is no more room for them. They move on and you continue to sell your wares.

Yet, there are ways to capture a customer's interest, sell them your product and continue to build the relationship, even after you have made the sale. We call this concept of engagement. You don't just want to put out products, you want to engage with customers. You don't just want sales, you want customers showing off pictures of their new purchase. You want to engage with them as people, acknowledging them and helping them. The more you engage with a customer, the more of a connection you will form with them. Over time, this connection will lead to a stronger relationship. And, if things go especially well, they may end up becoming more than a customer, they'll become a follower.

This might seem like it's a bunch of extra effort, but the truth is, it's fairly easy to work to create engagement with customers. It's really just a mindset that you need to hold to. When creating posts, when making content, focus on providing a great experience for Instagram users. Care more about what your customer personas want than what you want. Put people first. The more you can integrate this philosophy into your Instagram marketing, the better the chances you'll convert customers into followers.

Don't underestimate the value of word of mouth marketing. Nielsen states that 92% of people take more stock in a friend or family member's recommendation than any other type of advertising. It's one thing for a business to tell you that their product is great, but when a friend of yours recommends the product, then you know it is worth the money. By working to turn customers into brand advocates, simply by caring about them, you'll be generating significantly more sales than if you were to simply focus on promoting your products without much care of what the customer's want or need.

That's the fundamental core of Instagram marketing: you are building relationships. The more advocates and followers that you get, the larger your company will become. The ability to have a whole host of people who will excitedly recommend you via social media increases your growth potential significantly. And best of all, those customers often stay life-long! So not only do you get the benefits of the marketing for you, but you also get the benefit of them buying your new products! As long as you maintain an attitude of putting the customer first, you'll find tremendous success in building relationships. Now, with that philosophy in mind, let's move on to the nuts and bolts of building relationships through Instagram.

Finding Instagram Followers

While we mentioned followers as a concept to be people who are advocates, in this section we're primarily referring to Instagram Users who follow you on your Instagram Account. Followers are a necessary component of Instagram's success for a few reasons. The first reason is that when you make a post on Instagram, the post will show up in your follower's feeds. Then, if your followers like or make a comment on your post, their activity will show up in their friend's feed. This basically allows your followers to promote your profile whenever they engage with your account.

This will naturally increase the number of followers that you have, as users may come across one of your posts and like it enough to visit your profile page. When that happens, they'll have an opportunity to see previous posts. If they like what they see, they could even follow you, which will work to draw in more followers in a perfect cycle.

The second reason you want to have a high amount of Instagram followers is for social proof. When people come across a business that has sparked their curiosity, one of the first questions on their mind will be about the legitimacy of that business. The internet can be a sketchy place, with plenty of fraudsters and scammers about and most people are discerning. They want to be able to determine if the business they are looking at is real and trustworthy.

The more followers that you have, the better chance you have of gaining a potential customer's trust. After all, if 3,000 people are all following a business, they are most likely legitimate. But if a business has only a handful of Instagram followers, it's possible the potential customer might not trust you enough to explore further. That's why it's important to work to get as many as followers as possible in the beginning, to at least give people an understanding that you are an established company.

So how do we find Followers to begin with? When you're just starting out, you can generate more followers by simply working on converting your current fanbase to follow you on Instagram. For example, if you have a business that already has a following, you can run a promotion where if a customer follows you on Instagram, they get a special discount. Or, you can simply make an announcement on your home page and heavily encourage people to follow you on Instagram. Contacting friends and family, asking them to follow you is a great way to boost your initial numbers, even if those individuals are outside of your target demographic.

You should also take steps to include your Instagram feed on your home site so that people who are coming to your site from non-Instagram links are able to see what you have been posting. This will help passively increase the number of followers that you have. But passive generation isn't enough, at least not when you're just starting out.

Another way to build followers is to begin following people on Instagram who match your customer persona. Part of the Instagram etiquette is to follow back, so if you follow someone, they will generally follow you back. This is a great way to actively build up followers, but you need to be careful about a few things. The first is that not everyone will follow back, especially Instagram users who are extremely popular. Large companies, Instagram Influencers, and public figures often have a very small list of the people they are following. This is generally because when an account is that large, they don't need to work on generating followers anymore. Their fanbase has already grown to a significant amount and, unless they say something really bad, the numbers will remain fairly steady.

So, don't waste your time or energy on following major Instagram users in the hopes that they will follow you back. Instead, try to focus on following the regular people who use Instagram daily for the purpose of consuming content. The benefits of this are twofold, first, you get followers who are actually interested in the content that you are putting out. This means that they are more receptive to hearing your brand message. Second, you have a better chance of active followers actually engaging with your content. Remember, you want to find followers who are liking and commenting because this increases the likelihood of other people coming across your content.

So how do you find people on Instagram? The easiest way is to simply search for content that is relevant to your customer persona's interests. Then, look at the people who are liking and commenting on those photos and observe their profile. Do they match your customer persona? Are they similar enough to warrant the following? If the answer is yes, follow them! Hopefully, they'll follow you back.

You should be discerning with who you follow, of course. Make sure that you are following people who are only in your relevant demographic. Having followers is great, but you want to make sure that they are quality followers, who will respond to your marketing efforts. If you're selling hardcore hiking gear, there's no reason to follow accounts that are primarily focusing on the baking scene. Those people most likely won't convert and if they do, it will require a lot of convincing on your end. That is wasted time and energy. It's better to find a warm follower and heat them up than it is to find a frozen follower and thaw them out!

The last way to find Instagram users is to attract them through the Hashtag system. Instagram has a robust search and categorization system known as Hashtags. Hashtags, simply put, are keywords that when placed in an Instagram post, will be added to the search engine. Then, people who are searching for those hashtags will be able to find those posts. This enables a bunch of strangers, all who don't know one another, to share thoughts and ideas quickly between them. For example, if someone posts #mondayinspiration, they are joining thousands of other people who are all making different posts but with the same hashtag. They might not know one another, but they are all participating in the creation of a searchable, living index.

When you create posts, you will want to use hashtags properly. This will increase your chances of being discovered by other Instagram users who are searching for that hashtag. Your post will appear in the search section and they may end up interacting with it. If that's the case, it may result in you gaining a new follower! Hashtags are extremely potent and can help move a post out of obscurity into popularity rather quickly, especially if a lot of people are interested in searching for content related to that hashtag.

But there are some limitations to hashtags and discovery. If a hashtag is big enough to the point where it shows up in the trending section of Instagram, it is most likely spurring a lot of people to create posts with those hashtags. This, in turn, will create a flood of posts that will crowd out the search feature and could easily result in your posts being overlooked. If there are too many search results attached to a hashtag, you most likely won't be discovered.

The second limitation to hashtags is the fact that in order for a hashtag to be effective, people have to be searching for it. In other words, you cannot just create your own hashtags and wait for it to be discovered. People will not find your hashtags unless they are specifically searching for that phrase. So, until your Instagram account becomes large enough to set trends by getting followers to also post using your hashtag, you'll need to stick to using already established hashtags.

The trick is to find hashtags that are somewhere in the middle in terms of popularity. Too popular of a hashtag and you get lost in the avalanche of search results. Too few and nobody will bother to search for that hashtag. You'll want to find some hashtags that are trending upwards but haven't already hit their peak yet.

Finding Hashtags

Using hashtags is fairly easy to do, all you need to do is type # and then a phrase afterward. However, the difficulty lies in actually finding the right hashtags to use. As mentioned in the section above, you need to walk a fine line between obscurity and popularity if you want to maximize your results. So how do you go about finding hashtags and determining their popularity?

Fortunately, the process is easier than you might think. Thanks to websites like Hashtagify, you'll be able to type in hashtags and see how they are trending in terms of popularity, what the related hashtags are like, etc. These data points are extremely useful when it comes to planning outposts in the future. With the proper use of hashtags, you can greatly accelerate your Instagram account growth. Each post that you make will have a better chance of being discovered and engaged with. And, the way that Instagram works is that the more engagement a post receives, the higher up it will be in the search results. Success begets success.

The good news about hashtags is that you don't just get one chance. In fact, a post can have anywhere up to 30 hashtags! That means you are free to do research on multiple hashtags and incorporate them into your posting liberally. If you have two or three hashtags that are performing well, you can place them on the same post and watch as they grow! Of course, there is a caveat here. You want to make sure that any hashtag that you use in a post is both relevant and in the right context.

Relevancy matters because of quality control. You don't want to use irrelevant but popular hashtags because it can leave a bad impression on the viewers. For example, if you were to use a popular baking hashtag to attract people to your hiking post, you are accomplishing two things, both negative. The first is that you are bringing in people who are specifically looking for baking related things. Chances are they'll see in the search bar that the post is irrelevant and ignore it. This accomplishes nothing and wastes everyone's time. The second problem is that people who follow you may notice that you're using irrelevant hashtags and may begin to see you as being somewhat dishonest. After all, trying to widen your net with misleading hashtags isn't a particularly ethical thing to do. This can sour your relationship with your current followers.

Context is also highly important when it comes to using hashtags. Not all hashtags are straightforward in their meaning. There are sometimes concepts or ideas that surround why specific hashtags have grown in popularity. If you don't know the context of how a hashtag is being used, you could potentially create posts that are wildly inaccurate or worse, damaging to your company.

One great example of a hashtag gone wrong is when the hashtag #whyistayed began to trend on Twitter. A lot of people began using this hashtag as a means of discussing what kept them trapped in dangerous, abusive relationships. The purpose of the tag was to raise awareness of domestic violence. Yet, the pizza company DiGiorno had no idea that this was the point of the tag. All they saw was the fact that it was trending on Twitter and decided to use it without checking the meaning first. Their gaffe was "#whyistayed You Had Pizza." certain, of course, was wildly inappropriate and caused the company to receive a tremendous amount of flack for their tone-deafness.

In general, you'll want to do everything in your power to avoid this kind of behavior. Instead, make sure that you are 100% sure of the context behind the tag that you are using. Look at the posts that are using it and keep a note of the context, it's the only way to be certain that you aren't accidentally walking into a dangerous topic.

A Note About Buying Followers

While you are working on expanding and developing your Instagram following, you may end up coming across websites that offer to sell you followers for a rather reasonable fee. These followers, they promise, look completely real and will even fool Instagram's algorithms. These companies are often hoping that businesses purchase hundreds or even hundreds of thousands of followers, so they offer bulk discounts for their services.

However, it's important to know that purchasing followers from third parties will do absolutely nothing for your business. While some businesses might think that having a huge amount of followers will help improve their online reputation or give people a good first impression of their business, usually the opposite is true. It's fairly easy to tell if the bulk of an Instagram user's followers are real or not, and once you realize that the majority of a following are just bots or junk accounts made by some third party, the conclusion is fairly inevitable: this user paid for followers. This can damage your reputation.

Another problem with purchasing followers is the fact that these followers will not actively engage or interact with you. They will merely take up digital space. As a business you want your followers to be active as possible, interacting with you and each other, so that they can share your content and make purchases. A fake follower does none of that. All a fake follower does is waste your money. Besides, once Instagram's algorithms pick up the trail of these fake followers, they will purge the accounts, leaving you with nothing. If you want to spend money in the pursuit of getting more followers, you would be much better off using Instagram's ad system.

Posting Strategies

Instagram is a content publishing platform first and foremost. While people are enjoying liking and commenting on posts, having discussions about their favorite subjects, the reason they come to Instagram is to look at pictures in a steady stream. The app itself is heavily designed to create a seamless scrolling experience, allowing users to endlessly scroll down through the hundreds upon hundreds of pictures that are available to them.

Capturing attention isn't going to be easy. When you put a post up on Instagram, you will only be a small part of the Instagram user's feed. They'll have other pictures to look at, and, if your content isn't interesting enough, they won't engage with you. The less they engage, the less chance your posts have of showing up in their feed, to begin with, so that could create a dangerous downward spiral. Therefore, you must be willing to focus on developing the right content to share with your followers. There are three components to a proper posting strategy: timing, content, and frequency. Let's take a look at each one in detail.

Timing

Instagram focused on the chronological order of posts. That means if you put out a post at 5 pm and a hundred of your followers are on using Instagram at 5, they'll most likely see your post. This means being timely is of extreme value, as you will want to make sure that your posts are seen during the time that your users are most active.

Figuring out *when* your followers use Instagram the most is the hard part. Depending on your demographic, they may respond more during the daytime or during the night. Fortunately, there are social media tools out there that will help you to learn the patterns of your followers, so you can calculate an ideal posting time. Then, once you have your time, make sure you only post during that time period, to ensure that your posts show up in the maximum number of feeds possible.

Content

Developing content for Instagram is going to be the bulk of the work you'll have to do. In order to stay both interesting and relevant to your followers, you'll need to be putting out a number of posts a week. Without those posts, you won't be able to drive engagement and lead people back towards your link.

There are many different types of content that you can share on Instagram, but they all have one thing in common: they are primarily focused on the visual medium. This means, for the most part, you're going to need to either take pictures or find them online for distribution. But before we get into the visual aspect of Instagram photos, let's talk about the different types of content that are most popular on the platform.

Infographics

Infographics remain, to this day, as one of the most popular types of content that can be shared through Instagram. People are enjoying both the visual and written components blended together, helping them learn about something relevant to their interests.

Behind the Scenes

As a company, you will most likely have a majority of followers who are interested in your business. Some of them might even be loyal customers who are looking for an inside look at your company. Behind the Scenes photos are a great way to both generate excitement about your business, while also rewarding your followers with content unavailable anywhere else.

The best part of behind the scenes photos is that you'll be able to take them candidly throughout the day, without much planning required. This will allow you to organically share what is happening in your business while also providing you with content to frequently post.

Product Photos and Teasers

One great way to generate more buzz about your business is to show off high-quality photographs of your products. Or you can even take pictures meant to tease or hint at the nature of the next coming release. This will help to create more awareness of your products that are available, as well as increase the interest level in what is to come.

Team Introductions and Profiles

The biggest advantage that Instagram gives you as a business is the ability to form relationships with your followers. They don't have to see you as simply just some faceless corporate entity, but rather they can see you as a human company, full of regular, normal human beings just like them. This builds up empathy and a sense of connection. A way to help your followers see your company as more than just a sales platform is to use photos of your employees and team in action.

Of course, you'll want to make sure that your team is comfortable with being posted on Instagram. You don't want to end up in awkward situations where you have team members trying to cover up their faces during candid pictures. And in part of respect for privacy, you should never upload pictures of others on social media without their consent.

Customer Photos

While these photos are not necessarily created nor posted by you, having a call to ask customers to share photos of enjoying your product can be very beneficial. Those who respond and post their photos will be advertising for your product organically, and best of all, it will help to foster more loyalty to your company.

Instagram Stories

Instagram stories are a different type of content from other posts. Normally, when you make a post, you can select a picture from your phone's storage and when it's uploaded, it will be on your profile for good. Instagram Stories work on a fundamentally different level. First, Instagram stories only last for 24 hours from the time they are posted. After that, the story is deleted from Instagram forever.

This might seem strange, but it's a way for people to share highly exclusive content for a very short amount of time. Only those who are following your regularly Instagram will be able to access potentially important information through these stories. This rewards person for making an effort to check in to your Instagram Stories each and every day. In turn, this increases the chances of engagement from your followers. It can even add to more advertising opportunities for you as well.

Second, Instagram Stories are designed to be rawer and less polished. When making a story, you're recording a video or taking a picture to be uploaded immediately. You won't be able to upload a highly polished, well-rendered photo, instead, it will be more of an honest look at whatever you are recording. This is meant to allow people to feel as if they are experiencing the same thing that you are.

Stories grant a tremendous amount of options for businesses to create all sorts of interesting content. Let's take a look at a few different ways that you can use Instagram Stories to get maximum results!

Generate Buzz Through Slow Reveals

Your business may be working on a new product or some kind of special announcement, such as participation at a big event or convention. Rather than simply come out and announce the product or event, you could slowly work towards it. You'll warm up people as you show small snippets and posts throughout your Stories, generating excitement until you are finally ready for the reveal. Instead of just showing everything at once, you slowly build up to it in the hopes of generating enough of a buzz to warrant preorders or event sign-ups.

Create Flash Deals

Since Instagram stories only exist for 24 hours before vanishing, you have an opportunity to create what is known as Flash Deals. A flash deal is quick, lasting only for the time that the Instagram story is online. This will aid you in multiple ways. The first and foremost, it will help to increase sales in a product. As long as you are willing to offer a coupon code, a discount or free shipping, you will be able to get some people to finally make the purchasing decision. This will help your bottom line, and if they are new customers, it will help move them into following your business long-term.

The second benefit that Flash Deals provide to you is that you'll be able to create an incentive for your followers to check out your Instagram Stories on a regular basis. This will drive higher engagement as they might be waiting for a deal but could get pulled into other content that you have to offer.

Here's an important note about flash deals. While offering them can be a great way to increase sales and drive engagement, you shouldn't offer too many deals in too short a time. The reason behind this is that if customers miss a flash sale, but see another one just a week later, they'll come to the conclusion that these sales are very common. This conclusion will reduce the urgency of the sale and may lead to them not making a purchase at all, confident that they'll be able to buy later.

In general, you don't want to offer Flash Deals more than once or twice a month. You'll need to keep followers on their toes, never sure when you're going to be putting up a flash deal.

Create a Countdown

Instagram Stories have what's known as stickers, allowing you to add different fun, visual elements to your Instagram Story. One sticker, however, allows you to turn your story into a countdown clock. This will allow you to show customers that something interesting is coming down the pipeline, but they'll have to wait a certain amount of time before hearing the announcement.

On top of displaying a countdown, the followers will have the option to tap on the *follow* button of the countdown clock. Then, when the clock reaches 0, it will send notifications to those who follow the countdown, alerting them that the timer is over. Then, you can post a new story, with the announcement that people have been waiting for.

Countdowns are another invaluable tool for creating excitement about upcoming releases. If you have a wide customer base that is following you on Instagram, countdowns are a great way to reward them for checking out your Stories.

Exclusive Announcements

Another great way to use Instagram Stories is to use them for exclusive announcements, not found anywhere else. By using Instagram as the platform for these announcements you achieve two things simultaneously. First, you are rewarding your followers with exclusive content not found anywhere else. Second, you are encouraging people who aren't following you on Instagram to do so. This can be a great way to pull in new followers, especially if the announcement is of the utmost importance.

Contests

A lot of businesses use Instagram Stories as a way to host contests. These contests are usually some kind of giveaway that requires action on the part of the follower. For example, you can randomly select a customer from a list of people who use a specific hashtag or post a specific type of photograph as stipulated by the contest. This can considerably increase the number of followers that you have, as contests have a way of attracting new blood who are interested in getting something for free.

Of course, you'll want to be careful with the contest that you run. There are a few things to watch out for. First, you don't want the prize to be too generic, or else you risk people from outside of your target market following you in the hopes of winning. Instead, try to make sure that the product you are giving away is a part of the niche you're selling in. You want to attract followers who will eventually *purchase* your products later on. The cost of the free giveaway is just the cost of marketing.

The second thing to keep in mind is that Instagram does have specific rules for running contests. You must adhere to your local government's laws about promotions and giveaways, as well as make sure that "You must not inaccurately tag content or encourage users to inaccurately tag content (example: don't encourage people to tag themselves in photos if they aren't in the photo)" as stipulated by their website.

Frequency of Posts

Now that you've got a general idea of the types of content that is most popular on Instagram, all that's left is the question of how many times should you post in a week? In general, anywhere between one to three posts a day should be fine. Anything more than that and Instagram will begin to suppress those extra posts. Why? Because Instagram is a business first and foremost. They want to make money off of other businesses by selling ad space. Using Instagram for free, organic reach is entirely possible, up to an extent. However, posting too many times a day will cause your reach to diminish with each extra post. Instead, it's better to only post up to three times a day, in order for your content to reach the maximum number of feeds possible.

Crafting Captions

While it is true that Instagram is primarily a visual medium, that doesn't mean you won't have to write any words out. Below every Instagram picture is space of what's known as the caption. The caption can be quite short or quite long, depending on what you have to say about the matter. Captions are exceptionally useful for giving your followers context, story or insight into your post.

Captions also drive engagement. When a user sees a photo and likes it, their attention is naturally directed towards the caption section, where they will be able to get more insight on the matter. This space allows you to craft an interesting story for them, or even to ask them questions, prompting an opportunity for interaction with your followers.

So, what are some of the best practices when it comes to writing the perfect caption for your Instagram posts? Here are a few tips:

Support the Picture

Your caption should be in support of the picture that you post. This means that if you're showing a picture of say, an employee working on a project, you should be writing about the project they're working on. Tell a short story, help provide more context to the scenario.

Write the Important Stuff First

Instagram allows you to write up to 2,200 characters total in a caption. This lends to allowing you to write quite a big paragraph if you like. And, there's nothing wrong with writing a longer caption, either. However, you should note that only the first 125 characters will show up when people are scrolling through their feed. They will have to interact with the post in order to see the rest of what you have to say.

This means that the first 125 characters should be crafted in a way that will draw the viewer in. You will need to write a catchy hook that is able to pull them in so that they are willing to read the rest of the caption. So, when writing the first two sentences of your caption, try to think of those words as the "title" of your Instagram post. Will your title be able to draw them in to read more?

Things like hashtags should also go at the end of your Instagram post, not the beginning. The placement of hashtags doesn't affect your search ranking, so don't worry about that.

Create A Sense of Excitement

Remember, at the end of the day, you will want these Instagram captions to help motivate your followers to have some kind of experience. Ultimately, you will want to motivate them to make a purchase or engage more with you, so in order to do that, your writing has to convey a sense of excitement. Write with passion, use a strong call to action when appropriate. Don't just give a boring, bland description of what the viewers see, instead try to stimulate their imaginations and get them excited about what you're sharing!

Avoid being too salesy

It is true that you can use Instagram captions as a means of advertising for your products. And you absolutely should make the occasional pitch or mention that a specific product is currently on sale. However, what you absolutely want to avoid is pushing too hard in your captions. As a general rule of thumb, for every ten Instagram posts that you make, two of those should be geared towards advertising directly. Any more than that and people will start to get the sense that the only thing your business cares about is selling products to them. Any less than that and you won't be able to convert any of your followers into customers!

Get the Point

While you can write a very long paragraph if you so please, remember that people's attention spans are rather short. Everything else on Instagram is vying for their attention, and if you end up rambling too much in your post, they'll just go look at something else. There's nothing wrong with a long post, as long as your writing is both tight and focused. Get to the point as quickly as you can and then, once you've made your point, don't keep writing.

Each caption should really have only one focus, one topic. Trying to stuff too many topics into a single post can not only be overwhelming for the reader, but it can also affect the "punchiness" of your own writing. If you want to write about multiple subjects, make multiple Instagram posts. Don't try to put it all in one overstuffed post.

What to Avoid Posting

Before we conclude this section, let's talk a bit about the things that you'll want to avoid posting when using Instagram for your business. For the most part, you'll want to make sure that you are only posting high quality, good looking images. Blurry and poorly lit snapshots from your phone won't look particularly good and worst of all, may end up causing people to unfollow. After all, people come to Instagram to be wowed and impressed with the visual content in their feeds. An ugly photo could be a major turn off for some.

On top of quality control, you should also work to avoid posting anything *outside* of your target market's interests. You should be laser-focused, every post should be as relevant as possible to your customer persona. Any posts outside of those interests will only weaken your marketing efforts.

And last, when posting on Instagram, you should absolutely avoid any kind of controversial, political or inflammatory stances. While making a statement about some popular subject in the news might seem like a good idea, the fact is, people will take both sides of the argument. The last thing you want to do is end up alienating or irritating half of your follower base, just because you wanted to make an important statement. By staying politically neutral, you won't end up risking losing followers (and business) from either side. It's a best practice, especially in today's politically charged environment.

Summary

The best way to build a following through Instagram is to work on creating relationships. In order to create a relationship, you must be more concerned with providing value to your customers than for them to provide value to you. Building a proper relationship requires you to look at them as people and to honestly care about your customer.

Interacting and engaging with your followers on Instagram will help turn them into advocates for your brand. By paying more attention to their desires and giving them assistance when they need it, you are naturally creating advocates who will advertise on your behalf without any prompting.

The best way to gain followers through Instagram is to follow people that match your customer persona. Instagram etiquette dictates that they follow you back, allowing you to build your following over time. Make sure that you only follow the people who are relevant to your company, however, as you don't want to simply build a collection of followers. You want high-quality ones who will eventually convert and purchase your products.

Hashtags are some of the most effective ways that you can classify and sort data on Instagram. Through the use of

Hashtags, you'll be able to find ideas to plan content as well as help other people who aren't familiar with your businesses to find you. Doing the proper research on hashtags is necessary and you must make sure that you are fully aware of what hashtag actually means before you use it.

Content matters significantly more than most people initially realize when it comes to Instagram. You need to be aware of the kind of content that your followers want to see and then make a point to produce as much of it as you can. Always be innovating when it comes to making new content and most of all, make sure that you aren't coming across as too salesy. The last thing followers want to see is a constant barrage of Instagram salesmen, trying their hardest to make a sale when people just want something to entertain or inspire them.

Chapter 5: Step 4: Interaction, Raving Fans

Once you have a general handle on the type of content that you will be releasing on a regular basis, it's time to take the focus onto the most important part of Instagram: interaction. While posting is extremely important, the truth is, posting is only a means to an end. The end goal of social media is to help move fans closer to you so that they are able to engage more. The more engagement you get, the better chance you have of gaining their trust and later on, their company loyalty.

It's good to have fans, but as we've mentioned before, what you really want are raving fans. You want people who are so excited about your company and your brand that they are willing to go out and tell other people about it. You want the kinds of fans who will, unsolicited by you, advertise for your products without expecting anything in return.

And with a social media platform like Instagram, it is totally possible to work towards creating those types of fans. Note, that you don't really *find* those types of fans, rather, you actually work to create them by cultivating a strong, healthy relationship with them. Over time, those normal fans will develop into advocates for you. However, this requires that you be significantly more focused on your customers than your own company at first.

Remember, people are ultimately concerned with themselves first. It's all about the customer, not you. So, in order to get stronger fans, you're going to need to develop a content strategy that primarily focuses on increasing connection with your fans as well as driving engagement. This whole section will be dedicated to helping you learn different methods of increasing customer engagement, while simultaneously building more brand awareness in your followers.

Using Comments Properly

If you want to develop relationships through Instagram, you're going to need to spend time on the comments section of not only your posts but also the posts of others. It's all well and good to make as many posts as you like, but if you aren't commenting, you won't be able to have that personal interaction with others. The proper commenting procedure will enable you to not only maintain an online presence but also to move people towards your own Instagram profile page passively.

The first thing to keep in mind when commenting on other people's posts is that you want to keep your focus entirely on them. Feel free to praise their photo, talk about what you like about it, etc. However, you should definitely *not* try and move the conversation over to talking about you. You don't want to come across as simply spamming your own information inside of other people's comments. Instead, work to make a genuine effort in communicating with users.

In general, when interacting with others, you're going to want one of three things. You'll want to either encourage, inquire or solve a problem. Encouragement is easy enough, you just keep a positive, healthy attitude and spread love to others. Inquiring is really about asking the user a question or follow-up question about their post. Something to prompt the other person to engage in a dialogue with you and maybe even with others.

However, most likely the bulk comment work will be geared towards solving problems, often through answering questions. When you see a person in the comments ask a question that you know how to answer, you should make an effort to reply to that individual and share what you know. If they are a follower of yours, they will find you to be helpful and friendly and may be more receptive to your marketing efforts later on. If they aren't followers, your assistance might be able to motivate them towards following you.

Other ways to solve problems is to make recommendations for products, share helpful tips, give insight into what the problem is and, in some cases, even refer to your own products. Try to keep your sales pitches low, but if you are in a situation where you can genuinely help a person who has a problem with your products, you may even want to consider giving them a coupon code, to help them move along with the sale.

Responding to Comments

Posting a comment is a very proactive thing and can be useful for your business as you grow. However, while posting comments is optional, depending on how much time you have, responding to comments on your own post is decidedly less of an option. Why? Because, as a company and a brand, you're going to want to create as much of an appearance of being active and responsive as possible. When people comment on your own posts, they are taking time out of their busy day to make an effort. Whether they are praising your product, asking a question or just talking about their experience, your followers deserve to be replied to. In doing so, you show that you value and care about them. Ignore them and they might not comment on your posts after a while.

Of course, figuring out what to say can be a bit difficult, especially if a follower is just posting a simple, short word of praise to you. The easiest way is to just reply, short and sweet with a thank you. Other options include using Emojis as quick, easy replies. A heart emoji can go a long way and most businesses do use quick replies like that, so it wouldn't seem out of place.

When it comes to customer concerns or complaints, you should absolutely work to respond to those comments as fast as possible. However, it is important to remember that your conversation is not private when it comes to comments, everyone else can see the exchange. So, no matter what, you'll need to be both civil and diplomatic with your customer, even if you don't think the complaint is legitimate.

The best way to handle customer service complaints is to try and take the conversation private as quickly as possible. Either suggest that you carry on the conversation on in your direct messages, or request that they email so that you can handle the problem.

Social media is rapidly becoming a way of circumventing the drawn-out process of submitting problems to customer support. People are growing fed up with the fact that they have to submit tickets and then often get some kind of frustrating, automated message back to them. Sometimes they can't have their problems solved by the support team. What customers are finding, however, is that when they begin to complain about their issues on social media, it forces the company to respond quickly, or else they risk having their reputation damaged.

So, don't be surprised that if some of your customers who have problems take to social media such as Instagram to complain about you. They may even end up tagging you, as a hope of catching your attention. It's important here to remember that the reason for this behavior is usually born out of frustration and not maliciousness. Most customers just want their problems solved and when the products they use don't work as advertised, they often want to air their grievances. Taking an adversarial approach to these customers will only cause you more harm in the long run.

Even if a customer is malicious in their words against you, a harsh response will almost always prove to make you look petty and unprofessional. Remember, whatever you post online will stay online indefinitely. Even if you change your mind and take down the post quickly, someone will have already taken a screenshot of it and will distribute the post around the internet channels. That is why you must always keep your cool and stay diplomatic.

Handling Trolls and Moderating Comments

There are really two types of commenters online, people who are genuinely just trying to find solutions and interesting content and then there are trolls. The fact that one can be anonymous online combined with the fact that there are no repercussions for abusive or nasty actions has lent to creating a larger pool of people with nothing better to do than to harass and cajole others online. These people, trolls really, get a big kick out of causing trouble and making others suffer.

Part of working with Instagram is learning how to determine whether a commenter has legitimate complains and frustrations, or whether they are just trolling, trying to get a reaction out of you. A legitimate customer is usually looking for some kind of resolution, and while they may be upset or angry, you can generally calm them down once you are able to address the issue at hand. However, with a troll, you will quickly find that they will just say whatever it takes to get a rise out of you. In some cases, they may even devolve into slurs and inflammatory speech that has no place in your posts.

Trolls don't even have to target you, they can very well just put their aim at a follower of yours who posted a comment on one of your photos. If that's the case, you have options for handling these types of people. Thankfully, Instagram does grant you the ability to moderate comments, including putting together a language filter that automatically removes comments that use certain words or phrases.

All you need to do is go to settings and then go to the comments page. This will allow you to create automatic filters that delete posts based on certain words used. There are also manual filters that allow you to place phrases that you want to hide automatically. This is extremely helpful because it automatically moderates your comment sections and prevents the trolls from doing harm to your customer base.

You also have the power to delete someone else's comments on your own posts if you so choose. All you need to do is swipe right on their comment and you'll be given the option to delete it. This can be useful for when someone is clearly being inflammatory or a troll, but they aren't using slurs or phrases that would be picked up by the automatic filter. The cleaner you can keep the comment sections, the better!

However, you must be cautious when moderating the community that you are building around your Instagram profile. The ability to delete anyone's comment can be very alluring, especially if you see a customer make a negative comment about your product or customer service. However, in doing this, you are no longer simply working to preserve the peace, you are instead actively censoring your customer base so that you make yourself look good.

There are some serious problems behind this kind of behavior. The first and foremost is that it will signal to the customer who is complaining that you genuinely do not care about them nor their complaint. This will tell them that your company isn't worth trusting and that you would rather look good than admit fault. You will most likely lose that customer for life. And besides, nothing stops that customer from making their own posts talking about your censorship.

The second problem is that if your behavior gets caught by the community, a trust will rapidly diminish. The fact that a company is willing to actively censor and delete comments from people who aren't giving them glowing reviews is extremely shady. You don't want to risk losing your good reputation simply because you chose to remove a few bad reviews. It's just not worth it.

Addressing Criticism

So, if censorship is the worst possible thing you can do when a customer is criticizing your business online, what is the best option? Ultimately, you'll need to determine if there is validity to that criticism. If there is, apologize for their pains. This is an act of humility, but in doing so, you are demonstrating to the customer that they are more important than you. Then, once you apologize, take steps to make it up to them. This effort can turn even the most frustrated customer into an advocate for your company. It's one thing for a company to provide a good service or product, people generally come to expect that. However, when a company is willing to admit error and take steps to make things right, that is above and beyond what most people are expecting.

What do you do when the criticism isn't valid? Perhaps the customer's expectations weren't properly aligned or maybe their complaint is just kind of nitpicky? Just try to address their concerns without talking down to them. When people are having a problem, most of the time they just want to feel *heard*. Validating a customer by listening and responding, being as helpful as possible can go a long way. You don't have to apologize for something that your company isn't responsible for, but you should at least show the customer that you care and are paying attention. You'll find that most of the time, the customer will be happy with your response.

Sometimes, a customer will still be frustrated or make negative comments, but after you try to resolve it amicably, just stop responding. Some people will never be happy.

The Snark Trend

Recently, thanks to some aggressive snarkiness from Wendy's Twitter account, companies are beginning to treat certain critics with a degree of attitude. Some make wry, snarky comments that mock the poster, while others are absolutely ruthless in their treatment of the customer. This creates a bit of fun for followers, as they get to see these normally reserved companies suddenly act out of character towards their customer base. A lot of times, these snarky replies become viral and end up being circulated around on various social media platforms.

Being from the outside, it is easy to see the allure of using witty comebacks against negative commenters. First off, it's fun to watch and secondly, it allows you to give others their just desserts, especially if their negativity is uncalled for. But you should be cautious when considering whether to be snarky and dismissive towards commenters.

Most of the time, the companies that are so cleverly dismissing naysayers are quite large in size. Wendy's, for example, is a gigantic franchise that sprawls across the United States. They sell millions of burgers a year and most of their customer base doesn't come from social media. So, in a sense, they have the luxury to behave as they wish. Sure, there is potential for backlash, but Wendy's is large enough to where they can absorb the risk of such backlash. People are going to be stopping at Wendy's regardless of what they say on Twitter.

However, as a small business, you don't have the same luxury. When using your own Instagram account, you will most likely be advertising to people who aren't familiar with your brand at all. Many times, your Instagram posts will be the first point of contact for potential new customers. Their perception of you matters greatly. While you may believe that you're throwing out clever zingers at negative individuals, if a joke falls flat, or worse, looks like bullying, you could end up losing a lot of goodwill from your follower base.

So, while snarkiness has begun to trend on social media among the bigger companies, the question you'll need to ask yourself is if you can handle the backlash. If you lose even just one sale from a comeback gone wrong, is it worth it? Tread carefully, you don't want to take one step forward and then three steps back, just because you want to emulate what these multi-million dollar companies are doing.

Increasing Engagement

Engagement has tremendous value for your Instagram posts. First, it increases the likelihood that others will see your post. Second, engagement also increases the chances of a customer connecting more to your brand. The more familiar a customer is with your company, the better chances you have of converting them to a sale.

All of the above posts are really about how to engage properly on your end. Moderating comments, handling critics and answering questions are all great ways for *you* to engage with your followers. But now, we must bring attention to the question of how to drive your followers to engage more. Ultimately, you want every post you make to have plenty of likes and lots of comments. But how do you get there? There are a few different factors involved with engagement. Let's take a look at each one.

Relevance

Once you have a clearly developed customer persona, you'll need to focus completely on uploading posts that are relevant to your customer base's interests. Posting outside of those interests won't get you the results that you're looking for, and worse yet, may even end up hindering you. Remember, you have to anticipate the content that your customer *wants* and then distribute it for them. The more relevant and enjoyable quality content that you can distribute, the more engagement you will naturally get. This should really be the baseline for driving engagement. Put out what the people want and then watch them engage with it.

Popularity

Relevance alone, however, doesn't determine if a post will perform well. In reality, you don't really know how a type of post is going to do until you put it out there. It's possible that content that you think will do really well ends up getting no love while other posts that you didn't think would perform end up generating the most likes and comments.

You can use this information to determine what the best content is to release on your platform. Take a look at the elements of the most popular posts and do your best to try and replicate them. You may find that these posts continue to perform well, generating the most amount of likes and comments. If that's the case, you should continue focusing on releasing more content similar to the successful ones. Don't worry about the posts that fail to perform, instead, try to emulate the ones that are the most successful. Over time, this strategy will help you continually get more and more engagement from your followers.

Remember, it doesn't matter what content that *you* think is good. It's all about the customer's choices and tastes. If they don't like the type of post that you make, no matter how much you personally enjoy it, you have to stop making those kinds of posts. Go only towards what resonates with your followers. Leave everything else behind.

Asking Questions

As mentioned before, asking questions is one of the key methods of getting engagement from your followers. Creating posts that ask simple questions like "what's your favorite thing to do in the morning" or product-specific ones like "what's your favorite color of our product," will by default, lead your more interested followers in engaging with you.

But you need to find the right kind of balance when it comes to asking questions of your audience. You can't simply put out dozens of generic posts that ask questions. Too many questions in too short a timeframe will most likely end up being ignored by your viewers. Instead, try to ask one or two questions a week, but make them interesting enough to where the viewers will want to engage with you. This takes time to figure out, of course, as you'll need to ask questions that are relevant to your audience and capable of provoking intelligent discussion.

There are things to steer clear of when asking questions. First and foremost, you'll want to avoid the types of questions that are overly sales-oriented, especially if you have a small customer base. Questions like "what product are you most excited about buying," can be a little too much, as it assumes the customers are planning purchases.

In general, asking questions should be relegated to getting consumers to share their own thoughts and opinions, not as excuses to sell them on your products. You want to spark conversations that will get other people involved. A good, productive question will spark dozens if not hundreds of comments and will further your goals of increasing the overall range of your posts.

Another thing to avoid is any subject that could potentially become inflammatory. As we've mentioned already, things like politics and current events have a tendency to set people off and the last thing you want is to have a comment section full of people whose comments have been deleted by the filter. You should also pay attention to the attitudes towards specific subjects in the niche you've selected. If you know there are certainly strong opinions about one style vs another, then you should steer clear of asking people which they prefer.

Polls and Quizzes

A great and interactive form of asking questions on Instagram is to create polls or quizzes that ask what users prefer. Creating them is fairly simple to do as well, all you need to do is use Instagram Stories and then use the appropriate stickers to set these polls up. Generally, you can create two option polls that will let users select between two ideas. You'll be able to see how many users voted for option A and for option B.

Polls are a great way to not only get people to engage in simple preference questions but also to get a snapshot of what your customers find interesting about your products. Here, you'll be able to ask questions about what type of products or features that your customers would be most interested in. While it's not the most scientific method of data collecting, you'll still be able to get a snapshot of what your customers will be most excited about when it comes to making a new release.

Quizzes can increase the "fun" factor of a page as well. Asking silly, odd or even offbeat questions can provoke all sorts of great answers from the audience. People will see those answers in other feeds and perhaps even be motivated to answer the questions themselves.

Price Temperatures

There are plenty of barriers when it comes to making a purchase decision. One of the biggest can be the price point of the products you are selling. If you are in a niche, or a field that doesn't have a tremendous amount of competition, you will be free to set prices however you like. But, if your prices are too high, you may end up discouraging customers from making purchases. It can be difficult to tell what your customers are thinking when it comes to making these purchasing decisions and even with all the metrics in the world, it can be a bit of a guessing game.

Fortunately, you can just simply ask your followers directly questions about pricing. You can't make it terribly obvious that you're planning on adjusting the price to whatever the customers want, or else they'll just throw out the lowest number possible. But you can ask questions about theoretical deals or short-term sales and see if they respond. If you get overwhelmingly positive results from a question about dropping a price down a few bucks or creating a bundle deal that will increase savings, then you are taking the guesswork out of pricing!

Summary

If you want to have fans that are more than just followers, but advocates who follow you closely, you're going to need to put in both the time and the effort through engagement. Engaging with an Instagram follower means that you're willing to reply to their comments, like their posts and ask questions that provoke more discussion from your followers.

Not everyone on Instagram is an upstanding citizen who wishes you well. There are plenty of trolls online who only want to cause problems for both you and your followers. You should take time to build a language filter and enforce it on your posts, preventing trolls from using hateful speech and slurs against other commenters. You should work diligently to make sure that the comment sections are safe, free of personal attacks and calls for violence. There's nothing wrong with deleting comments of others that are inflammatory.

However, censorship is not the appropriate course of action when it comes to dealing with people who are legitimately criticizing your actions or your company. Rather, you should work to make things right with those individuals, trying your best to repair the relationship so that they walk away happy.

Asking questions and creating polls are a great way to get people to open up and begin a dialogue. The more you get people talking about the things they like, what they enjoy about their own lives, the more opportunities you have to learn about your customers. This will help you later on when it comes to creating or marketing new products.

Chapter 6: Step 5: Turning Followers into Profit

Using Instagram Ads for Increasing Followers and Engagement

Organic reach through Instagram is great but has its limits. While it is possible for you to build up a follower base through only free, organic use of Instagram, the truth is that it will take quite a long time to do so. As you've seen in the above sections, there are a lot of details involved with putting together a successful Instagram profile and running it does require a bit of a time commitment. As you keep at it and become more adept at using Instagram, you'll find that the time requirements grow less and less demanding, but at the beginning, if you're just using Instagram without paying for ads, you're paying with another currency: time.

Yes, Instagram is technically free and yes, you can technically grow your page nice and large without spending a dime. But that doesn't mean you aren't losing money. Your time is just as valuable as a dollar, more so if you consider that you can be using your time to generate more income for the business. Like with anything else, you have to learn how to calculate opportunity costs. The allure of free can be strong, but if Instagram takes 8 hours a week of your time, you have to be willing to determine what else you could be using that time for. If those 8 hours could have been used to earn your business say, $500 in income, perhaps by making cold calls, then those 8 hours of Instagram weren't free. They actually ended up costing you $500 in profit that could have been made.

One mistake that many business owners make, especially when they first get started with using Social Media is to see the low, low price tag of "free" and assume that they won't have to spend a lot of money in marketing. The truth is, organic, free reach through Instagram is like using sticks to light a fire. It will work, eventually, and only after some serious effort. Paid advertising, on the other hand, is like using a flamethrower to get a fire going.

Overall, the cost of using paid Instagram Advertising is significantly lower than the cost of doing it all yourself for free. You're going to get better results with Instagram Ads than you are with just using your own methods. Why is that? Simply put, because Instagram Ads use Facebook's targeting algorithms.

As individuals use Instagram and Facebook, the system itself is busy learning what the user likes exactly. It learns their behaviors by tracking their actions, the time they spend on specific content and most importantly, it learns to predict which behaviors the user will engage in. Then, using this data, they will place ads in front of people who are most likely to react positively to that ad. In other words, Instagram's targeting algorithms are entirely designed to put your ads in front of people who will most likely follow, engage or even make a purchase!

Instagram ads allow you to target the exact customer persona and then place your promoted posts in front of them. They are then free to engage with your post, either by liking it or even following your page. This will boost your numbers considerably. Best of all, since you're paying for the ad space, these posts are guaranteed to go in front of Instagram users. You don't have to worry about your post not showing up in other feeds, it is guaranteed if you pay for it.

Ultimately, the benefits of using Instagram Ads drastically outweigh the drawbacks. Even if you have a relatively modest advertising budget, you can still bring in a lot more followers using these ads as opposed to just going the free route. Because not only can you gain more post likes, you can also directly promote links to specific websites, as the one link rule only applies to unpaid Instagram profiles. You are free to create an ad for a specific product, run it on Instagram Ads and then link people to that product's landing page.

This means that over time, you will be able to build a direct link between how much you're spending on Instagram ads and how many sales you are getting from them. Eventually, you'll be able to calculate the cost of customer acquisition, which will then give you a key insight into how much it will cost your business in advertising before you are able to make a sale.

Those kinds of tools just can't be found outside of paid advertising. You may be wondering, if paid advertising is so powerful, then why bother with any of the advice found in the rest of this book? Wouldn't it just be more effective to only pay for ads and not bother about creating good content and building relationships? Not at all!

While paid ads are extremely potent for acquiring new customers and helping people become aware of your brand, that is only one half of the equation. The acquisition might lead to a one-time sale, but maintaining a relationship is what helps lead to more and more sales in the long term. A regular social media presence will ensure that those who have converted and are fans of your product and company, will still be able to interact with you and see what you're up to. More importantly, you'll be able to passively advertise to them on a daily basis.

So, there is the purpose of having both a paid advertising focus as well as having an organic marketing focus. The two together will achieve different goals. One will bring in more customers and increase your sales, while the other will help you keep the business of old customers, periodically reminding them of your products. With that in mind, let's go ahead and get into the specifics of how to make the most of using Instagram Ads in 2019.

Ad Campaign Goals

Running an ad on Instagram is easy to do. All you need is to pick a campaign goal, an appropriate picture or post and then find the target audience. The campaign goal is what determines how Instagram is going to be running your ad, how much it will cost per click and more importantly, what the end goal of the ad is going to be. You have a few options to select from, let's go over them quickly.

Brand Awareness

This option is primarily geared towards Instagram profiles that are trying to get more people aware of their business. If you're going to promote a post, for the purpose of simply making people aware that your product exists, without having an explicit call for action or the next step for the customer to take, this would be the right one to use. Why use the Brand Awareness option? Because you can get significantly higher levels of reach with it. While it's not explicitly calling for customers to take action, it helps increase brand recall. Brand recall is important when advertising later down the road, mainly because a customer who recalls your brand from previous ads has a higher chance of engaging. Think of a brand awareness campaign like planting seeds that you will reap later. Get the idea in their mind at first, warm the customer up and then, later on, reap the rewards with a direct ad campaign.

Reach

Reach is similar to brand awareness, but with one big difference. The reach goal is simply focused on maximizing the number of people who see your ad. Brand Awareness tends to focus on finding people who are the most relevant before showing them the ad. Reach instead looks to just get your ad out in front of as many people as possible, sacrificing some of that specificity. However, if the products you are selling aren't targeted and the general population would benefit from it, Reach is a great way to help potential customers become aware of its existence.

Traffic

Traffic is a consideration goal, meaning that you're actually aiming for more than just generating brand awareness. The traffic option means that you are looking to put your Instagram ads in front of people who are going to have the highest probability of clicking on the ad and visiting your website. This, of course, can lead to higher levels of sales if you're directing them to a specific sales page. However, you can also use this traffic goal to direct potential consumers to things like your website's blog or event page as well.

Engagement

If you're looking for page likes, comments and follows, then you're going to want to use the Engagement option. The Engagement goal essentially searches for and targets individuals who are most likely to respond to your content. Usually, this response is either liking or commenting on your post. You can use the engagement goal when you're looking to increase the amount of feedback on a single type of post of yours.

App Installs

If your business sells an app or has a custom app built for helping customers place orders, you can pitch the app directly to Instagram users with this option. Best of all, when the customer selects this option, they will be transferred to their phone's app store with the option to quickly download your app. This can be a great way of getting more downloads without making your users go through a bunch of hoops in order to find your app.

Video Views

If you have a video on your Instagram, you may want to consider using video views to promote them, especially if the video is a product announcement.

Instagram Story Ads

When users are browsing through Instagram stories, swiping through the various people that they follow, sometimes there are ads in between these stories. These Story ads are often short, quick and punchy. Most importantly, Instagram Story ads are unavoidable. While the other types of ads that you can run on Instagram can just be scrolled past quickly, an Instagram story user has no other option than to wait for the ad to run its course before they can move on to the next story.

This means that when you run an Instagram Story Ad, you have a captive audience for a short time. You can use Story Ads to directly sell to your target demographic, essentially running a mini-commercial for them to enjoy. However, just because you have their attention for a short amount of time doesn't necessarily mean that they will be interested in the products you are presenting. You'll need to work to put together a decent ad, one that will capture their attention past the initial few seconds of realizing they are looking at an advertisement.

Creating a Story Ad is a little different from other Instagram ads, in the sense that these story ads have to be well produced and put together like a min-commercial. You have the option to create either photo ads, video ads or carousel ads that let users scroll through multiple pictures. There are quite a few things involved with putting together a well-made story ad, so let's take some time to review the qualities of what makes for a good story ad.

Attention-Grabbing

In general, people don't like ads. Advertisements are just about everywhere, and they tend to be exceptionally invasive in our lives. When we see another ad for the one billionth time that week, we tend to be a little irritated. This puts the advertiser in a negative position automatically, as people are never relieved nor happy to see an ad pop up on their screen. Sure, they might not have any other option than to just let the ad play out, but that doesn't mean they have to pay attention.

You have a very, very short window of opportunity when you display your ad in front of the consumer. You must focus on trying to grab their attention as quickly as possible, through a combination of eye-catching visuals, a clear message and a hook that is interesting.

The hook doesn't need to be anything flashy or crazy, it just needs to spark enough interest to the point that the consumer is willing and ready to continue watching your ad. If you look at most of the successful short advertisements out there, you'll notice that they all have the same effect on people: they draw them in.

A hook doesn't necessarily need to be funny either. Some hooks focus on being mysterious, visually appealing or strange to look at. Some hooks use music or a catchy lyric to draw consumers in. You don't have to create a hook that is against the spirit of whatever product you are selling, you just need to be sure that you have something to pull viewers in.

Storytelling

At the core of advertising is storytelling. People respond to the stories that are being told to them through ads. A good ad incorporates a story of some sort. The story doesn't need to be overly complex, nor does it need to be spelled out, but it does need to be present. Simply saying "buy my product," isn't engaging or interesting. It doesn't hold interest and it certainly doesn't get people to remember your product for later on.

Fun Visuals

Ads don't always need to be garish, but they do need to pop out. Good visuals, a proper blend of colors and enjoyable typesetting will contribute greatly to getting people to pay attention to your ad. Try to stick with colors that pop out at viewers, while also avoiding the drab, boring colors. Of course, you do want to stay within the perimeters of whatever product you are selling, if you're selling business products to professional companies, you might want to stick to more neutral, inoffensive colors as opposed to if you were selling to a surfer crowd.

A Call to Action

It's all well and good to tell people about your product, but if you don't have a call to action that moves them forward, you are essentially wasting your ad money. You need to have a clear call to action that conveys both urgency and opportunity.

Consider using phrases that urge the user to commit action, such as "buy now," "on sale for a limited time," or "only while supplies last." These phrases can help a user make a faster decision, especially if they see the value of what they are gaining. Feel free to include discounts or special deals that would get them to make the proper decision, this will only strengthen your call to action and move them through the sales process faster.

Music

Music works well with advertising for two reasons. The first is that music creates and conveys specific moods, feelings or emotions. We, as humans, resound with certain types of music and can be greatly affected by it. Look at any serious, somber or beautiful ad, chances are, if you remove the music it's not nearly as serious or somber. Music allows you to set the tone that you want your customers to experience when they see your ad.

The second reason music works well with advertising is the fact that music creates an association. People often remember little songs or sounds from what they've heard in the day and sometimes it can get stuck in their head. If they're humming a tune from your ads, chances are they might remember your ad too.

Most Instagram users actually browse Instagram Stories with their sound on, which leads to a perfect opportunity for you to include music in your ad. In order to play music, however, you will need the commercial rights to that song. The best way to go about finding music to play on your ads is to look for royalty-free music that doesn't charge per use. You only pay a single time, flat fee to use the music and then you don't have to worry about paying royalties to the artist.

Fortunately, the process of finding royalty-free music has become greatly streamlined. There are plenty of websites out there that sell licenses to use those songs commercially. You just need to make sure that you check the copyright information, to determine whether you are able to use the song multiple times, whether you're required to credit the artist, etc. However, the process of acquiring royalty-free music has become much more streamlined in recent years and you should have little trouble finding music that goes along with the feeling you're trying to convey with your ad.

Putting it All Together

Combining music, visual appeal, good story, and tightly written copy will help to make an excellent story ad. Take your time when creating your ad, don't rush through the process. Customers won't be able to find your ad again, once it's out of their vision, it's gone for good. So, you have to make the right impression on them, or else you risk being forgotten. Take your time, develop a killer looking ad and then watch how well it performs!

Creating Shoppable Posts

If your company primarily focuses on selling physical goods, then you might have an option to create what's known as Shoppable Posts. Shoppable posts are like regular posts, except they display products and also show a price point, allowing for customers to quickly buy your products, using Instagram as the jumping-off point.

However, you can't just start creating shoppable posts, due to Instagram's policies. You'll need first to become an approved vendor, which means meeting the requirements that Instagram has for all of its vendors. These requirements, as taken directly from Instagram's support page, are below:

To use shopping on Instagram, your Instagram account and business must fulfill the following requirements:

- **Comply with our merchant agreement and commerce policies**

  Your business complies with our merchant agreement and commerce policies

- **Have an Instagram business account.**

  Your Instagram account must be converted into a business account.

- **Have a connected Facebook Page**

  Your Instagram business profile must be connected to a Facebook Page. Facebook Pages with the Message to Buy payment option will need to delete and create a new Shop with another payment option before they can use shopping on Instagram. Please note that country or age restrictions on your Facebook Page will not carry over to your Instagram account.

- **Primarily sell physical goods.**

  Your Instagram account must be a business that primarily sells physical goods. We are continuing to test this feature and hope to expand availability to more accounts in the near future.

- **Have your business account connected to a Facebook Catalog.**

  Your business account must be connected to a Facebook catalog. This can be created and managed on Catalog Manager or Business Manager on Facebook or through Shopify or BigCommerce platforms.

These are fairly easy to meet requirements and won't take much of your time. After you've taken these necessary steps to get your account qualified for shoppable posts, you'll need to go to the Business section of the Instagram Settings page on your app and then select the Shopping on Instagram button. This will take you through the steps to confirm an application for the ability to make shoppable posts. Once you've finished, you'll receive a notification from Instagram if you were approved.

Shoppable posts are highly useful when you want to create interesting, fun pictures that feature your products. Since you have the ability to highlight and tag specific images with a name and a price tag, you don't have to create a photo that only focuses on the product.

Finding Your Audience

As we've talked about extensively in this book, a keen awareness, and understanding of your customer persona is necessary if you want to be successful in using Instagram for marketing. The data you've collected and put together pays off when it comes to creating ads on Instagram, as you'll be able to create what are known as Audiences.

In advertising terms, Audiences are how Instagram is able to properly target the right demographic to place the ads. An Audience is composed of several different data points that you input when you create your very first Instagram ad. Generally, you'll be giving Instagram all of the information that you've collected, targeting an age group, country, gender makeup and then the interests and behaviors that you are looking to target.

Instagram makes it fairly easy to put together your first audience. As you input the data, you'll see the overall size of the group you are targeting on the righthand side of the page. You'll also be given an estimate as to whether your perimeters are broad or narrow. In general, you want to create audiences that are large enough to where you won't run out of people to advertise to, but not too wide, or else you may end up paying more for ads in the long run. You want to find an audience size that is closer to the middle, where you have room to grow, but the ad space isn't in so much demand that the cost of the ads increases.

Once you've created your first audience and run your first ad, you'll be able to look at the analytics that Instagram provides as to who engaged with your ad, who clicked on it and the general makeup of those who interacted with your ads. We will cover this in a later section, where we will discuss analytics.

You can create multiple audiences. This will help you greatly when it comes to running specific ads that will only appeal to one type of customer persona. For example, if your product appeals to customer persona A, who likes what you sell because it saves them valuable time, but it also appeals to customer persona B, who likes your product because of the price point, you should create two separate audiences, one for each customer persona.

This differentiation will allow you to run two completely different ads, targeting each Persona. You are then free to create one ad, extolling the virtues of how much time is being saved through the use of your product, and then another ad talking about how much of a bargain your product is. You can run the ads simultaneously, targeting two different groups at the same time. This will significantly increase your results than if you were to run just one ad for both groups.

Why is that? Because customer personas might not overlap as much as you would hope. While it would be great to have developed on "uber-persona" that encompasses all of your customers, but you won't be able to market to all of them at once and make it appealing. The more people that you try to please at the same time, the more disappointed they will become.

It's far better to use specificity as a means of capturing the right audience member. It will cost you no more to target only one specific audience at a time, but it will yield better results. The more appealing you can create ads to target one persona at a time, the better off you will be.

Audiences from Lists

If you have an email list that is already functioning, then you're going to want to import those emails into Facebook through the audience section. Those emails are then compiled, and Facebook begins to create a list of people who are similar to the habits and actions of those emails that you have collected. This gives you a big advantage when it comes to finding new customers, as a fully developed customer profile will help Facebook find the perfect people to put your ads in front of.

If you are unfamiliar with an email list, a list is simply a collection of emails that you gather from those who are in your target demographic. Generally, you gain emails from offering special deals or giving away free products. You can then use these emails to send direct advertisements to your customer base, helping move them along closer to converting.

Another term for collecting emails is known as "lead generation." A lead is a person who is relevant to your sales goals, but also interested enough to give you their personal data. A lead can be worth quite a bit of money because once you have them hooked, you'll be able to continuously market to them at a significantly reduced cost.

There are many ways to build an email list, so we won't go into all of them, but Instagram does offer an option to create a sign-up through their ads. This option is known as Lead Generation in the advertising goals section. Here, you can offer something of value to the Instagram user in exchange for their email.

Ad Pricing

The cost of ads is determined by how many other companies are trying to place ads in the same target market. Each company "bids" against each other, increasing the price of the ad space until the pricing evens out and a final price is determined by whoever has the biggest budget. So, if you're attempting to enter into a demographic that sees a lot of advertisers attempting to buy ads, the price of ads will be higher than if you were to find a niche that had a smaller number of advertisers.

In general, most of the types of ads that you'll run on Instagram will have what's known as cost per click. CPC simply means that you are only charged when an individual clicks on your ad. So, for example, you could run an ad to 1,000 people, but only 100 would actually click on that ad. With CPC, you'll only be charged for the 100 who actually engaged with your ad. This is helpful because it means that you're essentially only paying for the results you're looking for. While you might not be able to guarantee purchase orders or gaining new followers with CPC, you are still only paying for the people who exhibit interest.

Instagram ads run off of a specific budget that you plugin. Say you give them a maximum budget of $20. This means that Instagram will run your ad until it receives $20 worth of clicks. Depending on how crowded the ad market is in that sector, the clicks could be cheap, or they could be expensive. Instagram usually gives projections as to how much engagement or reach you'll receive based on the budget that you give them.

There will be room for experimentation when you're just getting started with running paid ads. There are things you can do to reduce costs, such a tweaking your target audience or finding a new target audience entirely. You'll have to spend time learning what your cost of customer acquisition is, and once that has been finalized, you can work to lower that cost.

Try, Try Again

One of the key principles behind marketing on Instagram is that you will see the best results the more times you run ads. Many small businesses make the mistake of running ads once, seeing no results and then chalking the whole thing up to be a waste of time. The truth is, Instagram advertising allows you to collect valuable metrics and data, giving you the ability to improve the effectiveness of your ads each time you run them.

In other words, it's not a sprint, it's a marathon. You will need to be disciplined to examine what went wrong after you see that an ad returned with very little results. You'll need to be willing to look at the analytics and data to see where you could improve. The more you work with ads, the better you'll get. It's a skillset, just like any other part of being a business owner. You just have to put in the effort and not give up just because there were no initial results. If you stick with it, you will get results through Instagram paid advertising.

Metrics and Analytics

One of the most powerful tools that we have in the advertising arsenal is data collection. When you run ads or even regular posts, Instagram is busy taking note of the behaviors, activities, and makeup of the people interacting with your posts. They aggregate this data and put it together for you to be able to study. Metrics and analytics are some of the most important components of running a proper Instagram advertising campaign because it will allow you to understand the actions that your customers are taking.

Without data, all of your efforts will essentially just be guesses. You need to have a clear understanding of how your ads, your posts and your Stories are performing each month, or else you won't be able to put together an effective strategy for the future. This requires that you spend time looking at the various data points provided by Instagram Insights.

Instagram Insights is your first tool when it comes to data collection. With Insights, you'll be able to see the overall behavior of individuals when it comes to interacting with your Instagram Profile. You'll be able to see how many people have visited your profile, see how many people are clicking on your website as well as what your audience is composed of.

These data points are important because they can help you understand the effectiveness of your actions. For example, let's say that you have a high level of engagement, perhaps your posts are getting an average of 100 likes a day. But your website visits through Instagram are nonexistent. No one is visiting your site. Clearly, this is an indicator that something is wrong. It will be on you to determine what is going wrong in this scenario and work to fix it, but without the data collection, you would have no way of knowing whether any of your efforts are working at all.

Basic Metric Types

There are four basic types of metrics to evaluate when looking at Instagram analytics.

- **Reach**: Reach represents how many unique people saw your content. For example, if you had a reach of 100, it means that 100 different users all saw your content throughout the post or ad's run.

- **Impressions**: While reach represents unique views, Impressions simply mean views. So, if you had 1,000 impressions in a single day, it means that 500 people could have seen the content twice, or perhaps one person saw it 1,000 times. Impressions are just a general way to gauge how many times your ad or post has been seen. You can combine reach and impressions together to get an idea of not only how popular your content is, but also how many people are coming back to see it again. For example, if you have a reach of 200, but impressions of 500, it means that 200 people viewed your content multiple times. This is a good indicator that your content is resonating with your current viewership. Pay attention to numbers like this, it will help you plan more content for the future

- **Clicks:** This is fairly self-explanatory. With clicks, you are able to tell how many people are clicking on your post links. Generally, you'll only see clicks when looking at the Instagram Ads analytics page, as normal Instagram posts do not allow for linking outside of Instagram

- **Engagement:** Anytime a follower takes a specific action such as liking a page, commenting or replying to a comment, that counts as engagement. Overall, you'll be able to see the engagement rate of your followers and calculate how much they are engaging compared to the number of people viewing your content. Generally, you want to see your engagement rate as high as possible. If you realize that your impressions and reach are quite high, but engagement is suffering, it is very possible that there is something wrong.

There are plenty of other metrics that Instagram has to offer when it comes to advertising. Most of these metrics are extremely specific and can help you determine just how much you have paid for ads, the price per click, what the cost of customer acquisition is and more. However, these data points are only available for those who are actively using Instagram ads. Fortunately, there are other ways for normal Instagram Businesses to gain deeper metrics.

Third Party Metrics

While it is true that Instagram offers quite a bit of metrics and analytical data, they don't always get the entire picture. If you're looking to find a more comprehensive way to analyze data, complete with easy to read reports, assessments and highly accurate pictures of your followers' growth and behavior, then you may want to consider working with a third party metric service. Oftentimes, these third parties allow you to gain access to even deeper, more specific analytics and provide suggestions as to how you can grow even more. The only downside to these services is that they often charge a monthly fee for their services. However, if you are growing considerably, you might want to use a third party that will help keep a bird's eye view on all of the data points you'll need to sift through on a weekly basis.

Instagram Conversion Metrics

After you've run ads on Instagram, you'll want to see how those ads are performing, not just in getting people to click on your ad, but also when it comes to making purchases on your site. The first step in this process is creating what is known as the Facebook Pixel.

The Facebook Pixel is a cookie, or tracker service, that attaches to people who end up on your website after clicking on one of your ads or links. This pixel can be customized to monitor specific actions or behavior on your website, triggering when that action is complete. Then, the information collected by the pixel is reported back to Facebook, and you'll be able to monitor the behavior in their analytics section.

This will allow you to track specific actions performed by your customers. For example, you can set it up so that if someone clicks to purchase a product you are directly selling online, Facebook will track that behavior. This will allow you to learn the actual conversion rate of your Facebook ads. Remember, just because a customer is willing to click on your website link doesn't necessarily mean they will make a purchase. You might be able to guess how effective your ads based on the number of purchases made in correction to the ads you are running, but Facebook pixels allow you to take the guesswork out of the equation entirely. You will be able to clearly understand not only how effective your ads are in getting a conversion, but you'll also be able to see what pages the average customer visits, how long they stay on the site, etc. All of this data will allow you to determine a more accurate cost of customer acquisition.

Creating a Facebook pixel isn't hard to do. You just need to navigate over to the Pixel section of the Facebook Business Manager area and follow the instructions they provide. After you finish that, you'll just need to follow the steps necessary to create all the events that you want. In general, you will want to make sure that the Pixel triggers every time a customer takes action on your website, such as purchasing a product, emptying their cart or even just clicking on another page. This will help you significantly in the long run.

Retargeting Campaigns

The biggest benefit that the Facebook pixel provides us the ability to do what is known as retargeting. When an individual visits your website, thanks to clicking a link on Instagram, they might be very interested in what you have to sell. They could potentially even be close to converting, but for some reason, they put it off. Perhaps they didn't have enough money to make the purchase immediately, or maybe they just got distracted by something else. The internet is a wide place and there are no shortages of things that are vying for your attention online. It's easy to lose interest in what's in front of you.

Not all interested customers will convert immediately. In fact, it's rarer to get an instant conversion than it is to slowly warm a lead up into making the purchase decision. But just because the client didn't make the purchase doesn't mean they never will. Rather, it means that for some reason they just chose to delay. If you're tracking the behavior of these customers with the help of the Facebook pixel, however, you will be able to run a retargeting campaign, reminding them of the existence of your product.

Retargeting simply means that you are running another ad set in front of a specific group of people, the ones who have clicked on your ad but didn't convert. Retargeting is a highly effective method of advertising, as these potential customers have already displayed that they are initially interested in your product. All you need to do is run another ad set, perhaps even offering some kind of discount or motivator, retargeting a custom audience.

Building a customer audience using retargeting data is fairly easy to do, all you need is to visit the audience section of Facebook Business Manager and use the data provided by your Pixel. This will create a specific audience, composed entirely out of the people who have visited your website before thanks to your advertising efforts. Of course, you will need to have a large enough group size in order for this to work. If the group size is too small, Instagram won't be able to run the ads, so you'll most likely need to collect data over a larger period of time, or run bigger campaigns before you can retarget.

However, once you have enough audience size to run a retargeting campaign, you will see much higher conversion rates than before. Why? Because those who decide to engage with the ad a second time are most likely going to convert, or else they wouldn't have bothered to click on the ad. This can lead to a higher conversion rate as well as cheaper advertising costs. Best of all, it will help you get a better picture of how much effort total it takes to convince a customer to make a purchase.

Summary

Organic advertising is free but it still has a price attached to it: your time. It's much better for you to spend money and get guaranteed results than it is for you to spend hours upon hours of your life trying to get free publicity. Opportunity cost is a real thing and your time also has a cash value, so make sure that you spend it wisely.

Instagram Ads allow you to have unparallel reach through Instagram. You can gain significantly more followers, product sales and even more email sign-ups if you are willing to pay Instagram to advertise. Instagram Story Ads are also extremely effective, allowing you to capture the undivided attention of an Instagram user for a few seconds, without giving them the option to simply scroll past your work.

Experimentation is a major part of running ads on Instagram, especially when you're new. It is possible that the first few attempts to make money through Instagram will fail, but that's perfectly normal. It takes time to learn how to master the system and how to hone your advertising efforts so that you make the most amount of money possible.

The data collected thanks to Instagram's advertising system allows you to calculate your cost of customer acquisition, as well as learn which customer persona is responding the most to your ads. With the help of metrics, not only will you be able to improve your ads, but you will also be able to decrease the amount of money you are spending on ads by learning to retarget customers who are already warmed up to you. By investing your money in a retargeting ad campaign, you will be significantly increasing the chances of getting more sales.

Chapter 7: Instagram in 2019

Technology changes rather quickly. Thanks to the various innovations and changes that happen in the online space, we can never be certain about what is around the corner, especially when it comes to online marketing. The fact is, if you're going to be using social media marketing sites like Instagram, you're going to need to pay attention to trends, statistics and how things are shaping up in the future. Nothing is guaranteed to remain the same, especially since people's tastes can be fickle. What is true today may end up false tomorrow. With that in mind, let's take a look at the trends and snapshots of Instagram user behavior in 2019, as provided by The Preview App.

Photos vs. Videos

According to the statistics, 84 percent of Instagram users are primarily focused on looking at photos as opposed to the mere 15 percent who like to watch videos more. This, of course, should come as no surprise, as Instagram's major claim to fame is based entirely around sharing photos that people like. While it is true that Instagram provides the option to host videos, the fact is those videos aren't getting as much attention as the photos. Why is this? Most likely because there are already better competitors in the video market out there, YouTube.

This isn't to say that you shouldn't make videos, however. If you have a sufficient reason to do so, feel free to create a video, but just don't rely on making too many of them, as that is not the primary reason people are interested in using Instagram right now.

Instagram Story Performance

Instagram stories are growing significantly in the last year. One trend is that more and more people are using Instagram stories for themselves, in fact over 86 percent of Instagram users like to post their own stories. This indicates a strong trend of story content out there, but the question is, how many people are looking at these stories?

Truthfully, according to these statistics, most users still prefer to look at posts than to look at stories. 63 percent of users look at posts more than stories, whereas only 36 percent engage with stories more. This, just like the videos, shouldn't be terribly shocking news. Instagram Stories are still growing, but in general, people still prefer to engage primarily with photos.

What does this mean for your business? It means that if you have only one area to focus on, then photos are your best bet. Instagram stories are helpful means of boosting your popularity with your current fanbase and Instagram story ads can be helpful, but you shouldn't divide your time equally between the two. Over time, it is possible that Instagram stories will become more popular, but for now, photos are still the undisputed king of the medium. Therefore, it of the utmost importance that a significant amount of time is spent creating good photos and visual content to distribute. Stories shouldn't be neglected, of course, but they are just to be treated as supplements to the main event.

Hashtags

While Hashtags might not seem as relevant today as when they were first introduced, the fact is, on Instagram hashtags are still going very strong. Over 59 percent of Instagram users follow specific hashtags, meaning that they will be the first to see when new posts with those tags are released. On top of that, 83.6 percent of Instagram users still use hashtags when making their posts. When it comes to how many hashtags people prefer to use in their posts, there was a split in the results. 39 percent uses less than 15 hashtags, whereas 40 percent prefer to use 15-30 hashtags. The remaining 19 percent use a total of all 30 hashtags in their posts.

These numbers indicate that, for the most part, hashtags are still primarily used on Instagram with no signs of slowing down. When it comes to the question of how many hashtags to use in a post, it's a mix between 15 to 30. This points to the trend that people aren't really concerned with how many hashtags they are using, just that they are still using them in full force.

Consumer Decisions

When it comes to planning or preparing a purchasing decision, whether it's buying a product, visiting a location for a holiday or even visiting a restaurant, 62 percent of Instagram users say they use Instagram to make those decisions. They use Instagram for finding new places to visit locally, to decide whether they want to buy some new items or if they want to visit a specific store. This is a healthy trend that indicates that the majority of Instagram users look to the platform in the hopes of finding something that will interest them.

However, while it is true that Instagram users are looking to plan their consumer decisions via Instagram, shopping on Instagram is an entirely different story. The majority of Instagram users, 65 percent, have never made a single purchase directly through Instagram. However, this may simply be because Instagram is fairly newer to the scene when it comes to creating things like shoppable posts. As Instagram continues to grow and develop their support for direct sales, we may see these numbers increase considerably.

IGTV

If you're not familiar, Instagram TV, or IGTV, is Facebook's attempt to compete with YouTube. They released the video uploading and streaming service in 2018, as an entirely separate app from Instagram. Their hopes, it would seem, would be to provide a platform for Instagram users who want to expand more into video production. While IGTV is attached to a different app, the program is still being pushed through Instagram, as videos from IGTV can be viewed on Instagram.

The fact that Instagram Videos from IGTV will now be appearing in the feeds of users will undoubtedly increase the number of people who decide to use IGTV, but according to the study, only 17 percent of the IG community is actively using IGTV. The rest are most likely watching the streaming giant that is YouTube, a platform that is showing zero signs of slowing down in size and scope.

So, is IGTV worth it? It's hard to say. Instagram TV is brand new to the market but has been developed by the people who have made both Facebook and Instagram very successful. There is simply no way of knowing right now whether it will be able to compete effectively with YouTube or to offer a replacement app for the people who want to watch videos through Facebook. But for a small business, it's important to know that IGTV has potential.

IGTV allows you to upload full-length videos, upwards to an hour-long. On top of that, the fact that IGTV will also push content to feeds on Instagram means that you have a built-in support network that YouTube cannot offer you. So, if for some reason, you have a need to be releasing long-form video content, IGTV might actually be the best platform for you, especially since it synergizes so well with Instagram right now.

Only time will tell whether IGTV will be a success or not, but sometimes there is a tremendous reward in being an early adapter!

Ads

The question on many advertisers' minds is whether or not Instagram ads will continue to be relevant in 2019. Will people still be willing to click on ads, despite the sheer rise in the number of ads they encounter on a daily basis? The answer to that question is a resounding yes! According to the study, 81.6 percent of Instagram users click on ads. A number this large is extremely exciting, as it signals that people are becoming more and more accepting of the value that ads do provide to their lives. With such a large amount of people clicking on ads, it means they are finding new and interesting content or products that are compelling enough to get them to interact. This is a good sign for the future!

Image

Another question that the poll asked Instagram users was whether they cared about how many followers an Instagram Profile had. 72 percent stated that they did, in fact, care about how many people were following an Instagram user. The reason for this is most likely because of social proof. An Instagram user who only has a few followers is seen as small, less trustworthy and perhaps even boring. Consequently, a profile with a large number of followers is seen as having already established themselves. When it comes to these types of things, perception can be a reality. If 72 percent of people are concerned with how many followers a profile has, then it would be in your best interest to work towards building enough followers to make you credible!

Time Spent

One of the most important questions that we need to be answered is how much time the average Instagram user spends on Instagram. The answers to this question vary, based on the interests, hobbies, and needs of each individual and the poll reflect four different answers. 50 percent of users reported using Instagram for 1 to 3 hours per day. That is about the average makeup of the Instagram user, they tend to use Instagram in the evening, or during downtimes such as lunch.

23 percent of users report using Instagram for only an hour a day, 17 percent admitted to using IG for 3 to 5 hours per day. And 8 percent stated that they used Instagram for more than 5 hours per day.

These numbers are more or less to be expected. There will always be a small portion of the population that overly engages with an app, as well as a portion that underutilizes. But for the majority of users, spending 1 to 3 hours seems reasonable enough.

So, what do these numbers mean for a business? Frankly, you don't have to worry too much about people not seeing your content because they weren't using Instagram. Rather, you need to worry about working with the Instagram algorithm to get it on your side.

Instagram Algorithms in 2019

One of the things that all social media marketers are going to have to contend with is the fact that all social media platforms operate through the use of algorithms. These algorithms can be changed at a moment's notice, to better improve the user experience, or to punish unethical practices that are causing problems for the social media platform itself. You must always make a point to stay on top of understanding how the current algorithm sorts content, how it displays said content and what behaviors it rewards and what behaviors it punishes. These are extremely necessary if you want to stay on the cutting edge of Instagram.

Let's take a look at some of the elements of the Instagram Algorithm that are present in 2019. Fortunately, unlike a few other social media engines that prefer to keep their information about how the algorithms private, Instagram has gone on the record with sharing exactly what their algorithms are looking for when sharing your content to relevant audiences.

Relationship

Instagram's algorithm is able to recognize the interaction between two different profiles, enough so that it can recommend content based on their relationship. For example, if a follower is greatly interacting with you, leaving comments and liking pictures, Instagram will take notice of that. The algorithm will then make a point of providing more of your content to that follower since they have an established relationship with you.

What this means for a business is that you can't just have your content pop up in a follower's feed just because they follow you. Rather, you need to have some kind of established relationship in order to have your content more frequently show up in front of them. Fortunately, this is not the only factor involved in how Instagram determines where your content shows up.

Interests

As we've stressed greatly throughout this book, relevancy is extremely important, not just so that your followers will get what they are looking for, but also because Instagram wants to put the most relevant content in front of those followers. With the power of photo recognition abilities and machine learning, Instagram is able to look at the actions and behaviors of a user and then predict what kind of content they would like. Then, the algorithm works to make sure that more of the relevant content will arrive on their Instagram feed. If your content is deemed relevant by this algorithm, you have a better chance of your posts showing up in your follower's feeds. If it is not deemed relevant, you will most likely end up passed over in favor of other content.

Frequency Updates

Each time an Instagram user logs in to the app, they will be greeted with content that is the most popular on their feed. However, if an Instagram user likes to log in multiple times per day, there will be a better chance of other, less popular posts showing up in their feed, as Instagram is also focusing greatly on providing new and interesting content to show their user. Therefore, if you target primarily active users who like to use Instagram multiple times per day, you will have a better chance of your content being seen, even if it isn't the first thing shown in their feeds.

Tools to Use in 2019

Instagram itself is a tremendous platform that gives you a wide range of options and tools at your disposal. However, this doesn't mean that Instagram's tools are the end-all, be-all of the markets. There are a wide variety of specialist programs out there that will help you supercharge your Instagram career, boosting your ability to get results as well as helping you generate more followers and better posts.

Let's take a look at a few different tools that remain popular to use in 2019 for businesses using Instagram.

Buffer

Buffer is a social media management app that does it all. It allows you to create posts through Buffer, tracks engagement as well as letting you run multiple social media accounts all from the same platform. The ability to schedule posts ahead of time is extremely valuable, as you can spend a shorter amount of time planning out your posting schedule. Rather than have to manually post multiple times a day and per week, you set one time aside to sit down and plan out all the posts that you want to make. You can put all of your content together in one session and then, schedule what days and times you want those posts to be published. Buffer will do the rest.

The only drawback to using a social media scheduler like Buffer is that it's not free. You will need to pay a monthly fee in order to use their services, but then again, time saved is money saved. Rather than struggling to come up with posts day after day, it's much easier just to sit down once a week and plan it all.

Hashtagify.me

Hashtagify allows you to do proper research on your hashtags. It will not only allow you to find relevant hashtags but will also recommend hashtags based on what you've been searching. This is an invaluable tool for research and planning. On top of that, there is a paid option that allows you to access their library as well as labs, providing you with even more tools to find the best possible hashtags.

Shorby

If you want to have more than one link on your Instagram page, you don't have any options within Instagram itself. However, by using Shorby's services, you can bypass that by adding more links to your Instagram page, taking users to any link you so choose. The downside here, of course, is that Shorby does cost a monthly subscription, but if you are looking to add more links to your Profile page, then this is one of the few ways to do so.

SocialRank

Analytics are extremely important and with SocialRank, you can get some of the deepest insights into not only your audience size and makeup but also about the audience members themselves. SocialRank works to help you identify your followers, learn more about them and even sort them into categories. This can be highly effective when it comes to learning new customer personas, as you'll be able to look at all of your followers and determine which persona they fall under. You may even end up learning about new personas entirely.

Boomerang

There is a type of Instagram video that seems to be in a constant loop, seamlessly moving back and forth from one action to the other. These are a special type of videos known as boomerangs. You can create these by downloading the boomerang app. It allows you to take ten photos in a burst, then creating a sort of stop-motion effect, allowing you to create a video that moves back and forth, like a boomerang. Boomerang is free to download and easy to use, and the videos can be fun and interesting, especially when you use them for product displays.

What Not To Do On Instagram in 2019

Tastes change, as we've already established. Some practices that worked well in the old days aren't nearly as effective as they are today. And, sometimes there are myths, bad ideas, and tips that are circulated by those unaware of the fact that Instagram is constantly changing. Here are a few things to avoid doing in 2019:

Ignoring Influencers

Instagram Influencer has become one of the most powerful types of marketer in recent years. With the rise of Instagram models and Instagram profiles with hundreds of thousands of followers, advertisers have taken notice of the fact that they can pay Influencers to promote their products organically.

Instagram Influencer marketing has become quite the industry, with many advertising companies finding ways to create links between influencers and businesses who are looking to expand their market through new and unique advertising methods. Some influencers are taking home enough money to live full time, others are even doing so well that they can go on expensive trips and see the world, all the while sharing their lifestyle with their following.

As an Instagram user, there are two different responses to these influencers that can be bad for your bottom line. The first response is to look at these Influencers, who are certainly doing well for themselves and come to the conclusion that it would be great if they could help you out somehow. Many times, a smaller profile will attempt to curry the favor of an Influencer, in the hopes of gaining more publicity and attention. This almost always fails, simply because the smaller profile has very little to offer to the Influencer. After all, if an Influencer has 300,000 followers, gets to post Instagram pics all day and gets paid from product sponsorships, why should they have to worry about someone with only 50 followers?

The second response is to look at how great these Influencers are doing and come to the conclusion that they would never be interested in a collaboration of any kind. Or worse, they come to the conclusion that Influencer marketing is all hype and isn't worth caring about.

Neither of these responses is the best approach when thinking about Influencers. If you're willing to make the right efforts, working with an influencer will pay off in spades. As we've talked about before, social proof is one of the most important things in the online economy. When an Influencer, who has a host of fans who adore and care about their opinion, recommends a product, it is almost on the same level as if a close friend had recommended that product. It is significantly more effective than celebrity endorsements and has incredibly high conversion rates, much higher than traditional Instagram ads.

The real difficulty in working an Influencer is figuring out the best method of approach. The first response we talked about, attempting to ride on their coat tails in the hopes of getting some recognition from them, isn't the way to go. Why? Because just like when marketing to consumers, it's a question of value. In order for an Influencer to want to be working with you, they must first perceive that it is advantageous for *them*. If they're doing you a favor by working with you, it's not a business relationship at all, it's a charity.

So how can you go about demonstrating that a business relationship with your Instagram will be advantageous? The easiest way to go about it would be to simply sponsor them. Provide them with free products, share sneak previews, even invite them to check out your business and see what goes on behind the scenes. Establish a relationship with them that provides them with enough value to motivate them to reciprocate.

Working with an Influencer takes time to figure out. You'll need to find an influencer who is popular and active within your customer persona's community. You'll need to determine what your budget is with them and then you will need to do the legwork to reach out to them. Chances are, if they are extremely popular, they might have very generous offers already, so be prepared for negotiations. But, if you are able to sponsor an influencer, or at the very least, get them to review or promote your products, not only will you be advertising to an extremely relevant target market, you'll also be drawing them towards your own Instagram profile!

However, it is important to note that if you are going to be sponsoring an Influencer, you will need to take the proper steps to make sure people know that the Influencer is being compensated or paid to endorse specific products. This is because the FTC requires that Influencers follow a specific set of guidelines so that consumers are aware of the compensation. This is known as disclosure and is an ethical thing to do. There's nothing wrong with sponsoring or being paid to review a product, but it is immoral to conceal the fact that they were taking money for doing so. The consumer has a right to know whether an endorsement came organically or if a deal was made.

Taking Bad Photos

The sheer fact that Instagram has become so popular has led to an arms race of sorts when it comes to photo quality. Most companies with Instagram accounts are focused not only on creating quality content but taking high-quality pictures as well. This raises the bar for anyone else who wants to be popular on Instagram. As vain as it might sound, people want to see pretty pictures, its why they come to Instagram in the first place.

There is no place for badly shot or poorly lit photographs on Instagram. While there's nothing wrong with the raw, honest types of photos that we get from Instagram Stories, the rest of the posts need to look great. And the best way to achieve this is to get a camera that is of decent quality. You don't have to spend a fortune on a camera, but you should at least try and get one that you can use for dedicated Instagram pictures. The better the photo quality that you use, the more people will enjoy what you are posting.

And besides, when it comes down to it, you're going to need a good camera for the purpose of taking product shots. You don't want to just take pictures of products with phone. While it is true that most phones take fairly decent quality, nothing can replace a good camera. If you're serious about using Instagram as your primary vehicle for marketing, then it's worth the expense.

Forgetting to Reply

We can all be busy, but unfortunately, customers don't have the level of patience that they used to. The fact is, we live in a culture of instant gratification. If a person wants to buy something online, they can get it the next day and, in some cases, the same day! We have the ability to access what we want when we want and that has created an unfortunate side effect of impatience. People who don't get instant gratification might even end up feeling frustrated or ignored.

This environment and expectation can lead to trouble with customers if they feel that you aren't replying fast enough. In general, you'll want to reply to any concerns or queries sent by your customers within a day, two at the most. This is prompt enough to show them that you care and are actively ready to assist them whenever they need it.

However, sometimes you may end up reading a message and then saying, "I'll reply later," only never to do so. This can be frustrating for the consumer, especially if they end up having to wait more than a few days for a reply. Or worse yet, you may have completely forgotten them and never reply to their message in the first place!

This is understandable, but from business, the perspective will only cost you both money and goodwill. The best way to prevent this from happening is to adopt a simple policy. If you read it, reply to it. Even if your reply is that you'll get back to them with more information, this will at least help the customer feel acknowledged. Saying that you'll read it later only delays the response and most of the time, questions can be answered fairly quickly.

Using Bots

There are some unethical, shady practices done within in the Instagram community, either by businesses looking to get ahead, or sold by companies looking to make some money off earnest business owners who don't know any better. We already covered one unethical practice, buying followers, but now let's talk about another one: using bots.

A bot is an automated program that performs specific tasks without any need for input from the creator. Bots are often used online as a means of collecting data, filling out forms and performing other tasks. A bot by itself is morally neutral, as it's just a program meant to do as its told. However, there are people online who have decided to create bots that are able to mimic human interaction on Instagram.

These automated bots are able to sift through content, using a type of machine learning similar to what Instagram's algorithms use, in order to find relevant content. The bots can like posts, leave comments and even follow other users. In other words, an Instagram bot can literally do all of the tasks that a human can do, although with varying results due to the fact it is just an artificial intelligence unit.

However, according to Instagram's terms of services, modifying the API in any way is against the rules. And bots do just that, they modify the way Instagram works, outside of Instagram's control. This creates a potential for all sorts of security risks and other problems. Using an automated bot for Instagram can lead to a permanent ban of your account.

But there are still companies out there who are willing to offer and sell these bots to the general public. They'll customize them to your specifications and then allow you to use them in exchange for a fee. Sometimes they'll even claim that their work is above board and completely within the rules of Instagram. However, it is important always to check Instagram's terms of service to see if this is actually true.

While it is possible for a bot to boost the results your company will see, by doing the majority of the legwork, there is a large chance you'll get caught by Instagram. Their algorithms have gotten better and better and this type of behavior is well on their radar. If they catch someone using a bot, they will shut the account down entirely. This will more or less destroy all of the hard work done on your business. You will always be hanging by a thread, hoping that somehow Instagram doesn't notice your bot's behavior.

In the end, while it isn't as advantageous to play within the confines of the rules provided, it is much safer. You might not gain all of the benefits of using a fully automated helper to

426

run your IG page, but at the same time, you don't have to worry about suddenly losing all of your hard work.

Does this mean that all types of automation are against the rules? No, not at all. There are certain types of automation that are perfectly acceptable to use, but these things will always plug into Instagram through the proper channels, requiring that you grant them permission to connect your Instagram account.

Tuning Out the News

A lot of things are happening in 2019 when it comes to discussions of advertising, data collection and online privacy. As companies like Facebook and Google continue to grow and become monoliths in their respective fields, people are beginning to wonder if the size of these companies is not growing into monopolies. Meanwhile, the outcry over privacy has led many advocacy groups to condemn the practices that Facebook uses for data collection.

2019 is going to be a turning point in how people view data collection in the United States. Congress is going to be getting involved at some point, potentially with anti-trust actions that could curtail the growth of these two companies. If it gets really bad, these two corporations may end up being broken up by the government.

Of course, this isn't meant to alarm you. There are a lot of changes happening and we are exploring brand new, unfamiliar territory due to the nature of the technology being so new. We didn't have social media to this degree 10 years ago. As a result, everything happening is a consequence of a brand new world, where the rules are being made up as we go along. There will naturally be growing pains.

Those who aren't in the loop are the ones who will suffer. Ignoring what is happening in the news, not bothering to stay abreast of current technological disputes and not paying attention can cause you problems in the long run. The internet moves quickly and platforms can change in an instant.

Those, however, who are able to pay attention to the trends and watch how the government handles these cases will be in a good position since they will be able to act proactively. Rather than being in a position where things are suddenly changing for the worse, the savvy marketer will be well aware of what is coming down the pipeline and adjusts to it ahead of time.

In many cases, those who are able to anticipate change and adapt to it quickly are the ones who make it to the top. Those who ignore or don't bother to pay attention to these changes can end up going under entirely.

This talk may seem alarming at first, but rest assured, this is the nature of working in online marketing. What works today might not work tomorrow. There is no guarantee. Even if it weren't the government to cause problems for your preferred social media platform, what would you do if a new platform was released that took 90% of your userbase? If you want to be truly successful in online marketing, you have to be prepared and ready to adapt. Many sudden changes weren't actually as sudden as most people think. They were simply unprepared for what was telegraphed ahead of time.

You may be wondering if perhaps with all these talks about the future of Facebook if it's worth investing the time and energy in learning how to use Instagram. After all, if the government comes at them, all is lost, right? Well, not exactly. First off, things move slowly at a governmental level. It won't be a sudden, swift decision. It will most likely be a few years before any kind of serious action happens at all. Second, the apps themselves aren't in danger. While there will be plenty of policies that do change if the government gets its way, the fact is, people aren't using Instagram for anything other than the fact that they like the app. It has become a way of life for many people. If something were to happen to Facebook, as unlikely as it is, the app itself will probably just be sold and continue to function as is.

As long as you keep an ear to the ground and an eye on Washington, you'll absolutely be able to take full advantage of all that Instagram has to offer. If changes start coming down the pipeline, you'll be in a position to pivot. Don't stay out of the water just because you're worried it might change temperature, because even if it does, there are always different pools to jump in!

Summary

Instagram is showing no signs of slowing down when it comes to both growth and innovation. Hashtags are just as relevant as ever and most people prefer to use upwards to 30 of them per post.

Instagram TV is brand new to the scene and does have some promise, although it is uncertain whether or not it will be a success. Large brands in the past have failed at major endeavors like IGTV and competing with YouTube is no small task. Still, the link between IGTV and Instagram is advantageous for those who are looking to branch into a long-form video.

There are a wide variety of tools out there that allow you to make the most of Instagram. Some of them are free, while others do have monthly subscription costs. There is nothing wrong with using a few tools to help you get a competitive edge, provided that these tools are approved for use by Instagram. While there are other shortcuts through the unethical territory, those shortcuts will only lead to problems for you down the road.

Instagram Influencers are continuing to grow as a major marketing force in 2019. It would be a tremendous mistake to ignore them, but it would also be a mistake to try and get them to help you out as a favor to you. Reaching out to them, establishing a professional business relationship and working to provide as much value to the Influencer as possible will bring plenty of rewards your way. It may end up being expensive, but the costs are well worth it, especially if the Influencer has an active following of your exact customer persona.

Chapter 8: Getting Ahead

In this chapter, we're going to be focusing on the various ways that you can get ahead in your Instagram endeavors. We'll be sharing tips, tricks and popular methods of developing a comprehensive content plan and minimizing the time you spend while maximizing the results.

Keep an Eye on the Competition

When it comes to getting ahead in the world of Instagram, you don't have to reinvent the wheel. There are already plenty of successful businesses out there who are using Instagram to get tremendous results. Fortunately, the nature of social media means that their work is entirely public, you can just go to any business's profile that you wish and see exactly how they are posting. You can watch their content strategy, see how they interact with others and more importantly, learn from them.

You should always be willing to keep an eye on your competition, as well as the larger companies, to determine if there is any way to emulate them. There's nothing wrong with copying a competitor, especially if that competitor is successful in their endeavors. Of course, there is a caveat to this. You should be willing to copy the successful strategies that your competitors are using, but you shouldn't be willing to take their photos and content and use them for your own. And you should also make a point to avoid plagiarizing their ideas for content as well. You want to keep your brand identity interesting and diverse. So, feel free to take their strategies, but make sure that you develop your own content.

Another benefit behind keeping an eye on your competition is that you'll be able to get a pulse for how they are developing as a company. Are they charging more or less for similar products? Are they getting a major buzz when they release a new Instagram story? You can also look at customer comments and reactions to try and gauge how consumers feel about their products. Perhaps you might even be able to glean a weakness, some kind of shortcoming that the customers are dissatisfied with. This can give you ideas of *how* to market your own products, perhaps even addressing the shortcomings of your competitors, without having to mention them.

Developing A Content Calendar

The biggest challenge that most businesses face when they first get started with Instagram is figuring out what kind of content they want to create. Worse yet, it can be troublesome having to sit down each day, thinking of what to post. Over time, it can grow exhausting and even frustrating. Fortunately, there are ways to prevent this type of fatigue and burnout from affecting you.

The easiest way to plan out your content is to use a content calendar. A content calendar is just a template with days and months, helping you sort out your ideas and plan what you want to create and release in the future. By sitting down and planning all of the content that you intend to make at once, you will be freeing up your mind to simply work according to the calendar. The more decisions that you cut out in the future, the easier it is to sit down and focus on the task at hand.

The first step to making a content calendar is to list out the different types of content that you want to release. For example, you could list infographics, behind the scenes and product photos as you want to release during Week 1. After you determine which content you want to release for the first week, you then select which days you will be releasing each type of that content. So, you could determine to release an Infographic on Monday, Behind the Scenes on Wednesday and Friday, and Product photos on Saturday. You list these plans out on those specific days on the calendar.

Then, from there, you just fill in the entire month with the appropriate content that you wish to release. It's good to have a monthly plan for a content calendar, but it's not a great idea to go past a month. Why? Because you'll need to analyze the metrics to see how all of your content has done at the end of the month. You don't want to schedule too far out ahead, or else you may end up having committed to a content strategy that simply isn't working. Taking it a month at a time will help you refine your process and eventually develop razor-sharp content that delivers every time!

Scheduling Out

After you have developed your content calendar, the next, bigger task will be going about creating all of the necessary content to release over the course of the next month. But the good news is that if you're going to use a content scheduler like Buffer, you will be able to do all of the scheduling in one sitting. After the content has been made, all you need to do is dedicate a day to follow your calendar, scheduling each specific post to a day and a time. Then, you're good to go for the month! All you need to worry about at that point is replying to your followers, making comments on others' posts and creating your own Instagram stories, which can't be scheduled in advance.

You will find that this process of planning everything ahead of time and allowing the scheduling program to handle the rest will greatly cut down on the amount of active time you use Instagram. And the best part is, even though you are doing considerably less work, you are still going to be getting all of the results of a regular poster! Even more so, when you consider that sometimes people end up forgetting to post or end up too busy due to business opportunities in the daytime.

The assembly line style of creating a calendar first, then content, then scheduling, will reduce the sheer number of time and effort that you will need to spend. But it does have a downside. Some of the work can be a little tedious, especially when it comes to creating posts ahead of time. However, it is a discipline worth developing, because soon you won't have to be worrying about whether or not you posted today. You get all of the rewards of being a regular poster, but with none of the drawbacks.

Managing Responses

Another reason you should be using a central content planner such as Buffer is that you will also have the ability to respond to direct messages or even comments from the website. This means that if you're dealing with a significant influx of people commenting or asking questions, you won't have to sort through them all using Instagram itself. Rather than sorting through and tapping out individual responses on your phone, you can simply use your computer to sort and then type replies, which is considerably faster than doing it all on your phone.

Create Teams

As a small business, you may not have a lot of employees working for you, but if you do have others involved in the business, you might want to consider creating team profiles. These profiles allow for others to create posts, edit or reply to your Instagram posts, all while using a social media manager. This can help divide the workload. Best of all, you can assign different permissions, depending on what role you want your team members to play. Some might be able to post, while others may only be allowed to reply.

Hire a Virtual Assistant

Creating content can be time-consuming and difficult, especially if you haven't done it before. Rather than simply go it alone, spending all of your time creating content, you may want to consider hiring a virtual assistant. Thanks to the power of online connectivity, more and more people are looking to find work online. Known as virtual assistants, these people can be hired to assist you in your online work, doing a wide variety of tasks in exchange for payment.

There are upsides and downsides to using a virtual assistant. Let's focus on the upsides first. Expertise is the biggest value that you get when it comes to hiring a virtual assistant. Thanks to the dozens of websites out there that let you find and hire the right kind of people, you can be assured that you will be hiring someone who clearly understands what you are looking for. If you want someone to create content, you will have a wide pool of experts who are able to sit down and put together great looking photos for your business.

Another upside to using a virtual assistant is that you are freeing up a major chunk of your time. By outsourcing these tasks, you are able to focus your efforts elsewhere on the business. You can do what you do best, while also getting good results from your assistant. It's a win-win situation.

Since hiring a virtual assistant is a contracting job, you also don't have to worry about paperwork or signing them on as an employee. These are work for hire positions that can be easily terminated if the employee isn't working out. You don't have to worry about being stuck with someone who isn't willing to do the hard work. If they are underperforming, you can just as easily find a new virtual assistant who is willing to do what needs to be done.

There are downsides, of course, to hiring a virtual assistant. There is the price factor. Most of the time, you're going to be paying them an hourly wage, which can stack up, especially if you have a lot of work for them. However, working with a virtual assistant is significantly cheaper than just deciding to go with a Social Media Marketing Agency, who often charges an arm and leg for services you could do yourself.

Another downside is that you'll primarily be working with a freelancer who might not have the same schedule as you. While they will still get the work done, they won't be available to talk immediately, especially if they aren't in the same time zone. This can lead to a message tag, so if you're expecting immediate replies during your normal hours, you may end up disappointed.

One thing you won't have to worry about too much is security risks. You can create team profiles for your virtual assistant, so they only have limited access to your accounts and they won't have administrative rights to do anything permanent. On top of that, most of the agencies or platforms that allow you to hire virtual assistances have ratings. You will be able to see the ratings that a specific virtual assistant has, how much they've worked and how many clients they've worked with. This should help to give you a picture of the employees' general skill set and how well they get along with their clients. Most importantly, you won't have to worry about hiring someone untrustworthy or unethical. If they have strong social proof and a high rating, you're in good hands.

Ultimately, a virtual assistant can supercharge your Instagram efforts, especially if you are limited on time. And, best of all, if they are truly good at what they do, they will ultimately end up generating you more money in the future, as their work will help bring in new followers and product sales.

Summary

Your time is extremely valuable and should be treated as such. Rather than treat Instagram Marketing as if it were a daily chore, it would be far better to plan everything out in advance.

Creating a content calendar will help you have the proper direction for when you create content. It will give you focus and reduce the amount of time you need to think about things other than content creation. This creates an assembly-line effect, where you aren't losing energy going back and forth from one topic to the other. Rather, you are able to stay focused on each part of the content equation until you are finished.

A social media managing program is necessary if you wish to take Instagram Marketing seriously. Scheduling posts well ahead of time frees you up entirely so that you are able to focus on other things during your business day. You won't have to worry about forgetting to post every day and most importantly, you will be free to focus on the things that matter: responding and replying to comments.

You don't have to manage everything by yourself, rather you can opt to create a team with the help of a social media managing program, putting other members of your staff in charge, all the while restricting access to admin rights, so they don't end up causing trouble. If you don't have the staff for such a task, you can also outsource a virtual assistant who will act as a dedicated assistant, well versed in picking up the slack where it is necessary. Whether you're looking for someone to handle customer service, create content or just simply develop the content calendar, a virtual assistant is well worth the money.

Chapter 9: Conclusion

As we come to the end of this book, it is our hope that you have learned a great deal about what makes for a successful Instagram marketer. Let's review a few of the major concepts presented here:

It's All About Them

Ultimately, a customer only cares about what they perceive to be valuable. You can have the best product in the world, but until you take the time to learn what speaks to your customers, you won't be able to market it to them. If you focus overwhelmingly on your customers and followers, learning what they value and providing them with content that lifts them up, you will be very successful in building a following.

Consequently, if you only talk about yourself and your own products, regardless of how great they are, you will end up being ignored. No one wants to have a conversation with a narcissist, both in the real world and online. Keep the sales talk to a minimum. Remember, nobody cares about what you know until they know that you care.

Engaging With Followers is Necessary

You can't just expect to rack up a large number of followers and then watch as the sales come flowing in. You'll need to cultivate real, honest relationships with these followers in order to gain their trust. Once they become familiar with you and trust you, it will be easier to show them the products that will help improve their lives. But without engagement, they won't know that you are honest and earnest with them.

Focus Beyond the Sale

A sale is a single transaction that happens once and then it's over. While sales are necessary for the lifeblood of your company, you're going to need more than just sales if you want to really thrive. You're going to want to turn your followers into advocates who are raving fans. This takes time and intentionality to pull off. You must be able to develop strategies that tell your company story to your followers while also bolstering their loyalty.

Contests, giveaways, and discounts for those who follow you closely are some of the best ways to reward them for their loyalty. Responding to their questions quickly and being honest when they are unhappy with your service will go incredibly far in helping fans turn into superfans.

Paid Advertising Is Important

Organic use of Instagram will aid you in maintaining the relationships and connections that you have made, but without paid advertising, your company will inch along. You can pick up the pace and save a lot of time by using the powerful advertising system that Instagram provides, either through doing traditional scrolling ads or story ads.

You simply cannot neglect to use the paid advertising system when it comes to Instagram. You will make significantly more sales than if you were to solely rely on organic reach. Both are important, of course, but in different respects. You have to spend money to make money, this principle never changes, no matter the business.

Always Be Learning:

When it comes to online platforms and social media, things are in a constant state of flux. We've done as best we can to provide a snapshot of what the current climate is for Instagram in 2019, but like all things online, the picture will soon change. Pay attention to what the trends are, look for what the news is saying about the future of Instagram and never stop learning. The more you learn, the better poised you are to not only adapt to sudden changes but also to thrive in the online marketplace.

Instagram is a powerful tool for marketing, but it's not the only one that exists online. Indeed, we've touched a lot on Facebook's advertising system, mainly because they are closely tied to Instagram due to being owned and operated by the same company. If you're interested in learning more about how you can incorporate Facebook into your overall marketing, check out *Facebook Marketing and Advertising for Small Business Owners in 2019*. Inside, you'll find all the necessary things for creating a proper Facebook page, how to use Facebook Business Manager and how to take full advantage of what Facebook advertising has to offer.

Or, if you're looking to develop a more focused way to convert customers, taking them from a cold state and warming them up enough to make a purchase and more, you should read *Sales Funnel Management For Small Business Owners in 2019*. Both of these books will provide you will all of the principles and ideas necessary to make money online, all the while building up a customer base that is crazy about you!

That's all that we have for you. We sincerely hope that you are able to get the most out of this guide and that you are successful in building the best Instagram profile possible. Good luck!

Dear Small Business Owner,

As

an independent author, and a one-man operation - my marketing budget is next to zero.

As such, the

only

way I can get my books in front of valued customers if with reviews.

Unfortunately,

I'm competing against authors and giant publishing companies with multi-million-dollar marketing teams. These behemoths can afford to give away hundreds of free books to boost their ranking and success. Which as much as I'd love to - I simply can't afford to do.

That's

why your honest review will not only be invaluable to me, but also to other readers.

Best,

Mark Warner

References

Horne, K. (2019). 9 Awesome Social Media Tools That Your Business REALLY Needs in 2019. Retrieved from https://digital.com/blog/social-media-tools/

The Importance of Knowing Your Customer | GROW. (2019). Retrieved from https://www.growbusiness.org/the-importance-of-knowing-your-customer/

Kolowich, L. (2019). 20 Questions to Ask When Creating Buyer Personas [Free Template]. Retrieved from https://blog.hubspot.com/marketing/buyer-persona-questions

Kirby, M. (2019). 5 Major Benefits of Creating Personas for Marketing. Retrieved from https://blog.roket.to/5-major-benefits-of-creating-personas-for-marketing

Marta, M. (2019). How to Measure Your Social Media Campaign. Retrieved from https://brand24.com/blog/measure-social-media-campaign/

Patel, N. (2019). The 5 Easy Steps To Measure Your Social Media Campaigns. Retrieved from https://neilpatel.com/blog/social-media-measurement/

Sukhraj, R. (2019). 10 Social Media KPIs You Should Track and Monitor. Retrieved from https://www.impactbnd.com/blog/social-media-kpis

Sutevski, D., & Foster, S. (2019). 4 Most Important Sales Funnel Metrics You Need to Follow. Retrieved from https://www.entrepreneurshipinabox.com/261/the-most-important-metrics-of-the-sales-funnel/

Tien, S. (2018). How to Create a Social Media Content Calendar: Tips and Templates. Retrieved from https://blog.hootsuite.com/how-to-create-a-social-media-content-calendar/

Bibliography

11 Principles That Need to Power Your Facebook Strategy. (2019). Retrieved from https://www.postplanner.com/blog/principles-to-power-your-Facebook-strategy

8 Strategies for Achieving SMART Goals. (2019). Project Smart. Retrieved 13 March 2019, from https://www.projectsmart.co.uk/8-strategies-for-achieving-smart-goals.php

Stec, C. (2019). How to Create Facebook Ads: A Step-by-Step Guide to Advertising on Facebook. Blog.hubspot.com. Retrieved 13 March 2019, from https://blog.hubspot.com/marketing/Facebook-paid-ad-checklist

Easy to Follow 7 Step Facebook Marketing Strategy That Works. (2018). Digital Marketing Blog. Retrieved 13 March 2019, from https://www.lyfemarketing.com/blog/Facebook-marketing-strategy/

Baker, J. (2018). 11 Best Social Media Scripts and Plugins to Streamline Your Workflow. Code Envato Tuts+. Retrieved 13 March 2019, from https://code.tutsplus.com/articles/best-social-media-scripts-and-plugins-to-streamline-your-workflow--cms-31941

Bullas, J. (2017). 21 Awesome Facebook Facts and Statistics You Must Check Out. Jeffbullas's Blog. Retrieved 13 March

2019, from https://www.jeffbullas.com/21-awesome-Facebook-facts-and-statistics-you-need-to-check-out/

What Do People Look for in Social Media? | Bearly Marketing. (2015). Bearly Marketing. Retrieved 13 March 2019, from https://bearlymarketing.com/what-do-people-look-for-in-social-media/

Trends, S., Daily, 5., & Guta, M. (2018). 52% of Small Businesses Post on Social Media Daily - Small Business Trends. Small Business Trends. Retrieved 13 March 2019, from https://smallbiztrends.com/2018/03/how-small-businesses-use-social-media-in-2018.html

StyleShare. (2019). Facebook Business. Retrieved 13 March 2019, from https://www.facebook.com/business/success/styleshare

Hawooo & Smartly.io. (2019). Facebook Business. Retrieved 13 March 2019, from https://www.facebook.com/business/success/hawoo-smartly-io#

Kakao Games & Wisebirds. (2019). Facebook Business. Retrieved 13 March 2019, from https://www.facebook.com/business/success/kakao-games-wisebirds#

PlayKids. (2019). Facebook Business. Retrieved 13 March 2019, from https://www.facebook.com/business/success/playkids#

15 ways to enhance your Facebook influence . (2011). Socialbrite. Retrieved 13 March 2019, from
452

http://www.socialbrite.org/2011/02/08/15-ways-to-enhance-your-Facebook-influence/

13 Quick Tips to Save Time on Facebook Marketing. (2019). Postplanner.com. Retrieved 13 March 2019, from https://www.postplanner.com/blog/13-tips-to-save-time-on-Facebook-marketing/

Us, A., Robert Cialdini, P., Biography, D., Publications, D., Vitae, C., & Services, F. et al. (2019). The 6 Principles of Persuasion by Dr. Robert Cialdini [Official Site]. INFLUENCE AT WORK. Retrieved 13 March 2019, from https://www.influenceatwork.com/principles-of-persuasion/

Influence — The Psychology of Persuasion — A Book Summary. (2018). Medium. Retrieved 13 March 2019, from https://medium.com/power-books/influence-the-psychology-of-persuasion-a-book-summary-7ae0ebf8950f

→, V. (2012). Summary of Influence: The Psychology of Persuasion by Robert B Cialdini. Ignition Blog. Retrieved 13 March 2019, from https://slooowdown.wordpress.com/2012/09/02/summary-of-influence-the-psychology-of-persuasion-by-robert-b-cialdini/

Book Summary: "Influence: The Psychology of Persuasion" by Robert B. Cialdini. (2014). ashishb.net. Retrieved 13 March 2019, from https://ashishb.net/book-summary/book-summary-influence-the-psychology-of-persuasion-by-robert-b-cialdini/

works, H., Agencies, F., e-Commerce, F., Businesses, F., Advertiser, F., Features, A., & Examples, F. (2016). Using Facebook Ads to Find Your Perfect Customer. AdEspresso. Retrieved 13 March 2019, from https://adespresso.com/blog/using-Facebook-ads-to-find-your-perfect-customer/

The Beginner's Guide to Creating Marketing Personas | Buffer. (2015). Buffer Marketing Library. Retrieved 13 March 2019, from https://buffer.com/library/marketing-personas-beginners-guide

How to Build a Buyer Persona (Includes Free Template). (2018). Hootsuite Social Media Management. Retrieved 13 March 2019, from https://blog.hootsuite.com/buyer-persona/

Kolowich, L. (2019). 20 Questions to Ask When Creating Buyer Personas [Free Template]. Blog.hubspot.com. Retrieved 13 March 2019, from https://blog.hubspot.com/marketing/buyer-persona-questions

7 Killer Tips for More Effective Real Estate Facebook Ads. (2019). Wordstream.com. Retrieved 13 March 2019, from https://www.wordstream.com/blog/ws/2018/02/06/real-estate-facebook-ads

Facebook Ads For Restaurants: 6 Killer Ad Strategies. (2019). 39 Celsius Web Marketing Consulting. Retrieved 13 March 2019, from https://www.39celsius.com/Facebook-ads-for-restaurants-5-killer-ad-strategies/

Adkins, T. (2018). How to Use Facebook Ads for Local Businesses. Social Media Marketing | Social Media Examiner. Retrieved 13 March 2019, from https://www.socialmediaexaminer.com/how-to-use-Facebook-ads-for-local-businesses/

The Importance of Facebook Marketing for Small Business - AMMEX. (2018). AMMEX. Retrieved 13 March 2019, from https://blog.ammex.com/the-importance-of-Facebook-marketing-for-small-business/#.XIh8WegzbIV

Get started with Business Manager: Free guide. (2019). Facebook Business. Retrieved 13 March 2019, from https://www.facebook.com/business/learn/how-business-manager-works/guide

How to Set Up a Fan Page in 5 Easy Steps. (2013). Heyo Blog. Retrieved 13 March 2019, from https://blog.heyo.com/how-to-set-up-a-fan-page-in-5-easy-steps/

22 Facebook Marketing Tips for Small Businesses on a Budget. (2019). Wordstream.com. Retrieved 13 March 2019, from https://www.wordstream.com/blog/ws/2018/07/02/facebook-marketing-for-small-business

Enterprise, F., Agencies, F., Business, F., Management, F., Marketing, F., & Care, F. et al. (2016). Facebook Fan Page vs. Profile: Know the Difference. Sprout Social. Retrieved 13 March 2019, from https://sproutsocial.com/insights/Facebook-fan-page/

How to Create a Facebook Business Page in 8 Simple Steps. (2018). Hootsuite Social Media Management. Retrieved 13 March 2019, from https://blog.hootsuite.com/steps-to-create-a-Facebook-business-page/

How to Create a Facebook Group (and Build an Engaged Community). (2017). Buffer Marketing Library. Retrieved 13 March 2019, from https://buffer.com/library/Facebook-group

Gurner, J. (2018). Top 25 Real Estate Facebook Posts from the Pros & Why They Work. Fit Small Business. Retrieved 13 March 2019, from https://fitsmallbusiness.com/real-estate-facebook-posts/

10 Ways to Use Facebook Groups for Restaurants - Social Chefs. (2016). Social Chefs. Retrieved 13 March 2019, from http://www.socialchefs.com/Facebook-groups-for-restaurants/

(2019). Retrieved from https://www.socialbakers.com/blog/219-top-10-biggest-mistakes-you-make-on-Facebook-pages

10 Common Facebook Marketing Mistakes (and How to Avoid Them) - dummies. (2019). dummies. Retrieved 13 March 2019, from https://www.dummies.com/business/marketing/social-media-marketing/10-common-Facebook-marketing-mistakes-and-how-to-avoid-them/

Haydon, J. (2015). 13 Super Creative Ways to Boost Facebook Page Reach - Without Facebook Ads. John Haydon. Retrieved

13 March 2019, from https://www.johnhaydon.com/13-ways-boost-your-Facebook-reach-without-spending-dime/

Bramble, J. (2018). 13 Facebook Engagement Tactics for Your Business Page. Social Media Marketing | Social Media Examiner. Retrieved 13 March 2019, from https://www.socialmediaexaminer.com/13-Facebook-engagement-tactics-business-page/

Garst, K. (2018). 17 Killer Facebook Post Ideas for Small Business Owners. Kim Garst | Marketing Strategies that WORK. Retrieved 13 March 2019, from https://kimgarst.com/17-killer-Facebook-post-ideas-for-small-business-owners/

22 Facebook Post Ideas for Businesses that Practically GUARANTEE Engagement. (2019). Postplanner.com. Retrieved 13 March 2019, from https://www.postplanner.com/Facebook-post-ideas-for-businesses-that-guarantee-engagement/

Trends, S., "Like", 2., & Pilon, A. (2017). 20 Facebook Post Ideas Your Small Business Fans Will "Like" - Small Business Trends. Small Business Trends. Retrieved 13 March 2019, from https://smallbiztrends.com/2017/04/Facebook-post-ideas.html

22 Facebook Marketing Tips for Small Businesses on a Budget. (2019). Wordstream.com. Retrieved 13 March 2019, from

https://www.wordstream.com/blog/ws/2018/07/02/facebook-marketing-for-small-business

5 Biggest Mistakes You're Making on Your Facebook Business Page. (2015). AP Digital. Retrieved 13 March 2019, from https://www.absoluteperfectionmedia.com/5-biggest-Facebook-business-page-mistakes/

Pelletreau, C. (2018). Create Scroll-Stopping FB Ads. Claire Pelletreau. Retrieved 13 March 2019, from https://clairepells.com/create-scroll-stopping-fb-ads/

works, H., Agencies, F., e-Commerce, F., Businesses, F., Advertiser, F., & Features, A. et al. (2015). 5 Ways To Get Your Posts More Attention In The News Feed. AdEspresso. Retrieved 13 March 2019, from https://adespresso.com/blog/5-ways-get-posts-attention-news-feed/

Kim, L., & Kim, L. (2015). The Science Behind Why People Engage with Facebook Content [INFOGRAPHIC]. Social Media Today. Retrieved 13 March 2019, from https://www.socialmediatoday.com/news/the-science-behind-why-people-engage-with-facebook-content-infographic/454653/

Enterprise, F., Agencies, F., Business, F., Management, F., Marketing, F., & Care, F. et al. (2018). How to Master Facebook Ad Targeting & Zero-In on Your Audience. Sprout Social. Retrieved 13 March 2019, from https://sproutsocial.com/insights/Facebook-ad-targeting/

Tariq, I. (2019). 5 Ways Your Business May Not (But Should) Be Taking Advantage of Facebook Marketing. Entrepreneur.

Retrieved 13 March 2019, from https://www.entrepreneur.com/article/325277

How to Use Facebook Business Manager: A Step-by-Step Guide. (2018). Hootsuite Social Media Management. Retrieved 13 March 2019, from https://blog.hootsuite.com/Facebook-business-manager-guide/

5 Reasons You Should Be Advertising on Facebook. (2019). Wordstream.com. Retrieved 13 March 2019, from https://www.wordstream.com/blog/ws/2015/10/14/advertising-on-facebook

How to Use Facebook Business Manager: A Step-by-Step Guide. (2018). Hootsuite Social Media Management. Retrieved 13 March 2019, from https://blog.hootsuite.com/Facebook-business-manager-guide/

Hubbel, A. (2017). 5 Benefits of the Facebook Pixel | AdvertiseMint. AdvertiseMint. Retrieved 13 March 2019, from https://www.advertisemint.com/5-benefits-of-the-Facebook-pixel/

How to Advertise on Facebook: The Complete Guide. (2018). Hootsuite Social Media Management. Retrieved 13 March 2019, from https://blog.hootsuite.com/how-to-advertise-on-Facebook/#howto

works, H., Agencies, F., e-Commerce, F., Businesses, F., Advertiser, F., & Features, A. et al. (2017). Mobile and Desktop Ads? Elevate Your Facebook Campaign and Use Both.

AdEspresso. Retrieved 13 March 2019, from https://adespresso.com/blog/mobile-and-desktop-ads/

9 Tips to Write the Best Facebook Ads Ever (with Examples). (2019). Wordstream.com. Retrieved 13 March 2019, from https://www.wordstream.com/blog/ws/2016/06/29/best-facebook-ads

West, T. (2019). 4 Reasons Why You Need A Content Calendar. Blog.scrunch.com. Retrieved 13 March 2019, from https://blog.scrunch.com/4-reasons-why-you-need-a-content-calendar

7 Ways to STOP Wasting Time & Money on Facebook Marketing. (2019). Postplanner.com. Retrieved 13 March 2019, from https://www.postplanner.com/ways-to-stop-wasting-time-money-on-Facebook-marketing/

How to Create a Social Media Content Calendar: Tips and Templates. (2018). Hootsuite Social Media Management. Retrieved 13 March 2019, from https://blog.hootsuite.com/how-to-create-a-social-media-content-calendar/

Gingerich, M. (2016). Get the Maximum Facebook Ad Results with Minimal Ad Management. Neal Schaffer-Social Media Speaker, Author, Consultant, Educator and Influencer. Retrieved 13 March 2019, from https://nealschaffer.com/how-to-get-the-maximum-Facebook-ad-results-with-minimal-ad-management/

Owens, R. (2018). How to Combine Facebook Ads and Email Marketing for Better Conversions. Social Media Marketing |

Social Media Examiner. Retrieved 13 March 2019, from https://www.socialmediaexaminer.com/Facebook-ads-email-marketing/

Hiban, P. (2019). 4 Tips For Effective Real Estate Email Marketing. Inman. Retrieved 13 March 2019, from https://www.inman.com/2017/06/05/4-tips-for-effective-email-marketing/

Chef, T., Chef, T., & Chef, T. (2018). Retrieved 13 March 2019, from https://upserve.com/restaurant-insider/quick-restaurant-email-marketing-best-practices/

Here Are 5 Reasons Why Email Marketing Still Matters. (2014). Inc.com. Retrieved 13 March 2019, from https://www.inc.com/peter-roesler/top-5-reasons-why-email-marketing-is-still-works.html

Thiefels, J., & Thiefels, J. (2018). 8 Straight-Forward Content Marketing Tips for Small Businesses. Jessica Thiefels | Organic Content Marketer. Retrieved 13 March 2019, from https://jessicathiefels.com/Organic-Content-Marketer-Blog/content-marketing-small-businesses/

Developing your USP: A step-by-step guide. (2019). Marketingdonut.co.uk. Retrieved 13 March 2019, from https://www.marketingdonut.co.uk/marketing-strategy/branding/developing-your-usp-a-step-by-step-guide

Stelzner, M. (2017). Using Facebook Ads to Turn New Customers Into Repeat Customers. Social Media Marketing | Social Media Examiner. Retrieved 13 March 2019, from https://www.socialmediaexaminer.com/using-Facebook-ads-to-turn-new-customers-into-repeat-customers-maxwell-finn/

Digital organizing 101: What is a ladder of engagement and why do I need one?. (2016). Medium. Retrieved 13 March 2019, from https://medium.com/@jack_milroy/digital-organizing-101-what-is-a-ladder-of-engagement-and-why-do-i-need-one-c523b5874e16

6 Ways to Use Emotional Storytelling as a Marketing Strategy. (2016). 3 Door Digital. Retrieved 13 March 2019, from http://3doordigital.com/6-tips-using-emotional-storytelling-marketing-strategy/

9 Great Tips for Stopping Social Media Scrolling in its Tracks. (2019). Solutionreach.com. Retrieved 13 March 2019, from https://www.solutionreach.com/blog/9-great-tips-for-turning-heads-with-your-social-media-posts

Marketing, C. (2017). How To Choose Scroll-Stopping Blog Images - Content Curation Marketing. Content Curation Marketing. Retrieved 13 March 2019, from http://www.contentcurationmarketing.com/how-to-choose-scroll-stopping-blog-images/

Facebook Video Tips: 12 Ideas for More Engagement. (2018). Search Engine Journal. Retrieved 13 March 2019, from https://www.searchenginejournal.com/Facebook-video-tips/238911/

Hutchinson, A., & Hutchinson, A. (2016). Facebook Adds New Tools to Amplify Word-of-Mouth Recommendations, Boost Response. Social Media Today. Retrieved 13 March 2019, from https://www.socialmediatoday.com/social-business/Facebook-adds-new-tools-amplify-word-mouth-recommendations-boost-response

Holmes, J. (2018). 10 Ways to Make Your Content Marketing Go Viral. Jeffbullas's Blog. Retrieved 13 March 2019, from https://www.jeffbullas.com/10-ways-make-content-marketing-go-viral/

11 Tips to Improve Your Facebook Ad Conversions. (2018). Hootsuite Social Media Management. Retrieved 13 March 2019, from https://blog.hootsuite.com/improve-Facebook-ad-conversions/

What Types of Content Are Going to Work Best in 2018?. (2018). Core dna. Retrieved 13 March 2019, from https://www.coredna.com/blogs/best-types-of-content

Johnson, W., & Johnson, W. (2019). 10 Ways to Find Inspiration for Your Social Media Posts | RankWatch Blog. Blog.rankwatch.com. Retrieved 13 March 2019, from https://blog.rankwatch.com/10-ways-to-find-inspiration-for-your-social-media-posts/#-for-your-social-media-posts/

CPSIA information can be obtained
at www.ICGtesting.com
Printed in the USA
LVHW081934240521
688349LV00002B/209